Young Researchers

Informational kinds of reading and writing are crucial in every lesson. This book looks at how we can encourage children from the very beginning to think of themselves as young researchers using skills and strategies for clear purposes. It argues that the creative practitioner nurtures children's sense of wonder and curiosity about the world and all its phenomena.

Packed full of advice on how to use the most stimulating and exciting texts and the liveliest approaches, the book celebrates the good practice of teachers and student teachers in a large number of classroom case studies.

The content includes:

- a summary of recent developments and a framework of principles to inform good practice in this challenging aspect of literacy
- chapters concentrating on particular age groups – beginning with the nursery and ending with the later primary years – and thus taking up an essentially developmental approach
- an assessment of recent research and how findings can be put to practical and creative use in the classroom.

A central message is that children benefit from collaborating with teachers and peers at every stage of finding out. The spoken language energises informational reading and writing, making the sharing of the fruits of children's research highly enjoyable. This book will inspire you and lead to the very best practice.

Margaret Mallett taught in primary schools before becoming involved in national research into English in the primary curriculum. Until recently, she was Senior Lecturer with responsibility for primary English courses at Goldsmiths College, University of London, where she is now Visiting Tutor. She is author of many articles in professional and academic journals, and of *Making Facts Matter* (Paul Chapman, 1992) and *First Person Reading and Writing in the Primary Years* (NATE, 1997).

Young Researchers
Informational reading and writing in the early and primary years

Margaret Mallett

London and New York

First published 1999 by Routledge
11 New Fetter Lane, London EC4P 4EE

Simultaneously published in the USA and Canada
by Routledge
29 West 35th Street, New York, NY 10001

Routledge is an imprint of the Taylor & Francis Group

© 1999 Margaret Mallett

Typeset in Sabon and Arial by J&L Composition Ltd, Filey,
North Yorkshire
Printed and bound in Great Britain by
Biddles Ltd, Guildford and King's Lynn

British Library Cataloguing in Publication Data
A catalogue record for this book is available from the British Library

Library of Congress Cataloging-in-Publication Data
Mallett, Margaret.
   Young researchers: informational reading and writing in the early
and primary years/Margaret Mallett.
       p.   cm.
   Includes bibliographical references and index.
   1. Reading (Elementary)—Great Britain.   2. Reading (Early
childhood)—Great Britain.   3. English language—Composition
and exercises—Study and teaching (Elementary)—Great Britain.
4. English language—Composition and exercises—Study and
teaching (Early childhood)—Great Britain.   I. Title.
LB1576.M3627   1999   99–13532
372.6—dc21   CIP

ISBN 0 415 21657 5 (hb)
ISBN 0 415 17951 3 (pb)

Contents

Illustrations

Figures

Tables

Preface

Helping children both to benefit from and enjoy informational reading and writing is a considerable challenge for any practising teacher. We do not want children trapped in tightly structured and essentially sterile learning processes. Rather we want them to become avid and curious readers, intent on finding out, and confident writers, practised in communicating understanding and meaning. If teachers can achieve this in the primary years they will have laid the foundations for a successful transition to the information-based learning of the secondary years and for a lifetime in which there will always be a need to acquire knowledge and skills.

In building these foundations, teachers need to introduce children to the whole range of sources of information from traditional books and journals to material published on CD-ROM and available on the Internet. Children also need to be taught library and study skills but we must remember these are only tools that serve bigger purposes and intentions. The challenge is to teach children to take control over their learning by acting as young researchers formulating worthwhile and insightful questions to take to the mass of material now available. They will then be in the driving seat when it comes to their own writing, not merely mechanical reproducers of other people's words but writing powerfully from within themselves, using the knowledge that they have obtained and assimilated.

Being in control is possible from the earliest stages. The nursery children learning about the topic 'Babies' (Chapter 2) were helped to look at the books and pictures to find out what babies eat and how they are cared for. But the teacher managed to create a learning context where they had not just acquired bits of information but became fascinated by the whole process of growth and development and their own stage within it. Heart, mind and imagination are involved in genuine learning. The Year 5 children studying 'The Tudors' bring their feelings as well as their intellect to their studies when they examine a sailor's shoe, raised from the *Mary Rose* and showing where the leather has been stretched and worn by the shape of the foot. As one of them remarked: 'This makes you realise they were real people that drowned using real things.'

This book addresses teachers, student teachers and all who are interested and concerned about reading and writing to learn. It adopts a developmental approach in the belief that teachers need to know what comes before and after their age phase if they are to be effective in the classroom. However, readers may, if they wish, turn first or mainly to the chapter concerned with their particular year group. The terms 'informational reading and writing' and 'non-fiction reading and writing' are used interchangeably since they have the same meaning. The former is used in the chapter and main titles as it has a more positive ring.

Chapter 1 provides a framework for the whole book, covering the recent history of informational reading and writing and setting out some principles about how children learn from secondary sources and produce their own writing. In doing this, the book looks at a relatively neglected aspect: how children learn from the visual aids that often complement and extend the meaing of the text.

At each age phase three things are important and they organise the structure of Chapters 2–5. First we need to recognise the range of texts children work with as readers and writers. From the early non-fiction picture books and first dictionaries or word books children progress to more challenging kinds of non-chronological writing and reference material. Sometimes this progression is a matter of introducing more demanding forms of the same text type – increasingly detailed dictionaries and encyclopaedias, for example. Sometimes new genres appear, for example the journalistic reading and writing introduced in the later primary years. Second, we need to have some criteria for judging the quality of the materials. From the huge array of publishers' titles we need to select books, computer software and other media like cassette tapes and video-film of the highest standard in both text and illustration. Third, in keeping with a developmental approach, we need to understand the needs, interests and abilities of each year group and to plan appropriate teaching strategies to enable children to use the reading materials and to do their own writing.

Becoming a successful reader and writer of informational material is not just a matter of controlling library and study skills, important as these are. It is to do with feeling a need to find out in more than a superficial way and of actually caring about what we discover, so that new ideas and information become part of our way of seeing the world. We must never forget that informational texts, like all other kinds of language, are created and used in a societal and cultural context. Thus we need to embed children's work as far as possible in contexts that recognise this. Often, as the classroom examples show, collaborative work round texts keeps alive this social aspect: the group of children producing the radio advertisement for prospective parents decided they needed an Urdu version to reach some of the local mothers (see Chapter 5).

Young learners with special literacy needs require extra support both in the kind of materials they are offered and in strategies to support their reading and writing. Chapter 6 considers these needs and how to provide for them.

Finally, Chapter 7 sets out what we need to keep in mind about assessing and making records of progress in informational kinds of reading and writing. Assessment is part of the whole learning process and will come into every chapter but it is considered in a systematic way here. At the end of each chapter some issues to consider and reflect on are suggested.

In keeping with the developmental organization of this work and for ease of reference, the lists of children's books and resources are placed at the end of the chapters in which they are mentioned. Children's informational books often go out of print within a year or two of publication. While trying to keep to books still purchasable, I have sometimes mentioned old favourites, like Aliki's *Welcome Little Baby*, which need to be tracked down in a library or from agencies, for example Bookfinders (0181 462 7331) or Fourshires Books (01608 651451).

Teachers in the United Kingdom face constantly changing requirements: National Curriculum Orders; the National Curriculum for Initial Teacher Training; the *Framework for Teaching* of the National Literacy Strategy. This book tries to help practitioners satisfy these in so far as they affect informational kinds of literacy, while remaining reflective and creative. I also have in mind my wider audience beyond the United Kingdom and have tried to provide insight into good practice which can apply in any educational context. The classroom case studies do not claim to be blueprints for perfect practice but show children being helped to enjoy and benefit from informational reading and writing activities.

Margaret Mallett
University of London, Goldsmiths College

Acknowledgements

The following teachers, student teachers and schools are thanked for allowing their own and the children's work to be used. I am also grateful to the many children I have worked with who allowed me to present their writing and drawings in the case studies.

In Chapter 2: Geraldine Flynn and Sarah Cook for the nursery case studies on 'Ourselves' and 'Journeys', and Penelope Hunter for the insights on computers. In Chapter 3: Rosslyn Carthay and The English Schools Foundation, Hong Kong, for the writing with the computer work, Angela Hedges for the 'Snails' work, Louise Grayson for the lessons on 'Drama and Writing' and Lisa Guy, Sarah Gardiner and Sherin Hassan for the hyperstudio printout. In Chapter 4: Carol Eagleton and Jill Hawkins for the 'Making Pizza' and 'Animals in Danger' examples. In Chapter 5: Jan McGillivray for the Tudor work and Bennet Sills for the work on *Brother Eagle, Sister Sky*. In Chapters 6 and 7: the vignettes of children's work are from the following schools: Castlecombe Primary School, Mottingham; Rowdown Primary School, Croydon; Crofton Junior School, Petts Wood; Kingswood Primary School, Norwood. Other schools which showed interest and allowed the author to include the work of teachers, students and children are: Christchurch School C. of E., Forest Hill; St Georges Primary School, Bromley; Horn Park Primary School, Greenwich; Brooklands (Nursery), Blackheath; Beatrix Potter (Nursery), Stockwell.

Publishers who gave permission for the use of illustrations from their books are: Franklin Watts for page 9 of *What's Under the Bed?* by Mick Manning and Brita Granström; Penguin Books for the illustration from Janet and Allan Ahlberg's *Baby's Catalogue* (© Janet and Allan Ahlberg, 1982); Frances Lincoln Ltd and Rajendra Shaw for the photograph from Kathryn Cave's *W is for World*; Walker Books for the picture of whale and baby from *The Big Blue Whale* by Nicola Davies and Nick Maland; Dorling Kindersley for the illustration from the CD-ROM *My First Incredible Amazing Dictionary*; Pavilion Books for the poster from Michael Foreman's *War Game*; The Mary Rose Trust for permission to use the photograph of the sailor's shoe.

My warm thanks are also given to all the students, teachers, children and colleagues at Goldsmiths whose work has inspired me – often making things at risk of being 'as dull as ditchwater, sparkle like diamonds'.

I would like to acknowledge the help my family have given, particularly David who has given unstinting encouragement and support.

Finally, thanks to Margaret Meek Spencer, who read the draft and made many helpful suggestions. Any faults that remain are of course the author's responsibility.

1 Informational reading and writing
A developmental approach

> We learn best when head and heart are engaged. It is important to be able to use reading as a knowledge resource, but for most children (as well as for me most of the time) reading for learning is primarily a means of triggering and satisfying curiosity, of helping to make sense of a constantly changing non-factual world.
>
> (Arnold, 1992: 133)

Introduction: some recent history

For a long time informational kinds of reading and writing were relatively neglected. It was assumed that once children had learnt to read and write they could transfer these abilities to all aspects of literacy. Now we recognise that different kinds, or genres, of reading and writing require different strategies. Even within the large divisions of fiction and non-fiction different reading strategies are needed. Novels, play scripts and poetry draw on different reading approaches and so do recounts, reference books and non-narrative texts.

Until recently, books about reading to learn either focused on the needs of older students or centred exclusively on relatively narrow aspects to do with study skills and library skills. Several recent studies have added considerably to our understanding of the demands this aspect of literacy makes. Alison Littlefair offers an analysis of the different kinds of writing children need to respond to as they make their way through the school years (Littlefair, 1991). The features of non-narrative text, and how they are realised in children's information books, are defined by Pappas (1986) and Neate (1992). Of course, teachers and writers do not speak with one voice nor should we expect them to. While Bobbie Neate believes we should produce information books of a consistent format and style for young children, Margaret Meek praises Walker Books' Read and Wonder series because each book is different and 'arises out of the diversity of reading and knowing' (Neate, 1992; Meek, 1996: 111). This is an issue that arises throughout this book and it is no secret that the present writer leans towards the second view: books written to a formula are unlikely to arouse and sustain young learners' curiosity and reflection. Two recent research studies have centred on prom-ising classroom practice. Both Mallett (1992) and Wray and Lewis (1997b) have started from the question: how do we help children feel in control of their informational reading so that they are less likely to copy wholesale from books when they write? In the smaller of these studies, but nevertheless one strongly rooted in the writer's classroom practice, Mallett recommends that children be helped to organise their prior knowledge by discussion at the beginning of a new project or series of lessons and then helped to formulate their own questions to structure their reading and writing (Mallett, 1992; 1994). In the much larger, national, Nuffield-funded project *Extending Literacy*, Wray and Lewis (1997b) have worked with primary teachers on strategies like 'genre exchange' (reading information in one format and writing it in another) and 'writing frames' (outlines to help children structure different kinds of writing). The project has given rise to a number of publications which are discussed at points in this book. The important thing is that teachers read critically and choose strategies that work well in their own classrooms. The present book adopts a devel-opmental approach and explains the issues as well as suggesting some solutions and case studies for reflection and discussion.

The literacy hour, designed by The National Literacy Strategy Team, requires systematic attention to reading and writing non-fiction, and sets out in the *Framework for Teaching* (DfEE 1998) much more detailed objec-tives than the National Curriculum. These objectives inform the develop-mental model set out in this book; however, requirements for literacy teaching will be changed and refined and therefore teachers need some enduring principles to hang on to. It is also true that success here, as in all initiatives, depends on the skill and imagination of teachers who translate lists of objectives into lively and appropriate tasks for particular groups of children. Everything we need to know about non-fiction for all age ranges can be organised under three headings which structure the first five chapters in this book:

- *the texts* and criteria for choosing them;
- *the children* and the developmental stage they have reached; and
- *strategies* for making non-fiction reading and writing purposeful, useful and pleasurable.

This chapter provides a framework for the whole book, beginning with non-fiction books and resources and arguing that they, like other language forms, are essentially social phenomena. Illustrations, which tend to be rather a neglected aspect, are carefully considered. Next, it presents a dynamic organisation of written language which can help classify texts, including the texts children produce. Then there is a brief account of how a develop-mental approach informs good teaching of non-fiction reading and writing. The analysis turns finally to promising strategies to help bring children and texts together, taking account both of non-fiction in the literacy hour and the kind of informational writing required in the key stage 2 English SATs.

The texts: informational reading and writing

The modern world is information saturated. More knowledge means publishers' output grows in specialist areas: we now have CD-ROMs carrying enormous amounts of information on disk while the Internet continues to spread its tentacles globally. Information Communication Technology (ICT) provides a vast world of information and poses new problems of how to find our way through it. To become clearer about this, we need to reflect more generally on the phenomenon we call language. Language is a human system of communication which uses structured vocal sounds; it can be embodied in other media such as writing, print and physical signs (McArthur, 1992: 571). Linguistic symbols can be used to communicate that which is not physically present, the past and the future. Importantly, it helps us to deal with abstract thoughts and feelings.

To control the different kinds of written language is a major aim of schooling. By putting texts (in the widest sense of the term, to include spoken as well as written forms) at the heart of things, children can be helped to learn about language as well as about subjects across the curriculum.

Texts, both spoken and written, surround us in everyday life. They can be 'as short as a single word (on a notice, for example) or as long as a book' (Sealey, 1996: xiv). Many kinds of language can generate texts – the telling of an anecdote, a retelling of a myth or legend, a novel, a radio commercial or a crossword puzzle. In the present book we concentrate on texts in the informational category. The global features of texts are important. In line with the *Framework for Teaching*, we need also to teach children about what linguists call the 'micro' aspects of language: phonology and orthography, lexis, grammar (morphology, word classes, syntax) and semantics. Non-fiction texts have distinctive formats and linguistic style as well as particular kinds of vocabulary and can usefully be considered in this 'micro' way. However, like many other educational thinkers and writers – for example Sealey (1996) and Graham and Kelly (1997) – I believe larger stretches of text or the 'bigger shapes' need to be kept in mind even when our attention is on these 'micro' elements. We must remember too that the illustrations – charts, tables, diagrams, drawings and photographs – explain, summarise and sometimes extend the written text and deserve our attention.

There is a potential problem with information texts. They can impart little bundles of information without a strong enough context for children to make full sense of what is offered. This applies also to the CD-ROMs that derive from information books. The authorial 'voice' is important and the interactive context which helps children makes sense of all that they read. Meek (1996), Barrs (1996) and Arnold (1995) all consider that authors of information books do not always anticipate the needs of the young learners well enough. The role of the professional, insightful and creative classroom teacher is paramount both in choosing books and resources of quality and in providing sensitive and thoughtful mediation.

Criteria for judging non-fiction

General criteria assume a different hierarchy according to both the kind of non-fiction being judged and the age group for whom it is intended. Most teachers would accept the following criteria as useful in selecting non-fiction stock:

- accuracy;
- attractive format and sound global structure;
- helpful retrieval devices appropriate to age range and type of non-fiction text: contents page, index, glossary;
- appropriate, useful and attractive illustrations that integrate well with the writing;
- avoidance of unwelcome bias;
- friendly but unpatronising authorial 'voice' and clear, interesting writing.

In addition, CD-ROMs need to yield the material in a clear and coherent way that facilitates an interaction between the child and a text which is not simply linear. Much more investigation about how to help children use all kinds of multimedia is required. Helpful information can be found in Loveless (1995), Jessel (1997) and articles in professional journals, for example Jones's 'Beware of the mouse' (Jones, 1997).

When we consider the accuracy of books and materials, we have to remember that not only is new information constantly discovered, but our attitudes to certain facts and bodies of information change. The viewpoint of the indigenous populations in the countries 'discovered' by the fifteenth-century explorers is now included under encyclopaedia entries like 'settlers' and 'explorers' (see, for example, *The Dorling Kindersley Children's Illustrated Encyclopedia*).

Some books lack several of the criteria mentioned and yet seem to have a star quality which makes them hugely enjoyable and inspiring. *Brainbox* by Steven Rose and Alexander Lichtenfels, has no contents page, index or glossary, but invites the reader in through excellent pictures and a text that explains challenging concepts clearly. Information books for the very young often need only feature some retrieval devices to avoid, for example, a more or less identical contents page and index. Factual narratives are to some extent a transitional genre, imparting information in a familiar story form, often about the life-cycle of a creature or the life history of a person; only some of the general criteria apply.

Illustrations

Visual aids, if they are of good quality and appropriate, make a text more interesting by providing variety on the page. Even the visually sophisticated children of today need help in interpreting them and producing their own. Surprisingly little is known about how children interpret illustrations and develop this ability through the primary years. In a recent study, Moore and Scevak (1997) used a 'think aloud' strategy as a window into what young learners did and did not understand. Teachers could use a modified version of this to check whether children understand how writing and picture combine to create meaning. Illustrations have an important role in identifying a text with a particular genre. When it comes to informational texts, charts and diagrams usually signal referential material while informational narratives, including biography and autobiography, tend to include photographs. Illustrations or visual aids are discussed in Chapters 2–5 as part of the consideration of texts for each age range. Here there is a brief discussion under the following headings: tables; diagrams; drawings and paintings; photographs.

Tables

These often serve a summarising purpose, bringing together information from different parts of a text. Information tends to be arranged in columns and there is often a numerical element alongside the writing. Tables are used in mathematics, science and geography books and materials and, to some extent, in other subjects like history and religious studies.

The reading and making of tables are best kept together. There is a good model of a table for children at key stage 1 in Claire Llewellyn's *My First Book of Time*, which summarises a short written introduction about the differing number of days in each calendar month. The young readers are then asked to make their own table of the current month using symbols like a ball or racquet for a games day and a balloon or piece of cake for a party day.

Early years teachers know that there is considerable scope for making tables in mathematics and science. Graphs can be made to show the results of mode of travel to school and of children's height and weight. Six year olds who had been testing how long it takes for jelly cubes to melt in hot, tepid and cold water enjoyed talking about the symbols they would use to make a table to set out their findings.

Too detailed a table can be off-putting even for older children. In fact, the more difficult the concept, the simpler the explanatory table should be. A very reasonably priced book, Dougal Dixon's *Dinosaurs* in the Ladybird Discovery series, copes well with the notion of vast stretches of time – difficult for all of us to comprehend. At the beginning of the book there are two related tables about the periods of the earth's history, which provide a conceptual framework for the whole book. One is horizontal, beginning with the Cambrian period 570 million years ago and ending with the present day; the other is vertical and communicates at which point the different animals appear. It is helpful to point out to children that these complementary diagrams are a reference point for the whole book and they soon learn to check back. The different subjects provide strong contexts for particular aspects of literacy including appropriate visual aids: in mathematics and science, the presentation of materials in table form; in geography, reading and making charts to show variations in temperature or population; in history family trees and time-lines.

Diagrams

While 'table' and 'chart' suggest a numerical element, 'diagram' suggests the showing of structures like parts of a vehicle or processes like food-chains and animal life-cycles. Computer technology makes possible moving diagrams to show parts of the human or animal body or machinery operating. Rather than replacing books, the new technology has had an energising effect, particularly in children's encyclopaedias which in many cases show clear, attractive and well-labelled diagrams. Clear labelling, of course, helps make good links between picture and writing as demonstrated in the work of David Macaulay, not least *The New Way Things Work*, which includes meticulously researched diagrams and pictures of machines including computers, vehicle engines and bicycles. For younger children, diagrams like the clearly labelled fish in *Chambers First Dictionary* – showing fish gills, scales, tail and fins – all mentioned in the writing, provide very good models.

Children may need help to interpret cross-sections and for an entertaining and useful introduction I recommend Manning and Granström's *What's under the Bed?* (Figure 1.1). Now in big book format, this would enliven a series of literacy hours on 'reading' cross-sections. This book successfully combines an imaginary idea – two children and their cat journey from under the bed through layers of earth right to the burning centre of the earth – with some useful diagrams like the cross-section of an ant colony with a numbered key. Double spreads, loved by many publishers, can make possible the setting out of large, carefully annotated diagrams.

David Macaulay shows how complicated structures and functions can be simply shown even if they remain conceptually challenging. Too much detail can give a muddled appearance. But there is an exception to every rule – you do not find more detailed work than Stephen Biesty's cross-sections – but they work extremely well. Perhaps it is because everything – pictures, labels, annotations and longer written accounts – are all beautifully interrelated. Whether in book form or on CD-ROM, these cross-sections make an excellent starting-point for discussion and reflection. One of my own favourites is Stephen Biesty's *Incredible Cross-sections: Castle*. In a huge diagram on page 11 even a small corner shows how castles were built

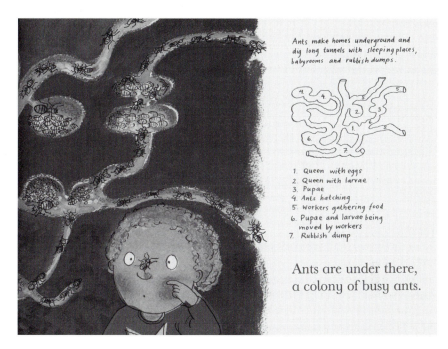

Ants make homes underground and dig long tunnels with sleeping places, babyrooms and rubbish dumps.

1. Queen with eggs
2. Queen with larvae
3. Pupae
4. Ants hatching
5. Workers gathering food
6. Pupae and larvae being moved by workers
7. Rubbish dump

Ants are under there, a colony of busy ants.

Figure 1.1 Ants' colony from Manning and Granström's *What's under the Bed?* (1996). Particularly in its big book format, this book helps the teacher explain to the class or group how a key is used to interpret a diagram.

and the workers' authentic tools. Opposite the large, full-page diagram are many written extensions about all the phenomena shown – the nature and origin of the materials used, the structure and function of many of the tools and the procedures necessary to get permission to build the castle in the first place. Biesty's work makes great demands on young readers; the information both written and pictorial is far from superficial and results from meticulous research. The sheer fun and wit of the pictures invites the young readers in. While we would not want to encourage wholesale copy-ing, children often find they can enlarge in their own way a small part of the cross-sections for their own purposes.

Research into children's writing often suggests that they tend to see its purpose as recall. In their study of children's perceptions of writing tasks, Bereiter and Scardamalia (1987) see the challenge as one of helping children transform rather than just repeat information. I believe that illustrations can play a part in this transformation of knowledge. They are often an excellent starting-point for discussion and provide information which children can express in writing. Older primary children are able to discuss the complementary roles of writing and illustrations and to give reasons why some diagrams are particularly successful in communicating information. Ten year old Scott remarked on looking through a book on Tudor buildings: 'Pictures can show us the materials – wood, wattle and plaster . . . but writing can tell us other details – where the material comes from, how old the house is and who lived there.'

Photographs and pictures

In my experience, quality photographs that integrate well with a text invite children into a topic and give rise to lively discussion and often to questions. They also have an important place in some of the books children make about visits and outings. Being required to think through where photographs fit with your own writing, and how much annotation is needed, makes you more likely to appreciate the role of photographs in your reading. Photographs can show us new ways of seeing familiar objects and can show us things that are difficult to express in words. For example, the picture of the bedraggled sea bird on a polluted beach in Claire Llewellyn's *Under the Sea* would take many words to explain. It is an example of a photograph with a strong emotional impact and in my experience never fails to stimulate discussion.[1] In Chapter 5 one of the case studies concentrates on children's response to photographs of items recovered from the *Mary Rose* wreck, including a sailor's shoe showing signs of where a particular foot stretched the leather. Other emotions are stimulated by quality photographs – wonder at something beautiful, fascination at something strange, and curiosity about something puzzling (Dalton-Vinters and Mallett, 1995).

If you want to compare the different roles of drawings and photographs, I recommend Michael Chinery's books in the Life Story series. *Frog*, for example, devotes the whole of page 15 to a wonderful photograph of developing tadpoles clinging to their jelly in the pond environment. The drawing on the opposite page shows more clearly than the photograph the suckers under the tadpoles' heads which enable them to cling to the sustaining jelly and the feathery growths tadpoles acquire at one stage in their development. The writing makes the link explicit: 'You can see the sucker in the drawing' and 'the tadpoles in the photograph are about two weeks old'. Drawings are useful when phenomena are difficult to photograph. The much praised Read and Wonder series by Walker Books features drawings and paintings of great aesthetic appeal. The poetic pictures in Davies and Maland's *Big Blue Whale*, for example, give a strong impression of the vastness of the ocean, even compared with 'the biggest creature that has ever lived on earth'.

Some teachers are concerned about transitional genres, like the books in the Read and Wonder series, which seem to be informational in purpose and yet have some of the features of a literary text – not least in the imaginative pictures that often seem to make the verbal visual. But there is every reason for regarding different kinds of books flexibly according to our particular purpose. In an interesting article 'Using illustrations as the bridge between fact and fiction', Judith Graham (1996) shows how pictures in story books can illuminate the real world as well as the world of the imagination. *Leila*, by Alexander and Lemoine, tells a very human story about the search for a lost Bedouin child in the desert, but as Graham points out, it also communicates much about the clothes, environment and lifestyle of the desert people through the illustrations (Graham, 1996). Thus children enjoying the story might extend an awakened interest – turning to information books to learn more about life in the desert would be a natural progression.

Kinds of reading and writing

There are a number of ways of classifying written material and I wanted to find one that would cover both the texts children read and those they produce as writers. Some categorisations deal with the finished products – this is a structural approach. Six main non-fiction genres can be identified: recount, report, explanation, discussion, persuasion and procedure. These link with work on genre by Australian scholars like Martin and Rothery (1986). Moreover they are the basis of the non-fiction element in the *Framework for Teaching* and are the genres selected for writing frame formats by the Exeter Extending Literacy Project (Lewis and Wray, 1996). In Table 1.1, literary kinds of non-fiction writing are added.

Texts can also be viewed more dynamically in terms of their purposes – a functional approach. Categorising according to function keeps the aims of the written or spoken text and the needs of the audience to the fore.

All too often official reports and statutory programmes do not explain how their recommendations for practice developed or offer any reasoned explanation for what is proposed. I suggest that the following way of categorising texts (see Table 1.2) fits the kinds of reading and writing mentioned in the National Curriculum English programmes and in *The Framework for Teaching* into a helpful overarching framework that draws on the work of Britton (1970), Beard (1984) and Wray (1995). The six non-fiction genres are located mainly under referential and persuasive language.

This classification allows for a less stark division between fiction and non-fiction. Some texts belong to more than one category. For example, *Anne Frank's Diary* is writing with literary aims, but it also imparts historical information in a different way to most referential texts. *The Drop in My Drink* by Meredith Hooper imparts much information about the water cycle but also becomes poetic when describing dynamic concepts like 'trickling, dripping, dribbling, swirling, leaking, condensing, evaporating, recycling, dissolving and polluting'.

Language as a social phenomenon

The great strength of a functional model is that it allows us to broaden our perception of language so that it is viewed as a range of discourses; these

Table 1.1 Kinds of non-fiction

Recount	Often the scene is set and then events are related in a time sequence. Includes writing about visits and newspaper accounts.
Report	Differs from recount as it is in non-narrative form, often starting with a general introduction, moving to an account of the main characteristics of the subject, and then finishing with a summary (topics might include 'Squirrels', 'Viking Ships', 'Volcanoes').
Explanation	Includes text which explains a structure like a building or a creature's body or a process like the digestive system or a machine working.
Discussion	These texts offer some different views on a topic like vegetarianism or homework, giving evidence and either coming down on one side or inviting the reader or listener to do so.
Persuasion	Close to discussion texts but, by their nature, urge towards one viewpoint. Examples include posters saying why an event is recommended, advertisements and writing the case for one view of an issue.
Procedure	Sometimes called 'instruction text', procedural writing sets out a series of actions, for example to follow a recipe or assemble apparatus in science.
Literary	Literary texts cover all the different kinds of fiction children enjoy. Two non-fiction types are autobiography (including the personal anecdotes children write) and biography. Some kinds of travel writing also fit here.

come into being as people use them to achieve their purposes as essentially social beings (Halliday, 1989; Sealey, 1996). Children learn actively to make meaning as well as to discover the subtleties of different kinds of language in use in their society. The intentions of the language user and the intended audience affect the way language is used. In the classroom the challenge is to find lively contexts for the different kinds of reading and writing we want children to control. Examples of promising contexts are found in the case studies at the end of Chapters 2–6.

The children: a developmental approach

Both the National Curriculum and *The Framework for Teaching* show a progression in children's work as they move through the primary years, thus implying that children develop intellectually and in other ways. There is recognition also – in the concept of differentiation – that children vary in their abilities and control over skills within their age range. However, teachers feel some concern that children's development as an interesting and necessary study has been marginalised in the face of many changes and

Table 1.2 Functional categories of texts

Expressive	Close to the interests and preoccupations of the writer; writing to help clarify thinking. Grammatically it is often like spoken language. Examples include: personal letters, diary entries and jottings; children's written anecdotes, news and personal writing; young children's first attempts at referential writing often have expressive features.
Literary	This is writing with aesthetic aims to do with shape and pattern and is where most fiction is placed. Examples of non-fiction literary writing include: autobiography, biography and the autobiographical anecdotes that children write.
Referential	Writing to describe, explain, inform and to get things done (termed 'transactional writing' by Britton [1970]). Examples include: recounts of science experiments, class outings and sports events; reports on topics across the curriculum; procedural kinds of writing, e.g. instructions for science experiments, recipes; lists, notices, signs, captions, labels, information leaflets, records, notes, writing on charts and diagrams, survey results; writing in encyclopaedias, dictionaries, thesauruses and atlases, narrative and non-narrative non-fiction-ICT texts as well as books and leaflets.
Persuasive	Writing to justify a request or to put a case to influence the reader. Examples include: advertisements, circulars, flyers; letters making requests to parents, friends of the school or outside agencies; journalistic kinds of writing to set out an argument; discussion texts setting out different viewpoints on issues for debate.

requirements aimed at raising standards of achievement. They worry that the attainment levels suggest a linear development that goes against their own experience and observations of children's progress. How time is used in initial teacher training courses is also more prescribed and many hours are required to be spent on teaching subjects and skills, leaving less time for important reading and reflection on how children develop and learn.

Nothing in the official documentation prevents teachers from using their knowledge of child development to create interesting and appropriate tasks within a favourable learning environment. What then do we need to bear in mind? One crucial awareness in a developmental approach is of the role of parents in children's achievement at school. The data collected during the Bristol Language at Home and School longitudinal study strongly suggested that the quality of children's understanding about literacy on starting school was the greatest indicator of future success (Wells, 1986). Some parents, regardless of their social group, seemed to have the ability to engage in the sort of conversations which developed the thinking of their young children. Many of these conversations occurred during the sharing of stories in books. Once at school, parents' continuing interest in what children were doing, and the kinds of models of reading and writing they provided at home continued to be of great importance in their children's progress.

Parents from different ethnic communities have a great potential role in sharing aspects of their language and culture with all the children. Young bilinguals bring special insights about language which can enrich the learning of all the children. Certain gender issues in developing literacy are of concern and we want both girls and boys to enjoy a wide range of reading and writing activities (see studies by Barrs and Pidgeon, 1993; Millard, 1997; Minns, 1991; Mallett, 1996/7; Graham and Kelly, 1998).

We must remember that a particular culture, its technology and ways of making meaning, greatly affect how children develop. Information Communication Technology will have a considerable impact on the developing mind and there is still much to discover here. Simple computers with basic word processing programs and words and picture keyboards, and sometimes a 'fried egg' type mouse which is hit rather than pressed, are available for very young children.

Above all, a developmental approach recognises that children do not learn or remember like a computer. Egan reminds us that learning is not just a matter of storing symbols in the mind for later retrieval. Children need to be initiated into the conventions valued by their culture, but as Bruner and Haste (1987) and Egan (1992) argue, they have the potential to be active meaning-makers, both imaginative and flexible. This has enormous implications for children's informational reading and writing. Just being told something by the teacher or reading it in a text is not enough. Rather than have knowledge and information transmitted, children need actively to transform new ideas and information to make it fit with their existing knowledge. Gordon Wells calls this 'the guided reinvention of knowledge' (Wells, 1986: 220).

Whichever age group within the primary years you teach, it is helpful to understand what has gone before and what will be achieved afterwards. Chapters 2–5 focus on children's development at particular stages as they journey through the primary years.

Teaching and learning strategies

While each stage has important and specific features, there are some general characteristics to keep in mind which help inform our practice. Children learn and make meaning actively; they are essentially social creatures capable of learning collaboratively; their physical, social and emotional development affects their intellectual progress; they need sensitive direction and support from adults at home and in school. The section below outlines the teacher's role, suggesting a framework of strategies, drawn from a number of studies and from good practice, to inform the non-fiction reading and writing element in the programme.

Nursery specialists are concerned that, while meeting the requirements for six 'desirable outcomes' (SCAA, 1996), activities for very young children should continue to be based in the right contexts and not distorted to meet narrow objectives. In their interesting book *Supporting Early Learning*, Hurst and Joseph (1998) give guidance on providing a developmentally appropriate and integrated programme. Nursery teachers might prefer to move straight to Chapter 2 which aims to fit non-fiction with all the other activities in the nursery environment.

Helping children organise prior knowledge

Children are active learners from the earliest stages and strive to make sense of their world. Organising prior knowledge through discussion helps create a setting for new knowledge acquisition. Teachers have always done this, sometimes calling it 'brain-storming', but it can be quite challenging to respond to a range of anecdotes and comments in a way that makes them a useful starting-point for learning. It nearly always helps to write down the contributions on the board or flipchart. The children could then be helped to make some brief notes on their existing knowledge. Making all this explicit helps the teacher understand the levels of sophistication of the concepts of individual children within the group or class and how far they are able to use an appropriate vocabulary. This indicates how much background information they need before turning to the books and materials.

Starting from the specific

I have often found it helpful to provide an interesting example of the new phenomenon before turning to the books and materials. Depending on the subject, this might be a display of historical objects to focus further discussion, an outing or visits from an expert, a dramatic enactment or a video-film. Seeing a real baby bathed and played with made nursery children excited about looking in the books and materials about babies (see case study 2.2) and the enactment of a story about environmental issues energised the writing of the children in the drama case study 3.3.

Children's questions

Taking their own questions to information books and resources keeps children's learning active (Mallett, 1992, 1994; National Curriculum English, Reading key stage 2, 1995; Lewis and Wray, 1996). There are different ways of approaching this and teachers will want to ring the changes. Sometimes all that is needed is a joint list on the board or flipchart of questions to bear in mind as they approach the secondary sources. While presenting children with a ready-made list of questions on a worksheet is a dull start, there is no reason why the teacher should not suggest some questions. Sometimes children have to be helped to make their questions realistic and manageable. Most children can think of a good number of questions, including some intriguing ones, but others benefit from working with a partner at this stage of the work. Older children can be asked to group questions from the joint list into topics and then into hierarchies within a topic (Mallett, 1992).

Later in the work, children can share the answers they have found to their questions. The children in the 'Snail' case study 3.1 made their own book structured round their questions (see Figure 3.5).

Modelling different kinds of non-fiction reading

Once the children have some purposes to take to the secondary sources, it is often helpful to have a display of some of the materials they will be using and to talk about them. Encyclopaedias, either in book form or on CD-ROM, are likely to play a part and the teacher can demonstrate their format and retrieval devices. This helps children take on the language of informational reading and writing: 'index', 'contents page', 'glossary', 'heading' and 'diagram'.

The features of the different information books can be explained – global structure, use of headings and subheadings, information boxes, illustrations and kinds of writing used (sometimes different kinds are used in the same book). There is no reason why one of the books being used in a lesson in any subject should not serve as the text for the week in the literacy hour. In fact, this kind of linkage between lessons across the curriculum and the literacy hour is welcomed in the *Framework for Teaching*. The purpose of reading as part of a topic in a lesson and that of scrutinising a text in the literacy hour are different. The literacy hour is a setting for looking at text on a word and sentence level as well as more globally. On a word level, looking carefully at the vocabulary of a particular passage that identifies it with a particular genre is helpful. At sentence level, the kind of syntax typical of non-narrative writing can be a focus. At an early stage in a series of lessons I often let the children know that I will be interested to have their comments on the relative merits of books with the same content and purpose later on. Feedback can be monitored either in discussion or on a book review sheet with some dimensions like:

- the format and general layout of the book;
- the retrieval devices;
- the illustrations;
- the writing;
- the degree of excitement and interest in the book.

Some teachers invite children to award the different aspects of the book up to five stars – from weak to excellent.

Of course, as teachers know, the modelling of reading and writing is not always neatly planned for a particular time. Opportunities for helping particular groups and individuals arise all the time.

Collaboration: creating a community of young researchers

Children are social beings and the first impetus into language and learning arises from the need to communicate and engage with others. The wish to collaborate and co-operate continues. Too often in the past 'finding out' reading and writing has been solitary. Talking and discussing the issues in information books and materials is motivating. Other children also serve as a good audience for listening to or reading what their peers have found out.

Books expressing different viewpoints or leaning towards one opinion are particularly good for encouraging discussion and leading to written accounts. Very young children can have views about issues if they have commitment to their work, for example four and five year olds became concerned about the slaughter of whales and their possible extinction (Doyle and Mallett, 1994). A Year 5 class greatly enjoyed some book-based detective work on whether the grey squirrel really was responsible for the falling number of reds. Different books gave different information (Mallett, 1992).

Integrating reading and writing with other activities

Outside visits, video-film, talks from experts, drama and art and craft all enrich informational reading and writing. It has been made clear that the literacy hour must focus on reading and writing and direct teaching, but other times across the curriculum can be used more flexibly. We only have to look at the children's work in the 'Giant' case study 3.3 to see how drama brought excitement and interest to children's work and energised their reading and writing.

Supporting children's organisation of their writing

It is difficult to produce your own account from the already organised writing of an information book. It certainly helps to bring questions to the reading as detailed above, and to make some notes from more than one book to inform the writing. This makes direct copying less likely. Of course scaffolding strategies vary according to the kind of writing to be done.

Changing the genre

Many teachers have asked children to write in a different genre to the book they have been reading. *The Extending Literacy Project* directors (Wray and Lewis, 1997b) call it 'genre exchange' and give examples of children writing advertisements, newspaper reports, diary entries and faxes in order to use rather than copy what they have found in books. The children whose work on 'Giant' is presented in case study 3.3 created posters after reading about environmental issues; and the ten year olds in case study 5.3 write letters to express their feelings on environmental issues. This is a good way of helping children stay at the centre of the writing task. In my experience there needs to be some discussion of both the features of the writing genre and the kinds of information to be communicated, with perhaps some examples, to avoid a superficial response.

Scaffolding writing

There are a number of ways of providing support. First there is what Donald Graves (1983) calls 'conferencing' – a rather grand-sounding way of saying children and teacher talk together about the style, content and organisation of a child's piece of writing. This approach is consistent with all we know about the benefits of adult and child interacting closely, so that the more mature person's thinking patterns are made explicit.

Second, where the writing is substantial enough to make a small booklet, children can be helped to make a contents page to provide a structure. The most useful kinds are differentiated – not just 'life-cycle' but also sub-headings 'Mating', 'The Squirrel Kittens', 'Diseases and Death' (part of a child's contents page for a book on squirrels [Mallett, 1992]). The contents page can be discussed with the teacher before being finalised. Another child involved in the same series of lessons asked if she could group her questions – all those on the squirrel's structure, all those on food and so on – and use these to organise her booklet. This seemed a good idea which had not occurred to me and in the end worked extremely well. Both the contents page and the grouping of questions give children practice in producing their own global framework.

One of the best-known strategies arising from work in the classroom in the course of the Exeter *Extending Literacy Project* is the use of writing frames (Lewis and Wray, 1996). These are frameworks provided by the teacher to structure the writing process but are not intended for the direct teaching of generic structures in study skills sessions. Children work their own ideas into the sentence starts and connectives provided. The frames can help get children started on writing with different aims: expressive, referential, literary and persuasive. There is no doubt that this kind of scaffolding helps some children, particularly the less confident writers. However, we want children to work towards organising their own written accounts and Wray and Lewis would be the first to say that the frames are a temporary aid and not to be used for too long or too mechanistically.

Making their own information books, as well as being satisfying and enjoyable, helps children put into practice what they have learnt about informational writing and illustrating, as well as what they have learnt about the topic. These can then be a classroom resource. One school I visited made some books by removing good photographs from out-of-date books and helping children to write a better text on the word processor to make a new resource.

Helping with the creation of illustrations

In history, geography and other lessons across the curriculum, the children can be encouraged to bring something of their own to their efforts rather than just copying the pictures. In history, for example, children can use the details in the illustrations of costumes, buildings, food and so on in the secondary sources to create their own composition, perhaps based on an incident described.

Another strategy is to enlarge one part of a picture in a book for a particular purpose. Stephen Biesty's cross-section books lend themselves very well to selective copying. The best features of two pictures of something similar can be combined. For example, a group of ten year olds interested in cross-sections of Tudor buildings created their own large poster drawing on the good labelling of one picture and the clearer outlines of another.

Terry, who found concentrating on reading and writing tasks difficult, enjoyed making a copy of a Tudor plague doctor with long cloak and nose cone from a history book. When asked how he could add something, he suggested labelling the different parts of the outfit with reasons for each item, drawing on the class discussion. Thus he wrote labels like 'nose-cone to protect from disease' and 'long boots to protect his body' (see case study 6.6).

With some encouragement, children can be inventive in creating their own pictures and diagrams. Ten year old Rakhee made a most individual, labelled diagram to show the differences between winter and summer dreys (Mallett, 1992). Where there has been a class outing, the children's own photographs are of course excellent illustrations for their accounts.

Sharing all that has been learnt

It has already been argued that informational reading and writing benefit from being shared. Where there has been a sustained study of a topic, it is satisfying to bring things to an end with a special presentation or display for parents or for another class. This creates an audience apart from the teacher who has been involved all along.

Assessing progress

Many schools use the *The Primary Language Record* (Barrs *et al.*, 1988) or a system based on it. There is scope for parents' comments about reading and the children's perceptions of their progress. Non-fiction texts can also be included in children's reading diaries or journals with evaluative comments.

Chapter 7 looks in more detail at ways of recording and communicating progress.

Statutory requirements

The National Curriculum

In the United Kingdom requirements are constantly changed and modified, not least in the area of English teaching and literacy. The full range of informational kinds of reading and writing indicated in Tables 1.1 and 1.2 is likely to increase in importance.

Key skills include using reference materials for different purposes and controlling retrieval devices (2d). At key stage 2 there is a checklist of key skills including posing pertinent questions, distinguishing between fact and opinion, and representing information in different forms (2d, key stage 2). All the requirements are included in the framework of strategies above.

The Standard Assessment Tests (SATs), particularly those at the end of key stage 2, assume knowledge of specific non-fiction forms and control over them as writers as well as readers. These include:

- *recounts*, including autobiographical kinds of writing drawing on experience of journeys, experiences at home and school, and challenges met. First-person writing has its own style and flavour and children need to experience models; for example, *Anne Frank's Diary*, Roahl Dahl's *Boy* and Martina Selway's *What Can I Write? Rosie Writes Again*. (See Mallett [1997] *First Person Reading and Writing in the Primary Years* for practical suggestions for encouraging this aspect of literacy.)
- *writing to inform and persuade*. In the 1998 SATs children had the option of writing a letter to parents informing them of a school event and explaining its importance. One child carefully included a tear-off slip at the bottom of the work with a can/cannot choice for parents to return – showing good control over this form!
- *answers to comprehension-type questions*, whether the passage is fact or fiction, demand a special kind of informational writing often including the expression of a supported opinion.

There is more about non-fiction in the SATs and the issues raised in Chapter 7. Adherence to the objectives of the literacy hour set out in *The Framework for Teaching* should ensure that all the kinds of reading and writing mentioned will be covered.

The National Literacy Strategy and the literacy hour

Non-fiction is fully integrated in the objectives for the literacy hour. The progression from early non-fiction texts and written recounts at the reception stage to the more challenging non-narrative texts to support learning across the curriculum and the persuasive and journalistic kinds of reading and writing at the end of the primary years are set out in detail. The range of reading and writing enlarges on what is mentioned in the National Curriculum English orders and the objectives are much more detailed.

I have much sympathy for those teachers who find the speed at which the new initiatives are to be in place and the prescriptive tone disquieting. However, I believe many of the strategies set out above can be carried out in the literacy hour. Others can be put in place at other times. Positive things about the literacy hour are, first, that it promotes the use of real texts; teachers can still enjoy choosing quality resources to suit their classes. Second, there can be mutually enriching interaction between reading and writing across the curriculum and the literacy hour and vice versa. Third, it encourages knowledge and understanding about language and offers a framework for looking at books and resources at text, sentence and word level. There is also welcome reinforcement of the importance of teachers' modelling appropriate reading strategies, which is most important in non-fiction reading.

Like all classroom initiatives, it is the skill, judgement and imagination of teachers which makes success possible. Being well informed about the required objectives, about the genres to be covered and the resources available on the market puts teachers in control. We can then use the literacy hour as an opportunity to promote children's progress in this important kind of reading and writing. (See Mallett's [1998] article 'Non-fiction in the Literacy Hour' in *Books for Keeps* for recommended books for the literacy hour.)

Non-fiction in schools' policies

The new initiatives will require some adjustment to school documentation. Many schools will already be covering something very like the objectives in the *Framework for Teaching*. Now it is a matter of showing how these will be achieved in the literacy hour in the school's English policy and in more detail in the English schemes for each year group.

Teachers have been quick to realise that sustained writing tasks, whether of the fiction or non-fiction kind, will not be possible within the time constraints of the literacy hour. This means that much non-fiction writing will still take place in the history, geography and science contexts which give it life and meaning.

Notes

1 See M. Mallett's article 'Engaging heart and mind in reading to learn: the role of illustrations' in *Language Matters*, CLPE 1996/1997 No. 3. Also, in Spring 1999, 'Words and pictures: the complementary roles of text and illustrations' in *English 4–11*, the journal of the English Association, Leicester University.

Further reading

Arnold, Helen (1992) '"Do the blackbirds sing all day?" Literature and information texts'. In M. Styles, E. Bearne and V. Watson, *After Alice: Exploring Children's Literature*. London: Cassell.

Bereiter, C. and Scardamalia, M. (1987) *The Psychology of Written Composition*. Hillsdale, NJ: Lawrence Erlbaum.

Bruner, Jerome (1986) *Actual Minds, Possible Worlds*. Cambridge, MA: MIT Press.

Egan, Kieron (1992) *Imagination in Teaching and Learning*. Chicago: Chicago University Press.

Graham, Judith and Kelly, Alison (eds) (1998) *Writing under Control*. London: David Fulton.

Hoodless, Pat (ed.) (1998) *History and English: Exploring the Links*. London: Routledge.

Littlefair, Alison (1991) *Reading All Types of Writing*. Milton Keynes/Philadelphia: Open University Press.

Meek, Margaret (1996) *Information and Book Learning*. Stroud: The Thimble Press.

Millard, E. (1997) *Differently Literate: Boys, Girls and the Schooling of Literacy*. London: Falmer.

Moore, Phillip J. and Scevak, Jill, J. (1997) 'Learning from texts and visual aids: a developmental perspective' in *Journal of Research in Reading*, Vol. 20, No. 3, October 1997.

Pappas, Christine (1986) 'Exploring the global structure of children's information books', paper presented to the Annual Meeting of the National Reading Conference, Austin, Texas, 1986.

Wells, Gordon (1986) *The Meaning Makers: Children Learning Language and Using Language to Learn*. London: Hodder & Stoughton.

Children's books mentioned

Alexander, S. and Lemoine, G. (1986) *Leila*. London: Hamish Hamilton.

Anne Frank's Diary (1960). Ed. G. Jameson. Unicorn Books. London: Hutchinson Educational.

Biesty, Stephen (1994) *Incredible Cross-sections: Castle*. London: Dorling Kindersley.

Chambers First Dictionary (1995) Ed. Angela Crawley and John Grisewood. London: Chambers/Larousse.

Chinery, Michael (1991) *Frog*. Life Story series. London: Eagle Books.

Dahl, Roald (1984) *Boy: Tales of Childhood*. Harmondsworth: Penguin Books.

Davies, Nicola and Maland, Nick (illustrator) (1997) *Big Blue Whale*. London: Walker Books.

Dixon, Dougal (1996) *Dinosaurs*. London: Ladybird Books.

Hooper, Meredith and Coady, Chris (illustrator) (1998) *The Drop in My Drink: The Story of Water on Our Planet*. London: Frances Lincoln.

Llewellyn, Claire (1991) *Under the Sea*. Take 1 series. London: Simon & Schuster.

Llewellyn, Claire (1992) *My First Book of Time*. London: Dorling Kindersley.

Macaulay, David (1998) *The New Way Things Work*. London: Dorling Kindersley (in book and CD-ROM form).

Manning, Mick and Granström, Brita (1997) *What's under the Bed?* London: Franklin Watts.

Rose, Steven and Lichtenfels, Alexander (1997) *Brainbox*. Illustrated by Mic Rolph. London: Portland Press.

Selway, Martina (1997) *What Can I Write? Rosie Writes Again*. London: Red Fox Books.

2   Pre-school and nursery years (0–5)
Entering the world of information

Everywhere we take our children we can find exciting free reading materials to point out, talk about and play with: from leaflets and carrier bags to road names and advertising posters . . . But our babies and toddlers do not just wait to be taught . . . they will show some interest in print and notice it everywhere.

(Whitehead, 1996: 116)

Introduction

Non-fiction should be a source of pleasure as well as information from the earliest years. Enjoyment should also accompany children's experiments with the very early writing and mark-making which is part of their general exploration of the world. Pressing of adult forms too soon on the very young can be counter-productive. This chapter offers some principles on which to base very young children's first experience of non-fiction reading and writing.

The first principle informing the practice of the good nursery team is that children bring with them many achievements and ways of dealing success-fully with new experiences. When it comes to literacy, the nursery pro-gramme needs to build on previous success in making meaning and to use children's own learning strategies to inform that programme. Early years educators are rightly concerned to hold on to aspects of their practice informed by knowledge of children's development in the early stages. Becoming literate is best established as part of a variety of ways of making meaning, through activities such as role play, art and craft and, of course, talking and listening in a wide range of contexts.

The second principle, linked to the first, is that books and resources of all kinds need to serve children's wider intentions and needs. Often the adult will see an opportunity to enrich and inform children's play by the carefully timed introduction of a book. Sometimes it is a story which can best energize the play and suggest new things to explore. On other occasions children need specific information to make their play satisfying; this became evident in the 'Journeys' case study 2.1 at the end of this chapter: What sort of things do ticket inspectors say? How are train doors opened? Children move easily from the world of make-believe to the world of information and very soon learn that we use different texts for different purposes.

A third principle is the recognition that partnership with parents brings considerable benefits. Early years educators welcome the continuity between experiences at home and school, including literacy experiences, that a culture of partnership makes possible (Hurst and Joseph, 1998). In my experience and that of my students, parents are willing to contribute in very practical ways to the work in hand. In the 'Ourselves' case study 2.2, parents brought into the nursery photographs of the children when they were babies for the 'Peepo!' book made by the teacher and children. The linguistic and cultural diversity of the families and communities from which the children come offers a valuable resource. This does depend, of course, on establishing good communication with the parents. Thus when it comes to reading and writing for information, some parents are willing to contribute to learning about other countries and cultures by demonstrating cooking, showing distinctive clothing and objects, and translating information books into home languages.

A fourth principle is to do with the quality of books and resources. Young children deserve the best quality materials available, and there is more about this later. Nursery teams are concerned to continue to operate on the principles described above and to make sure that their practice is compatible with what is known about how young children learn and develop. Although the nursery phase is not gathered into the National Curriculum framework, there are requirements for 'desirable learning outcomes' in all areas of children's learning and activities, including language and literacy, at age four. These requirements must not be allowed to distort the nursery programme (Whitehead, 1999).

This chapter follows the organization of the other chapters on particular age phases. It begins by looking at the range of non-fiction resources provided in the good nursery school and very often at home: non-fiction picture books; very early reference books; and computer programs. Then some appropriate ways to help young learners become involved in reading and writing are considered. Emphasis is placed on children's playful explorations and message sharing (Whitehead, 1997).

Information and reference books are appreciated more when they are based in strong and interesting contexts. We must remember that while they can be enjoyed for their own sake, they are also often tools to enrich learning, for this age group through play. The case studies that end this chapter, the classroom projects on 'Journeys' and 'Ourselves', draw on all the principles discussed and show how much young children can achieve when their interest and concern are encouraged. It is not a matter of introducing particular kinds of books and working through different genres. Rather, informational reading and writing must be integrated into children's wider purposes and intentions.

Non-fiction books and resources for the very young

Generally, it is easier to think about the texts for very young children as a whole without seeking to make a rigid differentiation between fiction and non-fiction. However, non-fiction in the nursery years has tended to be pushed into second place, even in excellent accounts like Dorothy Butler's (1995) *Babies Need Books*. As Butler says, story remains supreme as a source of language. But non-fiction has its appeal too and deserves careful consideration. Many early books defy classification and a flexible approach towards grouping them is best. The children in the 'Ourselves' case study 2.2 move easily from stories about babies to books and resources with a more informational focus. This is why the more dynamic approach outlined in Chapter 1, which looks at the functions and purposes of the books and resources, seems most appropriate. Young children soon find that different books meet different purposes. Here informational books and materials are mainly recognised by their ability to meet a need 'to find out'. Many of the best also entertain.

Very early books: alphabet, number and colour

Adults and children enjoy sharing these simple and colourful books which are often in board or cloth form. They can be introduced from the earliest stages at home and also have a continuing place in the nursery school. Favourite alphabet books include Helen Oxenbury's *ABC of Things*, Brian Wildsmith's colourful *ABC*, Dick Bruno's *b is for bear* and John Burningham's *ABC*.

Some of the same authors have produced number books, including Helen Oxenbury's *Number of Things*. Emilie Boon's *123 How Many Animals Can You See?* combines simple rhymes with the numbers in words with a clear numeral below and a picture of the named animals with the existing group opposite. Other favourite number books include Jan Pienkowski's *Numbers* and Caroline Bucknall's *One Bear All Alone*. Dorothy Butler recommends that the adult occasionally run a finger under the text as some of these books are read, commenting that by the time the baby is old enough to connect the black marks on the page 'the knowledge that the meaning arises from the writing will have lodged in her bones' (Butler, 1995: 16).

Colour and Size books, for example those by Jan Pienkowski and Shirley Hughes, link with young children's experience of the world, as do what we might call 'noise books', for example Julie Lacome's *Noisy Noises on the Farm* and Tony Wells's *Noisy Noises on the Road* both by Walker Books.

There are also more reflective books linking with children's experience like Aliki's *Welcome, Little Baby*, which tells about all the activities the newborn will enjoy, about learning to walk, talk and read. Tessa Dahl's *Babies, Babies, Babies* shows some different babies and their families and has children asking questions (the sort that sound convincing to parents) to which answers are given.

When looking at some books for the very young, the crudeness of a fact/fiction split becomes very evident. There is a kind of book difficult to categorise which reaches out to the real world of meal times, shopping and playing but which is also the forerunner of certain kinds of story. Dorothy Butler calls them 'descriptive books' and praises the work of Sarah Garland, whose titles include *Oh No!*, *All Gone!*, *Having a Picnic* and *Going Shopping*, and of course Shirley Hughes – particularly her 'Nursery Collection' for Walker Books: the pictures and text match perfectly in books like *Bathwater's Hot*, *All Shapes and Sizes* and *When We Went to the Park*. Under titles like these we could find the banal and uninspired but in the hands of imaginative writers and illustrators like Shirley Hughes, Sarah Garland and Jan Omerod, each stage of babyhood, with all the surrounding detail of young children's lives, is perfectly communicated.

Before leaving these very early books we should comment on books as toys. In a very interesting analysis of children's early experience with books, Marian Whitehead reminds us that they can be 'tasted, sniffed and stroked and this sensual delight in the texture, taste and smell of books may linger into adulthood' (Whitehead, 1997: 103). Some books are specially designed to encourage these sensory investigations: non-fiction kinds often have playful features like flaps (for example, Rod Campbell's *Noisy Farm*), materials to feel (for example, *Wild Animals* in Dorling Kindersley's 'Touch and Feel' series – the sticky pads on the feet of the tree pad are particularly satisfying) and pop-ups (for example, Catherine Felstead's *Creepy Crawlies* in HarperCollins Pop-up Surprises Series). The latter pop-ups are wonderfully three-dimensional – enlarged ladybirds, dragon-flies and grasshoppers spring up dramatically from the pages. The end pages have smaller flaps to raise with the name of each creature clearly printed. This encourages children to resavour the information. One of the first books to exploit the possibilities was Eric Carle's *The Very Hungry Caterpillar* with its famous holes through the pages. Here we have a highly entertaining book with poetic and fantasy elements which also manages to help with counting and learning the days of the week. It would be entirely inappropriate to start fussing over its status as information or story book.

Non-fiction picture books

These are a progression from the early books described above. Many well-designed and interesting picture information books are being produced. The best have bright illustrations and appealing text and a touch of humour is appreciated by the nursery school age group. *It Takes Two* by Karen Wallace and Ross Collins is a colourful and original book about having babies in the animal kingdom. It concentrates on how the sexes attract each other and how the young are born and cared for. The book is highly enjoyable and introduces children to notions of comparison and classification. Another factual picture book *How Did I Begin?* by Mick Manning and Brita Granstrom, concentrates on human mating and gives the right terminology to match the diagrams of conception and birth. It is detailed enough to answer the often quite searching questions of the very young.

Books organised round questions and an over-the-page answer generally appeal to children aged under five. Watts's *Who Are You? Titles* (Early Worm series) uses this format for animals on the farm, in the sea and in the rain forest.

The My World series, with titles like *My Night*, *My Day* and *My Seasons* by Siobhan Dodds, invites young readers in with a simple text and beautiful illustrations. *My Night* explores the world of nocturnal creatures like bats and foxes when children are asleep.

The joys and responsibilities of pet-owning are well explored in Jakki Wood's books *Puppy*, *Guinea Pig*, *Rabbit* and *Kitten* in the If You Choose Me series, also from Watts. A nice touch is to include the toys that a potential pet will like, as well as giving sound information on food, care and handling requirements.

Books about speed and noise are often favourites – fire engines, aeroplanes and cars. *Big Machines on the Farm* and *Big Machines in Town*, both by Steve Cox, show the machines in context. Young children like the speech bubbles and the touches of humour. *Big Wheels* by Anne Rockwell shows bright uncluttered pictures of cement mixers, dumptrucks and bulldozers. Other titles by the same author are *Cars*, *Planes*, *Trains* and *Boats*.

A book greatly appreciated by the nursery children in the 'Ourselves' case study 2.2 was the Ahlbergs' *The Baby's Catalogue*. They liked the labelling of successive pages under 'Toys', 'Brothers', 'Sisters', 'Dinners' and so on. This is a much more than superficial glimpse of the world of five very different families and their babies, two of which are twins. Another Ahlberg book, *Starting School*, pictures the experiences of a group of young children all about to embark on this rite of passage and this generally gives rise to much reflection and talk.

We tend to think of picture books as featuring drawings and paintings but there are some good photographic titles. Fiona Pragoff is a well-known name here; her *Starting School* picture book has a different flavour to the Ahlbergs' book of the same name featuring drawings. Photographs give a clear signal of a referential function. The children in the case study consulted Angela Wilkes's *See How I Grow!*, the photographic record of a baby's first 18 months, to answer specific questions.

Some nursery children develop special interests and these need to be nourished by appropriate books and resources. Claire Llewellyn's *My Best Book of Creepy Crawlies* is the sort of book which might awaken and sustain interest. All children of this age ask questions and would enjoy sharing with an adult the Oxford 'Why Is . . .' series, which includes

Books

Figure 2.1 'Books' page in J. and A. Ahlberg's *The Baby's Catalogue* (1982). This illustration shows the sheer enjoyment of sharing books from the earliest stage.

Ripley and Ritchie's *Why Is Soap So Slippery?*, *Why Do Stars Twinkle?* and *Why Is The Sky Blue?* But what about those questions not likely to be answered in books specially written for this age range? When the children are working with a particular theme like 'Food', 'Growth' or 'Creatures that Live in the Sea', nursery teachers often bring in books intended for older children and adults. The very detailed questions about breeding in blue whales asked by the children in the course of a project on whales were not addressed by the children's books available at that time and it was necessary to provide a specialist book on sea creatures (Doyle and Mallett, 1994). Case study 2.1 presents an action research study on nursery children using a challenging book, with help, to inform their play about journeys.

Early reference books

First picture dictionaries and word books have an important place in the collection. The best word books for the pre-school and nursery years have clear print against a white background and bright illustrations. Particularly inviting are *Garage*, *House*, *Tools* and *Wheels* all by Venice Shone (now sadly out of print) and *Fire Engines* by Anne Rockwell. There always seems to be an exception to every rule and Richard Scarry's hugely detailed and imaginative word books may be bright but are not really clear and are certainly not simple. Nevertheless children over three often become immersed in *Cars and Trucks and Things that Go*. Very different in style is *My Little Animals Board Book* designed by Helen Melville for Dorling Kindersley. The animals are arranged under categories like 'Powerful' (bear, gorilla, lion, etc), 'Climbers' (tree frog, bushbaby, squirrel monkey) and 'Armoured' (crab, tortoise and snail). *Collins First Word Book* creates a series of double-spread scenes like the kitchen and the garden and then surrounds them with words. Words are helpfully embedded in phrases in *My Oxford Picture Word Book*.

Perhaps the simplest book ever produced about genre is Anthony Browne's *I Like Books*. With great wit and imagination Browne shows some of the features of the different kinds of book with a small creature as guide.

While word books are often thematically arranged, early dictionaries are alphabetical. Most good early dictionaries surround every page with the alphabet; the *Ladybird First Picture Dictionary* highlights the letters dealt with on each double spread. It has a simple pleasing format and is good value at only £1.50 at the time of writing. Larger dictionaries which deserve a place in the collection include *Chambers First Dictionary* (clear format and good illustrations), Dorling Kindersley's *My First Dictionary* (1,000 headwords) and *My First Oxford Dictionary* (1,500 words). Young children quite often ask questions about phenomena not covered in dictionaries intended for their age group. Dictionaries, like for example *Usborne's First Dictionary* (2,500 words), which are recommended for age five upwards, therefore have a place in the nursery collection.

Encyclopaedias provide good browsing material and help with the many questions young children ask. Good first encyclopaedias will be helpful at home and in the early years classroom as well as in the nursery. Several publishers make early encyclopaedias and other reference material an important part of their output. *The Kingfisher First Encyclopaedia* and *DK Children's Picture Encyclopaedia* both have clear text and some well-labelled pictures. Dorling Kindersley have a number of beautifully produced encyclopaedias with clear retrieval devices and well thought-out entries.

Software

Nursery schools are strengthening their ICT provision and increasingly each class area has its own computer and colour printer switched on throughout the day. There are many software packages suitable for the under fives. *EasyPage* (1998, Windows 95 version) is an easy to use desk-top publishing package to help young children make their own books. *Smudge and Spaniel* (Storm Educational Software) is suitable for nursery and reception age children, and includes learning about the environment.

Children, when allowed to choose an activity, frequently select adventure and simulation games. Simulated situations in *Teddy* extend experience by providing imaginary and playful contexts in which to try out decisions and to see what happens. What would happen if Teddy tried to put his socks on after his shoes?

When it comes to writing, a co-operative, collaborative approach is sometimes of great value. The shared screen is much more conducive to sharing contributions than a pencil and paper. Collaborative talk helps children refine their thinking in the light of the contributions of others. The teacher will model how to go about this fruitful sharing. Penelope Hunter found in her small-scale action research study that children who found writing difficult enjoyed contributing verbally to what was to be written down. This sort of context provides an excellent opportunity for observation and for formative assessment of children's ability to contribute to the task of the group and to articulate their ideas through talk as well as writing (Hunter, 1998).

A word about illustrations

The different kinds of illustration children are likely to find in their informational reading are considered in Chapter 1 and are discussed in this part of the book alongside other aspects of each genre. Young children like bright colours but soon learn that there are different kinds and styles of illustration. Some writer-illustrators have a most distinctive style which children come to recognize and appreciate. Dick Bruna's bright primary colours and simple shapes, often outlined in black on a white page, are appreciated by the very youngest children. Writing of Bruna's apple, a bright red sphere slightly indented where a green stalk is attached in *b is for bear*, Butler comments: 'I have yet to meet a very young baby who is not arrested by Bruna's apple' (Butler, 1995: 12).

However, children delight in variety and they also usually like the more subtle colours of the Ahlbergs' *The Baby's Catalogue*. The detailed illustrations of the six babies and all the things they use, eat and play with perfectly match the text and lead to highly enjoyable discussion.

When assessing illustrations in any book for young children, whether it be a story or non-fiction, we look for accuracy and a good balance between picture and writing. In a most interesting article Judith Graham suggests that illustrations can sometimes be the link between fiction and non-fiction. Picture book illustrators often take great care over detail and accuracy; in Alexander and Lemoine's *Leila*, a story about a child searching for her lost sibling in the desert, the text is accompanied by pictures showing authentic plants and creatures and the clothes and cooking utensils used by the desert people (Graham, 1996). Graham goes on to suggest that enjoying the story and savouring the pictures might well lead to seeking out information books to answer particular questions. Case study 1 shows young children using a range of different books and resources to support their role play.

Involving children with the books and resources

In good nursery schools the principle of sharing books, audio and video tapes and software is well established. Information books as well as fiction can be shared and enjoyed in a relaxed way in book corners and language areas.

Children enjoy sorting through the collections of books and arranging them. Displays of all manner of things – shells, stones, animals, plants and even musical instruments – are a feature of good nurseries. Whitehead suggests that 'interest is further stimulated by placing appropriate reference books next to thematic displays or collections of materials and artefacts' (Whitehead, 1997: 175). Books matched with objects is an important element in the case study which helped children use and talk about the books and objects in the 'Things for Babies' display.

Having books close at hand leads naturally to the teacher beginning to model for the children, looking things up and scanning the contents page and index. The alphabetical order of indexes and early dictionaries and some encyclopaedias becomes evident. The purposes of information books and the flexible kind of reading appropriate to them can be shown. Children come to realize that their own questions can dictate the way they use the book and that often only one part of the book needs to be consulted. A light touch with all this seems best, since reading should not be presented as an anxiety-generating activity. The emphasis in the good nursery is on sharing and enjoying.

Early years teachers are well aware that very young children when motivated are committed to finding out and are tireless in their investigations. A group of children learning about whales was determined to find out why people killed whales and this led to the teacher reading out loud from books intended for much older children. Young children are also able to reflect deeply when their interest and concern are awakened. One of the children investigating whales remarked that future children might not be able to see whales because they had all been killed for their meat, oil and blubber. She added 'I don't think you could kill a whale if you looked at its face' (Doyle and Mallett, 1994).

The role of parents as partners in the educational process is becoming well established at all stages. Certainly it is helpful to liaise with parents over reading and writing so that literacy at home and school can be mutually enriching. In her interesting study of the parents' role in literacy, Jo

Weinberger found that three year old boys in particular often mentioned non-fiction books on creatures like sharks, whales and dinosaurs as being their favourites at home (Weinberger, 1996: 46). Nursery teachers often make a time for sharing books children are enjoying at home, and non-fiction deserves to be included.

Just as stories in addition to being pleasurable teach about characteristic narrative structures, early experience of information books shows the conventional linguistic structures typical of this genre.

Browsing is highly enjoyable and should be encouraged but children also learn much when information books are brought in to everyday work to meet particular purposes, as both case studies in this chapter show. The information books used in the 'Journeys' and 'Ourselves' projects linked with children's preoccupations and questions.

Information Communication Technology (ICT)

Children from a range of backgrounds often come to nursery school as experienced users of electronic media and communication technologies. The appropriate use of ICT is one of the desirable outcomes for four year olds in gaining knowledge and understanding of the world (SCAA, 1996). The majority of nurseries now use one or more computers to promote children's learning. The computer is, however, a tool and it should serve and extend the children's wider intentions and purposes as they go about their work.

EasyPage is like a desk-top publishing package for the very young and allows the creation of a text to match their pictures. This has much to offer book-making activities.

Early non-fiction writing

Children see people around them writing for all sorts of purposes and they soon begin to pick up pens and crayons to try to make messages themselves. These early attempts to write are different from children's early drawings; cross-cultural studies indicate that their scribble shows features of the written language in their environment. Vygotsky argues that cultural sign systems like writing have a considerable impact on intellectual development (Vygotsky, 1978). There are several studies that identify stages in learning to write. Marie Clay suggests that before children can reliably produce letters of the alphabet, some principles of their early efforts at mark-making can be detected and described. For example, the repetition of the same marks and letter formations is termed by Clay 'the recurring principle'; the way in which writing is orientated is the 'directional principle'; and the 'inventory principle' is to do with the way children start to arrange letters that have become part of their written repertoire (Clay, 1975, Chapter 3). More recently Tom Gorman suggested that we see the emergence of writing in seven stages; he is concerned to point out that this is only one way of looking at writing and that it is difficult to generalize about the ages when children control features of writing (Gorman, 1996: 8). Children encounter environmental print on signposts and billboards, on clothes labels and in shops. Their homes, too, are likely to be saturated with writing – birthday cards, notes, letters, instructions and so on. Of course, before they go to school children vary in their knowledge of how written language is represented (Wells, 1986). However, they are likely to have acquired some level of capability in ICT: programmable toys, video games, TV remote control and so forth.

As Case study 2.2 'Ourselves' shows, there is much to be gained from keeping reading and writing together as complementary activities. A first step might be to ask children to talk about textless books, adding their own comments to a sequence of illustrations. Next, the teacher might scribe their sentences to match their drawings to make a first book.

Most termly or half-termly nursery themes create strong contexts for writing. 'Food' topics invite the writing of menus and lists, 'Journeys' to making timetables, tickets and posters; and the 'Ourselves' topic to lists of baby items in categories, birthday cards and clinic appointment cards.

Using the computer to write

The computer does not replace the variety of surfaces used in the nursery (e.g. paper, card, boards, sand) nor does it replace the writing tools (e.g. pens, pencils, crayons, chalks, jumbo markers, paint brushes, sand markers and squirt bottles), but it is a powerful new tool for developing literacy. Penelope Hunter, a mature student, found during her teaching at an inner London nursery school where many of the children came from families for whom English was an additional language, that the computer greatly contributed both to autonomous learning and to the development of collaborative skills. Above all, the computer contributed to children's early writing development (Hunter, 1998). Penelope's account of her work makes it clear that she linked all the writing on the computer at her nursery school group with the writing practices in the children's homes. At home children saw parents and older siblings writing (a) *to maintain the household* (shopping lists, business letters and annotation of routine and important dates on the calendar), (b) *to maintain communication* (telephone messages, notes and letters) and (c) for more *personal communication*, e.g. diaries (Barton, 1994). In an increasing number of homes, writing on the computer and written forms on the Internet are becoming common. This cultural change widens the definition of literacy and will be reflected in schools, including the nursery school.

The computer can be a useful tool in helping young children become writers. We must remember the sheer physical effort which handwriting demands; it involves combining fine motor skills as well as intellectual ones. Children have to integrate controlling the writing implement, the handwriting style and page layout with the effort of composing sentences. There is no reason why traditional handwriting skill should not be acquired along-side learning how to type. Indeed, being freed from the labour of handwriting helps children concentrate on what they wish to communicate. At the same time, the interest that children often take in presenting their work in a variety of fonts and colours and in using the bold, italic, underline and tab functions may well, as Crompton and Mann (1996: 270) suggest, transfer to their handwritten efforts.

The four year olds Penelope was working with were helped to become familiar with the QWERTY keyboard by writing their names and then experimenting with some more adventurous graphic name displays. Correcting mistakes was introduced as 'drafting and editing' and became an enjoyable part of the writing activity. One child, who lacked confidence about word-processing her name at first, was greatly helped by a 'speaking' computer which brings together the communicative skills of reading, writing, speaking and of course listening. When she managed to type the letters of her name, the voice synthesiser provided immediate aural feedback. Of course the children were able to print out several copies of their work and to take home a copy to show their parents, thus encouraging parental involvement in this aspect of literacy. The children in this example went on to experiment with their addresses and to write stories. There are a vast number of informational kinds of writing that can arise naturally during children's play, and word-processed forms add authenticity to tickets, menus and notices.

Group work is a strong organisational feature of good early years work. The computer fits well with this and is used in a public setting conducive to collaborative work. However, the desired quality of reflection on ideas for writing together often requires the skilled intervention of the adult. This support is needed for most young children to understand the potential of the computer as a tool for writing (Jessel and Matthews, 1993; Jessel, 1997; Hunter, 1998). *HyperStudio* from TAG is a multimedia authoring tool which enables teachers to create interactive books for particular individuals or groups of children.

CASE STUDIES

A main theme in this chapter with regard to the learning of the under-fives, is that texts and materials of different kinds need to serve bigger purposes. Two case studies follow which take up this holistic approach. First we join three to four year olds using both fiction and non-fiction to support their learning through play about 'Journeys'. Of special interest here is the need for quite an advanced information book to help answer the children's questions. The children are clear about the purposes of the books they use and enjoy. Second we follow stages in a nursery project about 'Ourselves'. Again, the books and materials meet children's genuine needs to find out and they also show how reading and writing can interrelate. In both case studies the important role of the teacher in observing children's progress and supporting their learning with a variety of resources and activities is recognized.

Case study 2.1: Journeys

Three to four year olds use books for different purposes to inform and extend their learning through play

The context of the work

The children attended a nursery attached to a primary school in South East London. Open for eleven years, the nursery intake draws on families of different economic status and from different ethnic roots. The children flow freely into the large outdoor play area which has trees and grass. The nursery benefits from books and resources provided for particular topics by the Greenwich Project Loan scheme and the nursery walls are filled with pictures and environmental print. The nursery team plan within the framework provided by the Desirable Outcomes (SCAA, 1996) and an assessment breakdown has been devised to ensure development of the whole child.

It was the practice here to use a story, often a picture book, to provide a focal point for exploration of a topic in the play area. Sarah Cook, a final year Goldsmiths student, carried out small-scale action research to find out how a non-fiction text might be used to promote children's play and how this was used differently from a story. The work is based on the recognition that play can be a vehicle for kinds of complex learning. It is often symbolic and much play is interactive and social. There is not space here to set out the arguments for the value of play for young children in detail. These arguments are well understood in good nurseries and can be read about in Bruner, Jolly and Sylva (1978); Moyles (1991; 1994); Bruce (1996); and Guha (1996). Sarah C's observations are based on six afternoon sessions over the two-week project.

Talking about trains

Before the topic started a train structure had been created out of the Design Technology Quadro equipment. The children, who were aged between three and four years, had tended to use the structure as a climbing frame and the teacher decided to talk to them about journeys as the introduction to a topic. It soon became clear that the children were particularly interested in journeys by train. Many of their parents used the train to get to work and some of the children had gone on holiday by train. To focus the next discussion Sarah C brought in Dorling Kindersley's *Eye Witness Guide: Trains* by John Coiley. Although this book is intended for older children, it provides a detailed account of all aspects of trains and train journeys – types of trains, structure of trains, stations, trains from stories and the roles of people who work on trains. The illustrations are detailed and well annotated.

The children were particularly drawn to the photographs of steam and diesel trains and mentioned a favourite character *Thomas the Tank Engine* as an example of a steam train. They were delighted to find, after this had been mentioned, a picture of Thomas under the double spread on 'Trains for Fun'. The teacher paraphrased parts of the book in answer to the children's questions about how train carriages were joined together and how the lights were turned on and off.

Preparing for the role play

The children were excited about the prospect of role play on the train. They decided that it was to be a diesel train and that there needed to be a control panel and brake lever. Other decisions were jointly taken about the structure of the train – for example where the engine was, the driver's cab and how the seats, doors and windows were arranged. Some adult intervention was needed to establish the roles – driver, guard, ticket collector and passengers. Familiar phrases associated with train journeys were suggested such as 'stand clear of the doors' and 'mind the gap'.

Learning through role play

The teacher took up a role as a passenger so that new vocabulary could be fed in. The children were drawing on their previous experience of trains and stations and using some of the new concepts and ideas introduced through the book. A display was set up in the role play station area with artefacts like a driver's hat, a rail timetable clock, pencils and tickets. Posters showed an intercity train and diagrams and photographs of track construction. Coiley's book *Eyewitness Guide: Trains* was on display and much browsed through by the children. Parents took an interest and brought in objects of interest like models of steam trains, timetables and used tickets: Often what they had said provided a good introduction to the play sessions. For example, Jasmine's father remarked that there needed to be a ticket office: 'Can't go on a train without a ticket or you have to pay even more money!' This led to Jasmine looking up about tickets in the book and making some to be issued from a ticket office area. Jasmine's mother sent in some Japanese tickets and this led to a discussion about trains in different parts of the world and how the writing was different according to the country where the journey was taking place. Some of the children used the clock in their role play, making their own rules about when the ticket office was open and when closed.

The enthusiasm for the role play spread into other areas of the nursery – trains were being made in the construction corner and train noises were made in the outdoor play area. Kirsty suggested that they make lunch for the passengers in the playdough area. A particular incident shows the level of absorption the children invested in the role play. Kirsty brought the refreshments to the train but one of the cakes slid off her tray and into the 'engine area' of the train. Phelan the guard noticed this and blew the whistle to stop the train. The train was 'broken' and the cake has to be retrieved and the train mended.

The children would frequently come out of the role play situation to check something in the book or to ask the teacher for advice. The influence of the book was also evident in the new vocabulary being used – passenger, engine, track, refreshments, safety and junction.

Writing to develop role play

The children seemed increasingly eager to consult the display table and particularly the book on arrival at the nursery. Jasmine had already organized the making of tickets. In later sessions the children's attention was drawn to signs found in stations and on trains. The pictures in the book were studied and discussed and the children asked the nursery nurse to help them put up 'STASHUN', 'so that people would know where to catch the train' and signs for the platform and ticket office. The book was now being taken into the role play area and looked at by Hamish in his role as passenger.

Dilemmas and decisions: introducing another kind of text

By the fourth session the play was moving into more controversial and potentially confrontational areas. Whom should we let on the train? What was sensible behaviour on a train from a safety point of view? Whom do we want to sit beside? Sarah C, after careful observation of the children's interactions, decided that a story would help the children work through issues of compromise, empathy, acceptance and rejection. The children were ready to change the train from diesel to steam and to enjoy a fantasy journey inspired by John Burningham's *Oi! Get off Our Train*. The children brought much of what they had learnt from the information book to the new play theme, commenting that they had changed from diesel to steam and would need to burn coal to make steam. The rules about tickets and obeying the guard still applied in the fantasy situation which, in addition, allowed the children to explore some emotional and social issues when the different animals wanted to board the train.

Conclusions

Sarah Cook felt it was the book illustrations in the two different genres which enriched and extended the children's role play. They were invited into a challenging book *The Eyewitness Guide: Trains* by the detailed and colourful pictures. The storybook illustrations signalled a different kind of role play in which animals could talk and behave like human beings and face up to emotional issues and practical dilemmas. The illustrations contributed to the children's understanding of what they could get from different kinds of text. One short snippet shows how Tommy (3.9 years) had appreciated the purposes and registers of the two different books which had supported the project.

SARAH C: This looks like a good story. What's it about?

TOMMY: [reading the *Eyewitness Guide to Trains* book]: No it's not a story . . . it's a book about trains – look. [Points to pictures of trains on the different double spreads.]

SARAH C: [Showing Burningham's *Oi! Get off Our Train* book] Is this a book about trains then?

TOMMY: No it's a story about one train and lots of animals [indicates by pointing to the same train pictured on each page and stating 'same' each time he points].

The displays had also been extremely motivating and had interested the parents as well as the children. Above all it was the adults – teacher, nursery nurse and parents who had helped encourage the children to make their play creative by drawing on their experience as well as on books. The teacher, in particular, modelled the use of an information text which children would have otherwise found very difficult.

Case study 2.2: 'Ourselves'

Four year olds enjoy reading for information and producing their own writing in a rich motivating context

This example is a realisation of all that has been recommended throughout the chapter. The books and resources were carefully integrated with interesting and appropriate practical activities: the topic was one likely to engage young minds and hearts; and children were encouraged to link their own experience with what was presented on screen and in books. The teacher's role as provider of exciting resources and introducer to themes and activities was emphasised, thus keeping up the momentum of the work by responding to children's interests and comments. Parents were involved in the work, for example bringing in photographs of the children as babies, to make a special book.

The context of the work

The nursery school in Earlsfield where the work was carried out is attached to a well-resourced primary school which has the benefit of a large playing field and garden. There is a large indoor area, well equipped with sand, water, construction toys, reading area and home corner. The outdoor play area is spacious, with a wooden chalet and climbing apparatus. Interestingly, the teacher often shares information books with the children at 'storytime' by taking a book from a display, reading it through and showing the pictures, and then entering into a dialogue with the children based on its contents. By introducing information books at a time traditionally reserved for fiction, non-fiction is given the status that it sometimes lacks. The work on 'Ourselves' arose out of a more general exploration of growing, and particularly the children's observations of eggs hatching into chicks in the nursery garden. Using Angela Royston's book called *Chick*, from Dorling Kindersley's See How They Grow series, the teacher talked to the children about the ways in which the book related to their observations of the actual chicks in the nursery school garden. Conversation then changed to how they thought they themselves had changed since babyhood. This is a good example of how 'we can build bridges between experience and school learning' in the context of reading 'finding out books' as well as stories (Whitehead, 1997). The 'bridging' metaphor is pertinent to good early years practice in general and to this example in particular.

Books like *Chick*, which follow a natural life-cycle in a time sequence, are a sympathetic and appropriate way of providing information for the very young (Mallett, 1992). Children seem to sense very soon that the narrative form does not necessarily signal fiction.

Those who consider narrative and non-narrative forms should be kept separate may be mistaken. Bobbie Neate, for example, believes 'finding out' books should be organised in an agreed format and kept distinct from fiction (Neate, 1992, 1994). On the contrary, the security of a familiar narrative framework helps consolidate knowledge gained from experience while opening up new ideas and possibilities. This was certainly the case here: reading about the stages a chick goes through to become a hen helped the children to reflect on the changes common to all living creatures, including themselves. Thus a shared reading of a text relating to children's recent observations of a phenomenon, proved to be a bridge to the 'disembedded' kind of learning our school system demands of older children. Margaret Donaldson argues powerfully that young children can begin to achieve this kind of thinking if we begin by anchoring the learning in something familiar (Donaldson, 1979).

Introducing Matthew

Watching and talking about real chicks emerging from eggs before looking at the books proved to be worthwhile, and in extending the project to a study of babies and young children's growth and development, an equally exciting start was sought. A student teacher, Geraldine F, a mature student, had a very young baby and brought him in to be bathed, fed and played with in the nursery. The children's interest in observing, touching and listening to Matthew during several visits he made to the nursery provided an ideal setting for using a range of books about babies.

Creating a learning environment

There were several interactive displays featuring objects that babies use: bottles, rattles, safety pins, nappies and so on. The children were invited to classify them into different groups – things to keep baby clean, things for baby to play with. A baby clinic was set up for role play. We would expect all of this, of course, in good nursery practice. Where the provision differed was the way the books, labels, notices and charts were brought into the learning rather more systematically than is usually the case. The aim to help children experience and use information books was made explicit.

Using the books

Different kinds of books were provided, including picture book stories, information stories, playful interactive texts like the Ahlbergs' *Peepo!*, simple non-narrative texts and books that defy classification, like the Ahlbergs' *The Baby's Catalogue*. Margaret Meek describes this as 'the picture book version of the one from Mothercare' (Meek, 1996). It has a welcome multicultural flavour and, like Angela Medearis's book *Eat, Babies Eat*, shows babies from different cultures.

Books structured round photographs of babies were particularly liked and often provided a reassuring narrative of a baby's daily experiences and activities. *Babies*, by Nicola Baxter, has an interactive element which was appreciated, while *Baby Days* by Fiona Pragoff provides beautiful photographs showing the pattern of a baby's day and making the baby's voice heard – 'I'm hungry' and so on. All these books helped give the children's talk about babies a focus and were brought in at points where the teacher judged they would link with the children's preoccupations.

The children enjoyed stories about babies, particularly John Burningham's *Avocado Baby*, in which the first part of the story portrays life with a young baby quite accurately while the second part, in typical Burningham style, enters the world of the fantastic. The gender of the baby is never made explicit. The children were amused by the baby's response to a series of challenges after becoming very strong after eating avocado pears. Jan Ormerod's *Eat Up Gemma*, another favourite, is about a baby frustrating its parents by refusing food. The family's culture and lifestyle is conveyed by Jan Ormerod's distinctive illustrations and the way babies can rule the life of others is very clearly shown. Another Ormerod book – *Messy Baby* – invites the children to 'read' the pictures of a father clearing up after a baby only to find the baby has messed everything up again. An older child's point of view is effectively shown in John Burningham's *The Baby*; sometimes the baby is liked and sometimes it is found irritating – making a mess with its food. Above all, the sibling wants the baby to grow up! Picture books often home in on children's ambivalent feelings about little brothers and sisters more successfully than informational books.

A very detailed account about the birth and growth of babies (which even includes a facsimile of a scan) is found in Michael Foreman's *Ben's Baby*. The baby's growth is set against illustrations of the changing seasons described by Ms F as 'rather Hockneyesque'.

The children enjoyed the interactive format of *Peepo!* and their own version was made with baby photographs provided by the parents. The children were not yet able to appreciate the subtle reference to family life in the war years, but they liked the playful aspects.

The children learnt both about how babies grow and are cared for and, in the course of this, they also learnt about the materials and resources. Often in projects of this kind one or two books are central. Most time was spent using *See How I Grow*, partly because Ms F had integrated it into the work, but also because the children liked it. They found the increasing size of the basket in the illustrations showing the baby's rate of growth an intriguing idea.

Talking about growing

One of the books most used to help inform the children's observations of Matthew was Angels Wilkes's '*See How I Grow*. Geraldine, student teacher, showed the pictures in the book and read the text while Matthew sat in a little chair near the children. As we would expect, there was interplay between the children's use of their own experience, their observations of the baby and ideas from the book. Victoria, for example, began to forge connections between Matthew and the information contained in the text.

TEXT: My hands look really tiny next to Daddy's (page 10).
VICTORIA: Matthew's hands are tiny, 'cos I held them!

Daniel also questioned Matthew's development in relation to the baby in the text.

TEXT: My favourite game is trying to sit up (page 12).
DANIEL: Can Matthew sit up?

The children show signs of becoming able to use the language of the text, thus expanding their vocabularies. In the following exchange Edward seems aware that baby Matthew is bigger than the baby shown on page 10 of the book, but is initially unable to explain that his reasoning is based on the fact that Matthew is no longer lying flat. Later he manages to use the word 'propped' correctly.

Ms F: This baby is six weeks old.
  Is Matthew bigger than this?
EDWARD: Yes . . . but he's not *big*.
Ms F: How can we tell that he's bigger?
EDWARD: He's . . . the one in the book . . . is lying down.
Ms F: [reading text]: 'I can just about keep my head up now though it is still a bit wobbly. I like to be propped up in a seat so I can watch what is going on' (pages 10/11).
VICTORIA: Matthew is sitting up.
EDWARD: He's *propped* up.

Edward continues to adopt the language of the book, later asking of Matthew, 'Is he wobbly?' Edward also uses the language of the book in his play, asserting 'My legs feel a bit shaky'. Later Ryan, Edward and Victoria crawled round the nursery, experiencing again what it felt like to be babies through role play.

Writing together: making the 'All about Babies' book

The children had been drawing their own pictures of babies throughout the work. They were asked to think of some aspect of a baby's development they would like to write about. It was made clear that their writing and pictures would be made into a book which would become part of the nursery collection, to be read and enjoyed by the other children and the teachers and nursery nurse. This provided the children with an

We can climb in the playground, but babies
have to be held by their mummies.

Figure 2.2 Annecy's picture and scribed sentence in a book made by nursery
children, 'All about Babies'.

audience they could understand and also gave their efforts extra purpose. As they move through the education system, both 'audience' and
'purpose' will be important aspects of all the writing they do. Of course,
at this stage the children needed the teacher to scribe for them, but they
were involved in all the decisions about how the pictures and writing
would be organised in the book. They drew on the discussions they had
enjoyed in the context of both using the books and observing the baby.

Experience at home was also included; Annecy made frequent references to her baby brother in her talk and composed the following
sentence for the book: 'We can climb in the playground, but babies have

to be held by their mummies.' This seems to be her attempt to make sense of respective sizes of babies and children.

Ms F noticed as she scribed the children's sentences for the book that their language had taken on the more formal register of the information text, influenced particularly by Angela Wilkes's *See How I Grow*. Some of the children prefaced their sentences with 'This baby is/can. . .' Annecy and Victoria, who had previously referred to their own growth, used personal pronouns to begin sentences.

Daniel had been very interested in the food the babies in *See How I Grow* ate and in Ms F's comment that 'We don't need to have our food all sloppy because we have teeth to chew it with.' Daniel asked for the following comment to be put below his picture: 'This baby is trying to eat, but he hasn't any teeth yet.' The reading from the book, the talk about the pictures and observations of the real baby all contributed to his formulation of the sentence. Perhaps the most interesting thing is how easily the children take on the language of books when contributing the sentences to accompany their pictures. They take on this form of language to serve their purposes, using the grammar of formal written language to clothe their own ideas taken from observation and experience as well as from books. As Margaret Meek observes, 'Book learning is both life-to-text as well as text-to-life' (Meek, 1996: 26).

Another book was made for sheer fun and enjoyment from photographs of the children as babies brought in by the parents. Ms F constructed a keyhole book modelled on the Ahlbergs' *Peepo!* The children enjoyed using this playful and very personal book. The word processor was used to make the print look like a real book.

Conclusion

Reading for information and early non-fiction writing can be an exciting part of the early years programme. It needs its own resources and strategies but must be integrated with the whole learning context. As the case studies show, children move easily from fact to fiction and vice versa and soon make progress in understanding the purposes of particular books and resources. Books and resources enrich learning through play and help increase children's control over language so that they can communicate increasingly complex ideas and messages.

Nursery teams make careful records based on observation of all aspects of children's development including literacy. Informational kinds of reading and writing are one important aspect of literacy. Records based on careful observation of the non-fiction that children seem to enjoy, their understanding that the illustrations and writing link, and their first explorations of informational writing, are helpful in showing teachers how to extend achievements.

Issues to discuss and consider

1   Young children may bring certain gender-based attitudes towards computer technology to nursery school. How can the sensitive nursery team make sure both girls and boys have equal opportunities to explore and extend their computer literacy, particularly in the area of informational reading and writing on the screen?

2   What role does spoken language play in understanding informational kinds of reading and writing at this early stage?

3   What insights about supporting children's very early progress in informational kinds of literacy can inform the practice of teachers working with other age phases?

Further reading

Bruce, T. (1996) *Helping Young Children to Play*. London: Hodder & Stoughton.
Doyle, K. and Mallett, M. (1994) 'Were dinosaurs bigger than whales?' *TACTYC Early Years Journal*, Vol. 14, No. 2.
Hurst, V. and Joseph, J. (1998) *Supporting Early Learning*. Milton Keynes: Open University Press.
Matthews, J. and Jessell, J. (1993) 'Very young children and electronic paint: The beginning of drawing with traditional media and computer paintbox', *TACTYC Early Years Journal*, Vol. 13. No. 2.
Weinberger, J. (1996) *Literacy Goes to School: The Parents' Role in Young Children's Literacy Learning*. London: Paul Chapman.
Whitehead, M. R. (1996) *The Development of Language and Literacy*. London; Hodder & Stoughton.
Whitehead, M. (1999) *Supporting Language and Literacy Development in the Early Years*. Milton Keynes: Open University Press.

Children's books and resources mentioned

Alexander, S. and Lemoine, G. (1986) *Leila*. London: Hamish Hamilton.
Aliki (1987) *Welcome Little Baby*. London: Bodley Head.
Ahlberg, J. and Ahlberg, A. (1981) *Peepo!* London: Penguin.
Ahlberg, J. and Ahlberg, A. (1982) *The Baby's Catalogue*. London: Penguin.
Ahlberg, J. and Ahlberg, A. (1988) *Starting School*. London: Picture Puffin, Penguin.
Baxter, N. (1995) *Babies*. London: Franklin Watts.
Boon, E. (1996) *123 How Many Animals Can You See?* London: Orchard Books.
Browne, A. (1991) *I Like Books*. London: Walker Books.
Bruna, D. (1971) *b is for bear*. London: Methuen.
Bucknall, C. (1985) *One Bear All Alone*. London: Macmillan.
Burningham, J. (1964) *ABC*. London: Jonathan Cape.

Burningham, J. (1974) *The Baby*. London: Jonathan Cape.
Burningham, J. (1982) *Avocado Baby*. London: Jonathan Cape.
Burningham, J. (1989) *Oi! Get Off Our Train*. London: Red Fox Books.
Campbell, R. (1994) *Noisy Farm*. A lift-the-flap book. London: Penguin/Puffin.
Carle, E. (1974) *The Very Hungry Caterpillar*. London: Penguin/Puffin.
Chambers First Dictionary (1995). Ed. Angela Crawley and John Grisewood. London: Chambers/Larousse.
Coiley, J. (1992) *Eyewitness Guides: Trains*. London: Dorling Kindersley.
Collins First World Book (1997). Ed. E. Goldsmith; illus. S. Donnelly. London: HarperCollins.
Cox, S. (1997) *Big Machines on the Farm* and *Big Machines in Town*. London: Puffin/Penguin.
Dahl, T. and Dodds, S (illus.) (1991) *Babies, Babies, Babies*. London: Kingfisher.
Dodds, S. (1998) *My Day; My Night* and *My Seasons*. My World series. London: Franklin Watts.
Dorling Kindersley Children's Picture Encyclopaedia (1997). Ed. Claire Llewellyn. London: Dorling Kindersley.
Felstead, C. (1998) *Creepy Crawlies*. Pop-up surprises; What Am I? series. London: HarperCollins.
Foreman, M. (1989) *Ben's Baby*. London: Beaver Books.
Garland, S. *Going Shopping* (1985); *All Gone!* (1991); *Oh No!* (1991); *Having a Picnic* (1995). London: Penguin/Puffin.
Hughes, S. (1999) *Bathwater's Hot* and *All Shapes and Sizes*. London: Walker Books.
Kingfisher First Dictionary (1995). London and New York: Larousse/Kingfisher/Chambers.
Lacome, J. (1992) *Noisy Noises on the Farm*. London: Walker Books.
Ladybird First Picture Dictionary (1997) London: Ladybird.
Llewellyn, C. (1998) *My Best Book of Creepy Crawlies*. London: Kingfisher.
Manning, M. and Granstrom, B (1998) *How Did I Begin?* London: Franklin Watts.
Medearis, A. (1995) *Eat, Babies, Eat*. London: Walker Books.
Melville, H. (designer), Lily, K. (illus.) (1998) *My Little Book of Animals Board Book*. London: Dorling Kindersley.
Mitchell, S. (ed.) (1998) *Wild Animals*. Touch and Feel series. London: Dorling Kindersley.
My First Dictionary (1993). Ed. B. Root. London: Dorling Kindersley.
My First Oxford Dictionary (1993). Ed. E. Goldsmith. Oxford: Oxford University Press.
My Oxford Picture Word Book (1994). Ed. S. Pemberton, illus. V. Biro. Oxford: Oxford University Press.
Ormerod, J. (1985) *Messy Baby*. London: Penguin/Puffin.
Ormerod, J. (1989) *Eat Up Gemma*. London: Walker Books.
Oxenbury, H. (1992) *ABC of Things* and *Number of Things*. London: Heinemann.
Pienowski, J. (1983) *Numbers*. London: Puffin.
Pragoff, F. (1994) *Baby Days* and *Starting School*. Toddler and Baby series. London: Collins.
Ripley, C. and Ritchie, S. (illus.) (1997) *Why Is Soap So Slippery? and Other Bathtime Questions*. Oxford: Oxford University Press. (Other titles include: *Why Is The Sky Blue? Why Do Stars Twinkle?* and *Do The Doors Work by Magic?*)
Rockwell, A. (1986) *Fire Engines* and *Big Wheels*. London: Hamilton Books.

Royston, A. (1991) *Chick*. See How They Grow series. London: Dorling Kindersley.
Scarry, R. (1995) *Cars and Trucks and Things that Go*. London: Collins.
Shone, V. (1993) *Garage*; *Wheels*; *House* and *Tools*. London: Orchard Books.
Usborne First Dictionary (1995). Ed. R. Wardley and J. Bingham. London: Usborne.
Wallace, K. and Collins, R. (1997) *It Takes Two*. Wonderwise series. London: Franklin Watts.
Wells, T. (1992) *Noisy Noises on the Road*. London: Walker Books.
Wildsmith, B. (1995) *ABC*. Oxford: Oxford University Press.
Wilkes, A. (1994) *See How I Grow: A Photographic Record of a Baby's First Eighteen Months*. London: Dorling Kindersley.
Wood, J. (1998) *Puppy*; *Guinea Pig*; *Rabbit*; *Kitten*. If You Choose Me series. London: Franklin Watts.

Software

EasyPage (1998, Windows 95 version) an easy-to-use, desk-top publishing package for young children. They can be helped to make their own book combining their own text with illustrations (0114 258 2878).

Smudge and Spaniel with clear graphics from Storm Educational Software, is suitable for pre-school and key stage 1 children (0193 581 7699).

Teddy My World Software package. Granada Learning/Semerc (0161 827 2927).

HyperStudio is a multimedia authoring tool which enables teachers and student teachers to create interactive books. TAG (01474 357350).

Star books for the under-fives

Ahlberg, J. and Ahlberg, A. (1982) *The Baby's Catalogue*. London: Penguin/Puffin.
Llewellyn, C. (1998) *My Best Book of Creepy Crawlies*. London: Kingfisher.
Parker, V. and Collins, R. (1998) *Who Are You?*; *In the Polar Lands*; *In the Sea*; *In the Rainforest*; *On the Farm*. Early Worm series. London: Franklin Watts.
Wilkes, A. (1994) *See How I Grow: A Photographic Record of a Baby's First Eighteen Months*. London: Dorling Kindersley.

3 Informational reading and writing at key stage 1 (5–7)

Enjoying and learning about finding out

> Children are born as learners; their longing to *grasp* things, physically and mentally, is almost insatiable, especially in the early years . . . Books make most impact when they add to what experience offers, confirming and extending in various book ways, what children are already aware of.
>
> (Meek, 1996: 98)

Introduction

Good nursery practice and good practice in the early years[1] of statutory schooling are informed by the same principles. Whatever the current legislation in England and Wales, literacy learning and teaching in these years 'must remain part of a distinctive early years tradition' (Whitehead, 1996: 72). Making progress in becoming literate needs to be embedded in a number of ways of making meaning – ways that include music, art, role play and scientific investigations and which require talking and listening as much as reading and writing. By the time formal schooling starts, children have lived in the world a little longer and have experienced more outings and visits. They know more people outside the immediate family and friends are becoming increasingly important as they discover the social aspects of being a growing human being. Increasing control over the spoken and written forms of their mother tongue will have made a considerable impact on cognitive development. For example, they will have made headway in classifying phenomena and in reflecting on all that happens to them.

All this has considerable implications for children's learning about the informational aspects of literacy because it is best grounded in their broader preoccupations and concerns. In a favourable environment children become young researchers seeking answers to their questions. Increasingly they use writing as well as spoken language to explore and communicate their thinking.

There are many books and resources to interest and inform this age group and children deserve the best quality materials we can provide – more about this in the next section. As well as selecting texts directed at this age group, teachers can introduce and paraphrase from materials intended for older children but which answer a need in the children's learning. Different kinds of genre, factual and fictional, can be used flexibly as we see so clearly in case study 3.3, where environmental issues are explored through drama.

Another principle to keep in mind is the continuing importance of communication and co-operation with parents. *The Parent's Charter* (DES, 1991) gives parents new rights as customers in the educational 'market', but the emphasis is so much better placed on partnership. Children's progress across the curriculum, not least their developing literacy, depends partly on parents' knowing about their children's school activities and teachers' knowing about children's experiences at home. Many children attending schools in Britain's cities are young bilinguals whose foothold in two languages and cultures can teach us much about language and learning. Help from parents in translating stories into home languages is well established and, in many schools, this kind of support extends to informational kinds of material.

There need be no incompatibility between these principles and the requirements of the National Curriculum and the National Literacy Strategy *Framework for Teaching*. Nevertheless, early years specialists need to make their voices heard to ensure that what is known about children's development and how it is nourished continues to inform practice. Above all we must keep learning creative and avoid being pressed into a narrow and mechanistic approach to reading and writing. New knowledge is taken into existing meaning structures, as Piaget's powerful model of learning as adaptation shows so well, but it is essentially a dynamic process.[2]

Children are at the centre of their own learning and actively construct meaning in both spoken and written language, as a number of researchers including Marie Clay (1991), Donald Graves (1983), Lucy Calkins (1986), Gordon Wells (1986) and Pam Czerniewska (1992) have shown. Seeking information is not just about acquiring facts: it is also about feeling concern about those facts and becoming able to imagine the possible as well as the actual. It is when intellect, feeling and imagination are engaged that learning becomes enjoyable (Bruner, 1986; Egan, 1988). This is the principle on which the Walker Books' Read and Wonder series is based. How different people feel about spiders, for example, is regarded as part of the truth about them in French and Wisenfield's *Spider Watching*.

Study skills, library skills, retrieval devices and the computer are all tools to serve but not control a lively mind that sees facts and information in new combinations making new meanings. This is why some of the best early years work is structured by children's questions. The children learning about snails in case study 3.1 made the books serve their purposes and were able to see the limitations of the secondary sources they used.

This chapter begins by setting out the range of non-fiction books and resources which have a place in the collection for five to seven year olds. What we offer needs to be of good quality and to keep up with children's wider range of experience both in school and at home. Then we move to strategies to support children's informational reading and writing across the curriculum. Account needs to be taken of the National Curriculum programmes and the literacy hour objectives – there will undoubtedly be changes and new requirements after this book is published. Some things, however, are unchanging: non-fiction will always be best situated in strongly motivating contexts; the teacher's modelling of reading and writing strategies will always be important; and the purpose and audience for writing will be a major consideration. Above all we need to ensure that the four language modes – speaking, listening, reading and writing – work together as interdependent processes.

The chapter ends with some case studies that embody the principles of good practice. In case study 3.1, five year olds integrate their first-hand learning about snails with what they find out in books and are found to be critical readers right from the beginning. In case study 3.2, six year olds in a Hong Kong school are helped to use the computer as one aid to their writing progress alongside other approaches. Finally, in case study 3.3 we follow the progress of seven year olds in writing for real purposes within the context of drama.

Range issues: materials that are 'individual, strong and alive'

Many of the books and resources recommended for the nursery school stage will also be enjoyed in reception classes and beyond, so readers might find it helpful to look through the lists in the previous chapter. Similarly some children will be ready to use and enjoy some of the materials mentioned in Chapter 4 on seven to nine year olds. Our multicultural society needs to be reflected in both fiction and non-fiction resources in the classroom and this will benefit all the children. A good classroom collection will include information books about food, customs, history and religions across the world.

Chapter 1 suggested some general criteria for choosing information books and resources. It is generally agreed that we look for a clear format with helpful retrieval devices, accuracy, and lucid and interesting text which links well with illustrations and the absence of unwelcome bias and stereotyping. Margery Fisher's desire to find books that are 'individual, strong and alive' is a good starting-point for choosing materials for five to seven year olds (Fisher, 1972: 25). Information books have a shorter life than stories and need regular updating. However, some favourite writers are emerging. Claire Llewellyn's science and mathematics books hit just the right note for this age group. So do Michael Chinery's nature books, sadly out of print at present. Books with a touch of humour are liked, and those books that touch on some of life's rawer and more uncomfortable aspects; the bland and cosy rarely appeal. Teachers know best what the children in their classes will respond to and learn from, but it is hoped that the books and materials recommended in this section will be a helpful reference point.

Picture books and early information books

Picture books with a realistic flavour are still important for this age group and children continue to enjoy those illustrated with photographs like the Dorling Kindersley See How They Grow series and those about children engaged in everyday activities by writers and illustrators of the quality of the Ahlbergs, Shirley Hughes and Sarah Garland.

Gradually the writing becomes greater in amount and more challenging in terms of vocabulary and syntax. Often different kinds of writing are included in the same text. In Martina Selway's *What Can I Write? Rosie Writes Again*, children are shown, in an amusing way, that their everyday experiences are worth writing about. We hear about the people and things in Rosie's life through her first-person writing for the teacher and direct speech brings in voices other than Rosie's. These books flow easily from fact to fiction; Baker and Freebody (1989) would view them as 'transitional genres'. Many of them could be described as 'recounts': a description used in the *Framework for Teaching* and, not surprisingly, mentioned as a kind of reading and writing important at key stage 1. Reading or listening to accounts about everyday experiences leads naturally to children's anecdotes and then to their writing about a sequence of events.

Two new geography alphabet books meet one of the objectives in *The Framework for Teaching* for Year 2, Term 2 – learning about alphabetic formats. Ifeoma Onyefulu's *A is for Africa* and Kathryn Cave's *W is for World* introduce interesting vocabulary and ideas in the strong context of the photographic alphabet. Both books explain about our shared world in a warm and sympathetic way, and children would enjoy browsing through them and talking about the photographs.

Early information books often retain a familiar narrative organization, particularly in the natural time sequence in a journey or the life-cycle of a creature. The authors and illustrators of Walker Books' Read and Wonder series bring a human dimension to non-fiction which often strikes a chord with young readers. How people feel about a range of phenomena – spiders, pigs, the only partially known life-cycle of the eel, and personal memories of apple trees through the seasons – all feature. Great care is taken over the illustrations – for example, the wonderful transparency of the elvers is shown in Karen Wallace's *Think of an Eel*. The use of imagery to make the verbal visual is a feature of all the books: in Davies and Maland's *Big Blue Whale*, for example, we learn the whale's skin is 'smooth like a boiled egg, and as slippery as wet soap'. These are not conventional information books, although they do have some of the features associated with them – the index and often carefully labelled diagrams – for example in French and Wisenfield's *Spider Watching*.

The questions we need to ask about these and other less conventional information books include the following: Do they, through both verbal and visual means, share some careful observations? Do they excite curiosity? Is

Ss

is for Sunrise, time to yawn,
and stretch, and get moving.

In India, some people are
on their way to work when
the sun comes up. Early
morning is the coolest time
of day in a hot country.
These women and children
are off to pick jasmine:
when the sun is high,
the fields will be too hot.

Figure 3.1 'S is for Sunrise' from Kathryn Cave's *W is for World* (1998). This exceptionally fine alphabet book shows the environments and people of more than twenty countries using beautiful photographs and clear text.

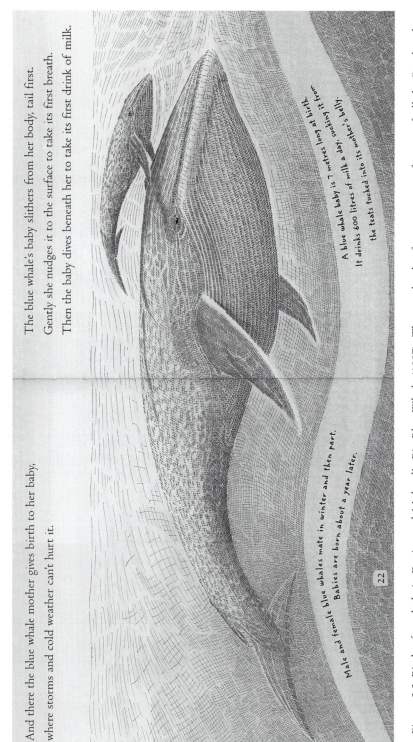

And there the blue whale mother gives birth to her baby, where storms and cold weather can't hurt it.

The blue whale's baby slithers from her body, tail first.
Gently she nudges it to the surface to take its first breath.
Then the baby dives beneath her to take its first drink of milk.

Male and female blue whales mate in winter and then part. Babies are born about a year later.

A blue whale baby is 7 metres long at birth. It drinks 600 litres of milk a day, sucking it from the teats tucked into its mother's belly.

22

Figure 3.2 Birth of a whale in Davies and Maland's *Big Blue Whale* (1997). The two levels of text, a strong feature of all the Read and Wonder series, work particularly well here. The large text tells the story of the whale's birth in poetic language, while the small text provides the sort of precise facts about the baby's size and diet which children often ask about.

the heart as well as the head engaged? Kingfisher's 'Animal Lives' series scores well. Before leaving chronological kinds of non-fiction writing, mention should be made of procedural accounts of simple science experiments, menus and instructions. There are a number of good cookbooks on the market including the Dorling Kindersley series and the Longman series of books about food, including Jane Asher's *Round the World Cookbook* which includes step-by-step instructions for dishes from China, Uganda, the Middle East and the Caribbean. Experience of this kind of procedural text helps with the text level work for Year 2, Term 1.

Non-narrative texts

Non-narrative or non-chronological books are what most people understand by the term 'children's information book'. These are often colourful, elaborately illustrated books on one topic like 'Mini-beasts', 'Rivers' or 'The Vikings'. Information is presented hierarchically rather than in story form and there is often a technical language to introduce new concepts. In an interesting research study Christine Pappas read a large number of information books and arrived at some features that she considered to be 'obligatory elements' of the genre. Teachers would recognize these in many of the information books in the classroom and library. The first element, *topic presentation*, introduces the subject matter, whether it be butterflies, ships or volcanoes. The second attribute, *the representation of attributes*, describes the different parts of the subject. The third element is *characteristic events* and, in the case of a plant or animal, this aspect of the book would describe the main events in the life-cycle.

Pappas believes that the clearer these elements of a book are, the more easily will a young reader understand it (Pappas, 1986). Objectives in the National Literacy Strategy for the final term in Year 2 include the need to help children become familiar with the format of information books, with their subheadings and retrieval devices. In the past information books have sometimes been criticised for their inaccuracy, for featuring banal language that failed to integrate well with illustrations, and on social grounds for not reflecting the full range of families from which children come. Publishers have taken note and there are now many worthwhile and attractive information books and multimedia packs. Some classics are emerging and there are some gifted writers of children's information books. Nevertheless they have limited print runs and need constant updating – sometimes publishers prefer to commission another book on a topic rather than update an existing one. This makes it more helpful to offer some criteria for choosing books rather than just listing good examples which may soon be out of print.

If you were to press me, I like *Dinosaur* by Hooper and Kitchen for reception and Year 1 mainly because it has a simple, clear text perfectly integrated with wonderful illustrations (also in big book form). This book, like others for the five to seven age range, introduces children to the conventions of informational writing one step at a time.

Two information picture books by Mick Manning and Brita Granström have a light touch with the text and again introduce gradually the features of mature exposition. *Wild and Free,* structured round questions, brings home the plight of endangered species like tigers and whales with inviting illustrations. *Out There Somewhere It's Time To* adopts an imaginative approach to time differences across the world, creating contrasts in the different environments which include Guilin (China), New York, Moscow and Newcastle upon Tyne. Both books have two levels of text: the main text is bold and conversational while the smaller print is more like conventional information book writing.

Some publishers specialise in non-fiction or at least include it in their titles, for example Dorling Kindersley, Usborne, Wayland, Collins Educational, Ladybird, Franklin Watts, Belitha Press, Frances Lincoln, Longman, A. & C. Black and Kingfisher. Most reading schemes include non-fiction titles with suggested reading levels, for example Oxford Reading Tree, Cambridge Reading, Longman Group Project, Ginn Science Story Chest, Heinemann Sunshine Books, Wonder World, Evans Rainbows and Nelson's Voyages (see below under 'reading schemes' for more information). There are several good journals which review current titles including *Books for Keeps, The School Librarian, Primary Science Review, Language Matters, Signal, Child Education, Junior Education, English 4–11* and *The Times Educational Supplement.* Keeping an eye out for these disinterested opinions will help teachers make appropriate choices from a mass of publishers' publicity material.

Reference materials

Five to seven year olds continue to enjoy and value the dictionaries and encyclopaedias recommended for the nursery collection for example, *My First Oxford Dictionary* and the *Dorling Kindersley Children's Picture Encyclopedia.* I would also place here the best of the many books on language – not the terrifying work books that seem to be returning to book shops but the entertaining ones like Shirley Hughes's *Make Hay While the Sun Shines: A Book of Proverbs,* Jan Pienkowski's *1001 Words* (under sections like 'Home', 'Farm' and 'Fun'), Patricia Macarthay's beautifully illustrated *Herds of Words,* Black's Buzzwords Series (Karen Bryant Mole's *Is It Shiny?* and *Does It Bounce?*) and Sunshine Books' *Word Books.*

Younger children at key stage 1 will still enjoy the alphabet books mentioned in the book list at the end of the previous chapter. *Letterland ABC,* by Carlisle and Wendan, has detailed annotations and illustrations that are likely to inspire discussion. Many reception teachers and children also like the *First Alphabetic Frieze* by the same authors. Ladybird and Kingfisher books have large collections of early dictionaries and word books.

Children also enjoy using the increasing number of dictionaries, thesauruses and encyclopaedias on CD-ROMs. In a swiftly changing world, reference material in book and software form needs regular updating. Collins, Kingfisher, Oxford University Press, Usborne and Dorling Kindersley are amongst those publishers producing good reference material. The same criteria that we use for information books apply. Before making an expensive purchase I would check that items I knew the children would be using right across the curriculum were included; that diagrams were clear, bright and well labelled; and that the language was inviting and new vocabulary well contextualised. I would also ask myself if the book or software item would be inviting for browsing. Two lively examples are *The Oxford Children's Encyclopedia*, in eight categories, beginning with 'My Body' and ending with 'The Universe', and *The Usborne Animated Children's Encyclopedia* which features clear, simple text, a wealth of coloured drawings and an accompanying CD-ROM. Some children will be ready to enjoy *DK Children's Illustrated Encyclopedia* with the teacher's help.

Wayland's *Big Book of Mapwork 1* begins with fairytale journeys and mazes and continues with simple map-making (the children's streets). Then the topics of aerial photographs, following a route, compass directions, using a grid, and understanding signs and symbols are all clearly explained and accompanied by suggestions for children's work. This book is an excellent model for using a contents and index page, a glossary and bibliography. Other good books about maps for this age range include Wayland's *First Picture Atlas*; A. & C. Black's *Going Places: Finding the Way* by B. Taylor and Richardson-Jones, and *Roundabouts: Maps and Journeys* by Kate Petty; Usborne's *How to Draw Maps and Charts* by Pam Beasant and Alastair Smith; Longman's *Keystart First Atlas*; Scholastic's *Sticky Maps* by Nick Arnold and Jan Lewis; and Franklin Watts' *Step-by-Step: Maps and Globes* by Sarah Crewe.

There are some books that do not lend themselves to easy classification, and yet they are often the very books that invite young readers in through an original approach and unusual illustrations. *Aunty Dot's Incredible Adventure Atlas*, written and illustrated by Eljay Yildirim, uses letters to involve children in a journey round the world. But there are good, clear maps of countries in each continent together with photographs and pictures of items and phenomena that give a glimpse into the different cultures. One of my students used this book for a range of imaginative activities with her Year 2 class, including letter-writing. The book crosses the fact/fiction boundaries but the children did not seem to find this a problem.

Big books

Big books have been with us for a long time and teachers have used them to model reading strategies as well as to provide an enjoyable shared experience for the children. Until recently big books tended to offer stories, songs and nursery rhymes. More recently, publishers have brought out non-fiction big books and some of these are of good quality. For use in the literacy hour a big book must be able to sustain children's interest over several days and offer a shared text that reveals relevant aspects of literacy. In addition to meeting the usual criteria for good information books – clear, inviting language; good match between illustrations and texts; and so on – the most obvious requirement is that the print be large, clear and sufficiently well spaced to be seen from a distance. Illustrations need to be sharp and inviting with just the right amount of detail. Very subtle colours may be too indistinct for whole-class use so good information books of standard size do not necessarily make good big books. A. & C. Black's Stopwatch series – very well-liked science books for key stage 1 – has adapted well to big book format and makes particularly good use of photographs in showing animal life-cycles.

A touch of humour is appealing to both teacher and children. *Splish, Splash, Splosh* (about the water cycle) and *What's Under the Bed?* (about the structure and content of the earth's layers) both by Manning and Granstrom are set, in my view, to become much loved, big book classics.

Pelican Big Books from Longman are designed partly to teach progressively about retrieval devices – subheadings, glossaries and indexes – and partly for sheer enjoyment. Sallie Purkis's *Looking at Teddy Bears* and Witherington and Neate's *What Babies Used to Wear* are intended for younger key stage 1 children while Coltman and Sparks-Linfield's *The Human Body* and Johnson's *You Can Make Your Own Book!* would be of interest for the younger end of key stage 2. Progression is also built into Cambridge Reading's Big Books Literacy Packs, but their books for reception and Year 1 do not overwhelm with too many information book conventions all at once. *Dinosaur* is an information story about one particular species – the Maiasaur – from egg to adult but with information boxes to introduce non-narrative text.

Non-fiction wordless big books allow children to write down information alongside illustrations. SRA McGraw-Hill's series Stick-on Story Books: Wordless Books to Read includes non-fiction and allows teacher and children to write a text and then remove the sticky paper so that a new piece of writing can be done (see Rowe and Routh [1997] and Mallett [1998] for more about choosing and using big books).

Non-fiction in reading schemes

Non-fiction is invariably part of the newer reading schemes and programmes pouring out of the publishing houses. They have heeded past criticism and the quality of books has improved considerably. New literacy initiatives stimulate the children's books market and the number of collections offered to schools as the full answer to the literacy hour from reception to Year 6 can be overwhelming. It is best not to get locked into one publisher's system. One reason is that, however good, there are bound to be some titles that are stronger than others. Teachers are professionals and can formulate with colleagues their own lists of criteria for the books they purchase for each year group. We risk our status as reflective practitioners if we let others tell us what to think and buy.

Discovery World, which is the non-fiction element in Heinemann's programme (the other two are *Storyworlds* and *Rhyme World*), contains six packs of seven pupils' books (readability 4–7), two big books and a teacher's *Skills and Assessment Guide*. The topics of the non-fiction books link well with the National Curriculum and the books represent an appropriate range of genres. The Non-Fiction packs in Nelson's PM Library, which are in seven levels, have been praised by reviewers (for example by Cliff Moon in *Child Education*, July 1998).

The Oxford University Press were one of the first to bring non-fiction into the initial teaching of reading together with Longman (The Book Project) and Cambridge Reading.

Software

New software to support reading to learn is produced constantly. Many good information books and reference books are now available in CD-ROM form – for example the Dorling Kindersley encyclopedias. The same general criteria for choosing CD-ROM apply as those for books – accuracy, appropriate language, whether written or spoken, good linkage between illustrations and language, material to nourish children's need to know. Being on CD-ROM does not add to any work's intrinsic merit but it has an added dimension as highly visual and interactive material. While, as Chris Abbott (1993) points out, a book dictionary is organised in one structure – alphabetical order – an electronic dictionary is a database which can be displayed in many to meet the requirements of the reader.

Computers also make possible the storage of great numbers of still pictures, sounds and video sequences as well as written text. An example of this flexibility is found in *Through My Window*, from Anglia Multimedia, supplied as a triple unit CD-ROM. The narrator invites the children to explore aspects of nature in her garden through the seasons. Spoken information can be activated by clicking on particular objects, and key words in the explanation are written and illustrated on the screen. Clicking on the storm icon produces information on thunderstorms, hurricanes and snowstorms with sound effects. The language is appropriate and the illustrations are clear. Increasingly teachers are combining the use of software with other class work. *Through My Window* offers considerable flexibility; it can structure most of the classroom work for a few weeks or it can be used on a season-to-season basis to help children understand the changes around them as it is divided into four parts each corresponding to a season. With help, the children could use it as a factual reference source.

Sherston's *Look! Hear! Talking Topics* offers six reference topics – 'Body', 'Dinosaurs', 'Homes', 'Land Transport', 'Pets' and 'Seashore'. Dorling Kindersley's *My First Incredible, Amazing Dictionary* has 1,000 words and sound and animations to reinforce alphabet and dictionary skills. TAG's *Picture Dictionary* helps children match text to pictures and can be used with any word processor.

As is always the case with large software packages, the teacher needs to help the children use it for clear and constructive purposes. Browsing is enjoyable sometimes, but as part of organised class work the children will need clear instructions about how to use the resource. For successful integration the teacher needs to spend time on becoming familiar with how the software operates and what it contains.

There are commercial programs providing series of linked words and illustrations on topics like animals and household objects, and often these are in a range of different languages (Hounslow Language Support Service 0181 570 4186). There is much of help and interest in Sue Walker *et al.*'s (1998) book *Write Round the World* about reading materials in other languages as well as English. The new word-processing programs, for example LETSS' *Allwrite*, in a range of scripts and languages, are a valuable resource for children and parents whose first languages are not English.

Software to help the writing process include Aztec's *EasyWorks*; TAG's *Expressions* which is an outliner tool for drafting; *HyperStudio*, also from TAG, which features a friendly animated dog which gives help in using this

Figure 3.3 Dorling Kindersley's *My First Incredible Amazing Dictionary* (1994). The 1,000 word multimedia dictionary is easy to use and includes games and puzzles to reinforce dictionary skills in an entertaining way.

Figure 3.4 Multimedia resource made by student teachers.

multimedia authoring tool; and *Kid Works 2*, which has a talking dictionary. Novell WordPerfect's *Write with Me* allows children to create their own signs, books and cards and has a talking text feature.

No account of resources is now complete without mentioning faxes, e-mail and sites on the World Wide Web – all of which have considerable relevance to the provision and communication of information globally. Christine Preston of Project Miranda at the Institute of Education has produced a regularly updated resource called *21st Century A–Z Literacy Handbook: Linking Literacy with Software* which can be ordered by telephoning 0181 686 8769.

Illustrations

We have to ask what purpose a diagram serves and how successful it is. If it is intended to show the structure of an object or creature, we should ask: is it clear and well labelled? If we also need to understand the function of a machine or animal or human organ this needs to come across. (One of the NLP objectives for text level work in Year 2, Term 2, is to introduce children to process diagrams.) Of course multimedia technology has contributed considerably to our ability to show processes and things happening simultaneously.

In French and Wisenfield's *Spider Watching* just the right amount of detail is given for a first look at cross-sections of creatures. Having said that, five to seven year olds often reach a stage in a project where they want more detail than is offered in the diagrams for their age group. After enjoying *Spider Watching* and Parsons and Young's *Amazing Spiders*, a class of six year olds needed something more detailed to answer their questions. With help from the teacher, they managed to learn much from a cross section of a spider in a book intended for much older children – Ted Dewar's *Inside the Whale and Other Animals* (Mallett, 1997). One of the annotations described the spinnerets as like 'tiny rubber gloves' and the children found this image helped them link the verbal and the visual. The quality of photographs and drawings is important; the best ones encourage a lively spoken and written response. The six year olds mentioned responded with a flurry of questions to a photograph of a huge cluster of golden and black baby garden spiders suspended from some privet leaves in Chinery's *The Spider*. These questions are often the bridge between the illustrations and the text and the starting-point for learning (Mallett, 1997).

Illustration can be the bridge between fact and fiction (Graham, 1996). Year 1 children learning about spiders were pleased to notice a little drawing of Miss Muffett on the edges of a page dominated by a picture of a huge garden spider in *Amazing Spiders*. Nathan found the classroom copy of Nursery Rhymes and all the children joined in the verse about Miss Muffett and the Spider. The teacher, Emma Richardson, noted that the children had no problem with moving from folklore back to science.

Children enjoy making their own pictures and diagrams. There is a strong case for drawing your own maps of the classroom, of the journey to school and so on before working with maps in books and on the screen.

Strategies to support children's reading and writing across the curriculum

Experienced teachers know that the classroom environment has to be well equipped and stimulating to encourage a positive attitude to all kinds of reading and writing. The range of non-fiction books of good quality available for five to seven year olds has been considered. This section looks first at how we can involve young children with the organisation of books. It then moves on to ways of supporting first reading non-fiction and then writing non-fiction. Although these processes are complementary, reading and writing need some separate discussion to cover all the necessary points. The section ends with suggestions for supporting young bilingual readers and writers of non-fiction.

Involving children with the organisation of resources

Children enjoy taking an active part in helping to arrange and set out the classroom books and resources, often in a special book corner (Graham and Kelly, 1997). Literacy role play can help young children learn a great deal about the conventions of organizing books. This sort of strategy is clearly described by Marian Whitehead; she suggests that children talk about how to arrange their classroom collection and include books made by members of the class. Visits to local libraries can help to show how librarians display books, and so furnish ideas for organisation under authors, or themes.

The role play can be extended to making borrowers' tickets and finding ways of issuing tickets and keeping a record of who has borrowed what. The skills and abilities developed in this kind of context include 'understanding of alphabetical order, reading and writing for practical purposes, the classification and retrieval of information and the nature of "subjects" and knowledge categories' (Whitehead, 1997: 176).

The writing corner or area is often an extension of the reading corner. It is discussed under 'Strategies for Writing'.

Supporting reading for information

A mix of strategies to help children enjoy and become familiar with the kinds of non-fiction reading is set out in Chapter 1. These will now be considered in relation to the five to seven year olds who are the subject of this chapter, but of course teachers choose a particular emphasis for particular lessons or series of lessons and it is not suggested that everything here will always be included or emphasised.

Organising prior experience

Whenever we begin a new topic it is helpful to think first about what we already know. Teachers usually talk over children's prior experience of the subject of new learning. This helps the children prime their existing knowledge ready for the new facts and ideas. It also indicates to the teacher where the children are in their conceptual understanding and contributes to the planning and resourcing of the work. Sometimes a brief discussion is all that is needed, but often it is helpful for teacher and children to set down some main points on a board or flipchart.

Starting from the specific

It can be best to begin with a specific example of what we are going to be teaching. For example, the student and teacher who planned and carried out the work for case study 3.3 on the Giant eased into environmental issues by looking with the children at an example of a community deprived of their mountain. A project on mini-beasts might well begin by looking at the life-cycle of one creature, perhaps shown on a video-film.

Children's questions

Sometimes these energise the beginning of a project and are a bridge between talking about what the children already know and seeking information from books. Often a specific example, as explained above, will awaken a genuine need to know. In two of the case studies at the end of this book the children's questions became important when the work was underway. The children studying mini-beasts made the vivarium and then wanted to know what snails eat and how to care for them. Observation of the creatures led to questions about what their shells are made of. In the 'Giant' case study 3.3 it is when the children have real concern invested in the topic – the result of lively drama and discussion work – that they want to find out about the harm careless throwing of rubbish can do to the countryside and particularly to animals.

Modelling of different kinds of non-fiction reading

When the children are ready to use the books and resources the teacher demonstrates how to use non-fiction. This is now built into the objectives of the literacy strategy and the literacy hour. It is not difficult to see how work with resources across the curriculum can give point to the modelling of reading strategies in the literacy hour, and how in turn what has been taught in the literacy hour can inform children's research in other lessons.

At key stage 1 children encounter a range of non-fiction with different purposes, for example: labels, signs, lists, instructions, reference materials like dictionaries and encyclopaedias, information books and software. The following list includes some of the main features of information books and resources that the good practitioner will teach children. The items link with the reading comprehension sections of *The Framework for Teaching* for five to seven year olds.

- There are different kinds of non-fiction text with different purposes, e.g. labels, lists, instructions, reference materials like dictionaries and encyclopaedias and information books and software programs on the computer.
- Looking at informational materials helps children to use the terms 'fiction' and 'non-fiction' appropriately.
- A non-fiction book does not need to be read in its entirety. Retrieval devices like the contents page and index can help find the required part of the text. Children can be helped to locate information by page numbers and words by the initial letter.
- Looking at the front, back, title page and at the format of headings and subheadings helps children predict what kind of genre and therefore what purpose a book has.
- Learning to use the index helps children to deal with the organisation of other alphabetically ordered reference material like dictionaries.

- Books on similar themes can provide different information organized differently.
- Some non-fiction has a time sequence – recounts, procedural pieces (science experiments, menus) and life-cycles of creatures. Words like 'then', 'next' and 'after' help us understand the generic structure of reading material and help us to follow written instructions about how to use the computer or other classroom equipment.
- Diagrams (including flow charts), pictures and photographs impart information as well as text. Children need help with the interpretation of processes shown in diagrammatic form (e.g. the Water Cycle).
- Teachers can model in context, scanning a text to find the name of a city or a date in history or skimming to get the gist of a few paragraphs.

Something needs to be said about the new kinds of literacy made possible by the computer. The user of CD-ROM can control the way the information is imparted much more than if a book is being read. Pictures, video extracts and sounds can all be stored and retrieved as well as written text. Developing Tray has made possible the reconstruction of texts; individuals or groups of children can make powerful predictions based on their knowledge about language in bringing a text to the screen from a given outline of symbols. There is more on the uses of computers in the sections on 'Writing non-fiction'.

Many teachers ask children to evaluate the books and software they have been using for a project or series of lessons. One of the objectives of the NLS *Framework for Teaching* is 'to evaluate the usefulness of a text for its purpose' (Year 2, Term 3). It is never too soon to be a critical reader. Some of the features set out above could be arranged as questions to aid the evaluation, for example: How useful was the contents page/index? Were the new words carefully explained?

While the reading comprehension sections of the *Framework for Teaching* list important features of books that children need to be taught, we must not lose sight of the fact that books and computers are tools to serve the purposes of the young readers and writers. We must encourage the excitement a young researcher should feel during the finding out process.

Collaboration: co-operating and sharing

At every stage learning is energised by collaboration: between a child and the small group he or she may be in or as a member of a class; between teacher and individual child, group or class. Much of the modelling of informational kinds of reading can be achieved in these collaborative contexts.

While talking about fiction is well established, reading out loud from and discussing informational kinds of material has had slower recognition as good practice. But what better way is there of making children aware of the distinctive pattern of a non-fiction text, the language rhythms and the authorial 'voice'?

Talk also keeps in mind those bigger purposes which extend beyond the classroom into the world outside and which give informational kinds of material their meaning and importance. Without these purposes and interests we risk having what Margaret Meek calls 'the world in bits' (Meek, 1996: 14). We may have acquired all sorts of strategies and procedures to access facts but have sacrificed the feelings of wonder and curiosity which give it point. The most productive kinds of talk feeds into further reading and into writing. Indeed, it establishes both purposes for writing and a sense of a community of readers and writers who will provide a meaningful audience for each other's spoken and written ideas.

Supporting children's non-fiction writing

Reading and writing are complementary, mutually enriching activities. However there are some particular points to be made about writing at this stage.

The writing corner

The need for a place – perhaps a corner of the classroom – starts in the nursery (as the previous chapter made clear) and extends to the primary years. The emphasis changes as children journey through the school years. At key stage 1 children appreciate an inviting wall display which might include photographs of themselves writing by hand and at the computer, examples of their best work, and some posters reminding them of writing routines. A similar range of writing tools to those recommended for the nursery stage – pens, crayons, pencils, writing brushes – are needed, with the addition perhaps of biros, felt tips and calligraphy pens. Paper and card of different sizes, shapes and textures continue to be important and some envelopes and ready-made sewn books of different shapes and sizes are useful. Children also like to have to hand useful items like sellotape, staplers, rulers, rubbers and glue. Word books, dictionaries and thesauruses are helpful, and of course a word processor and printer.

Stages in the writing process

First the young writer chooses a topic or is given one by the teacher. The task is greatly facilitated if the purpose and audience for the writing are made clear. While stories and personal accounts often gain momentum as the writer gets underway, informational writing, particularly a sustained piece, often benefits from a plan. This is where 'conferencing' – explored in detail by Donald Graves (1983) – the talk about writing between teacher and child, can help. Another way of scaffolding children's work at this stage is by providing a writing frame (Lewis and Wray, 1996). This offers a guiding framework of headings. Care has to be taken that this approach does not jeopardise a young writer's spontaneity and ability to structure their own work.

The next stage involves composing the writing, whether it is achieved by an individual child or a group – perhaps round the computer. When a draft is written, the advice of the teacher or peers may be sought about possible improvements (see Browne [1996] and Redfern and Edwards [1997] for helpful advice about encouraging children to look critically both at the organization of their writing and at grammatical points and choice of vocabulary). Once the piece has been redrafted, proof-reading can ensure that surface features like spelling, punctuation and handwriting are improved. Finally, the completed writing is ready to place in a folder, to be 'published' in a book or booklet or put on the wall for display.

Kinds of non-fiction writing

The NLS *Framework for Teaching* (DfEE, 1998) details the non-fiction writing objectives for each term of each year group for children at key stage 1. The list is what we might expect and includes in Year 1 writing captions, lists, labels for the classroom displays and for drawings, recounts, non-fiction book-making (including making dictionaries) and writing questions to take to book research. Some of these writing activities are returned to in Year 2, and this spiral curriculum approach (taking up the same aspect of learning or activity at different levels in the journey through school) is to be welcomed. Main non-fiction writing in Year 2 includes: fact files; writing instructions in impersonal language; making flow charts and other diagrams with labels; making simple notes from texts; writing non-chronological accounts with subheadings as appropriate. This is useful as required checklist but it is the teacher who is able to realise it all in an imaginative and worthwhile way.

At key stage 1 a lot of children's informational writing is not book mediated and there is much to be gained from becoming confident in writing from first-hand experience. Recounts of experience in and out of the classroom, procedural pieces on science experiments and cooking are structured chronologically. The first kinds of non-chronological writing include messages, labels and lists as mentioned in the *Framework for Teaching* (see Myra Barrs' account 'Mapping the World' [Barrs, 1987], which considers how children first begin to organise their world through writing). A very good context for using secondary sources comes about when book information can extend what has been observed first-hand (as in the 'Snail' case study, 3.1), or where it is used, with the teacher's help, to answer questions that have become important to the children (as for example those on environmental issues in the 'Giant' case study, 3.3).

Writing down the answers to the questions in note form, and then writing short non-narrative accounts helps children find satisfaction in composing.

It is important that children enjoy their writing. This account continues by considering some of the contexts for writing which are likely to motivate young learners – non-fiction writing in role, shared non-fiction writing and making non-fiction books. But first there is a discussion of the impact the word processor has made on writing in school.

Writing with a word processor

It is argued in the case study on introducing young children to computers that handwriting has not been replaced by typing – children can develop their writing in both media. However, computer technology has and is making a considerable contribution to supporting children's writing development.

Very young children, and older children whose motor skills have been slower to develop, thus making handwriting laborious, can develop confidence in their ability to compose using the word processor once they have acquired some keyboard skills. It is extremely satisfying for them to see the text created on the screen. There can be a much more constructive approach to making amendments both to content and to secretarial aspects, and of course several copies of a piece of writing can be made. Use can be made of easily accessed computer dictionaries and thesauruses.

Concept keyboard, now well established in primary schools, is of great help to young learners. The touch-sensitive surface enables the child to bring whole words and illustrations on to the screen. The words for a writing task can be provided by the teacher on the overlay and programs can also be purchased.

Desk-top publishing has made it possible for children to produce a range of professional-looking publications including leaflets, posters and their own books (see Walker [1993] for practical help in designing a range of materials).

There is more about writing with a word processor in the case study. Of course, all the suggestions for writing in the sections that follow can be realised using the computer if teacher and children wish. Three things are worth emphasizing.

1   Children need a clear purpose and a strong focus for their work on the computer (Jessel, 1997).
2   While there is a place for individual work, children's thinking and composing can be energized by talk with the teacher or other pupils. The potential of collaborative work has been vastly extended by the arrival of networked computers and the National Grid for Learning, which allow children to work on school-based projects and inter-school enterprises. Electronic messages can be sent across the world by children at the increasing number of schools who have an e-mail address, and the World Wide Web ensures a global audience for a school web site.

3   The computer's potential in children's learning can only be fully realized if it is regarded as essentially a tool, albeit a very powerful one, to encourage and awaken reflection. This means that the kind of intervention the teacher makes and his or her response to children's progress is of paramount importance.

Writing in role

The reading and writing activities arising out of the home corner in different guises – fire station, cafe, baby clinic, shop, travel agents and so on – are very often informational. They include labels, lists, menus, recipes, notes, work rotas, maps, routes, cards, tickets, posters, letters and prescriptions.

The teacher can sometimes write in role to the amusement and delight of the children. In a reception class known to me and my student group there is a bear called William who likes to go home with a different member of the class each weekend and school holiday. He has a small case with his overnight things packed ready. The children have to write him a letter formally inviting him to their home and explaining what he will be doing during the weekend or holiday. He often returns with a letter or diary about what he has been up to, which is read out to the class. There is a list of what he likes to eat and what he is less keen on. He has acquired a passport, a cheque book and a library card.

One of the most inspirational examples of how a teacher, Ms Pat Glen, created a rich and exciting writing context for her six year olds in Scotland is set out in detail in *Mr Togs the Tailor* (1987) published by the Scottish Consultative Council on the Curriculum. Mr Togs was a life-size doll in charge of the classroom shop. The children used their imaginative and creative abilities to create a life history for Mr Togs, who had birthdays, illnesses and setbacks in his business including a burglary. The work came to an end when the term finished with Mr Tog's retirement to the country. The present book has stressed the importance of children understanding writing and reading as having essentially social purposes. The Mr Togs project gave rise to a considerable amount of meaningful informational writing, including notices, labels, price tags, receipts, letters to customers, family tree of the Togs family, plan of the Togs' home, burglar alarm instructions (after the break in!), notice for the estate agent's for selling the shop.

For detailed suggestions for writing in role see Brian Woolland's book (1993) *The Teaching of Drama in the Primary School*.

Interactive kinds of writing

There are a number of ways in which writing can be made interactive. Many classrooms now have message boards on which children and parents can leave notes. Some role play situations can involve interactive writing, as in the William example which involved children, parents and the teacher.

Children's early news writing can be made interactive by bringing in a dialogue approach. The teacher can respond in writing to the children's anecdotes. This is one way of scaffolding children's work (see Mallett, 1997). There are good suggestions in *Keeping in Touch* by Nigel Hall and Anne Robinson (1994) and in *Practical Ways to Inspire Young Authors* by Angela Redfern and Viv Edwards (1997). The role of the teacher as interested audience to what children say and what they write cannot be overestimated. At every stage of the writing process, talking through developing ideas with an interested adult keeps up confidence and motivation. This is particularly evident in the vignette about Owen and his hen book set out below.

Shared non-fiction writing

Shared writing need not always be a story. Children can enjoy writing a joint news item, recipe, recount of an outing or activity, a description of a plant or creature, or a labelled diagram in the security of a class activity. Of course, teachers and children benefited from shared writing using OHP, screen, flipchart or board to set out their ideas before the advent of the National Literacy Project. However, many of the objectives in *The Framework for Teaching* can be achieved as the teacher scribes and models different kinds of writing, including explanation, procedure and discussion. Composing together, discussing what to write and then proof-reading helps children understand the writing process. There can be helpful talk about vocabulary and grammar as well as spelling and punctuation.

Non-fiction book-making

Making books continues to be an enjoyable way of learning about writing and reading at key stage 1. Where the context is shared, spoken language between child and child and between teacher and child makes explicit the choices a writer makes about organisation of the text, use of illustrations and book-making techniques. Paul Johnson's (1998) *You Can Make Your Own Book!* (Longman Big Books) provides step-by-step advice about making concertina books, origami books, books with pop-ups and enclosures and wallet books. Other useful advice is set out in Barry Wade's (1990) *Reading for Real* (see particularly the chapter on 'Information Books' by V. Cherrington), Smith's (1994) *Through Writing to Reading: Classroom Strategies to Support Literacy* and Redfern and Edward's (1997) *Practical Ways to Inspire Young Authors*. At first the teacher or other adult will act as scribe and often the child will help to produce a word-processed version. All four language processes are brought together in book-making; child and supporting adult discuss each decision and the writing is constantly reviewed by being read back to one another. Book-making highlights the content of what is being composed and draws attention to the options open to the author. It also brings into conscious focus the nature and conventions of written language. The actual words and sentences used can be considered as the work is reviewed and proof-read.

One of the most powerful accounts of a child's progress as a result of a book-making opportunity is Angela Redfern's about six year old Owen writing about his hens. Redfern notes that Owen's teacher was concerned about his lack of enthusiasm for writing. But when asked about his chickens: 'it was like switching on a light bulb. Once he got started, it became clear that Owen knew everything there is to know about keeping chickens and as he gathered momentum he positively glowed.' There was no good book about hens in the school library so Redfern acted as scribe as Owen planned the global structure of a book with sections on kinds of chickens, food, laying eggs and so on. Redfern and Owen reviewed each chapter and corrected spelling errors. They decided to have a word-processed version of the book and this involved decisions about fonts and the organisation of the text and illustrations.

CHAPTER TWO

The hens live in a big hutch and they have a perch inside.

They have four nesting boxes.

You have to put in wood shavings and straw.

You have to close the window at night because the foxes might get them.
(Redfern, 1994: 14)

This extract shows how a child's writing can gain vitality when there is a strong sense of purpose and audience.

For a long time teachers have helped children make their own alphabet books, friezes or posters. This is an enjoyable way of meeting the NLS requirement that children know the alphabet and about alphabetical order. Making attractive dictionaries or word lists with robust covers reinforces a growing knowledge of alphabetical order and introduces the idea of looking for spellings in dictionaries and other books that are available in the class (Brown, 1996).

Book-making can bring a whole class together as a community of young readers and writers. Children love to make flaps, pop-up pictures and covers in the shape of the subject of the book. At Goldsmiths College one of the first classroom projects students undertake as part of the Primary English Course is the making of a book with one young learner. Many of the books are delightful stories but a fair number of students and their pupils choose to make an information book, often with a contents page, an index, a glossary and an 'about the author' page. The input of a visiting tutor, Carol Eagleton, a primary teacher with a curriculum strength in art, provided practical help with these devices; we have had books in the shape of record players, houses, telephones, pizzas and all manner of creatures. There have been doors that open, animals that spring out of pages and machines that 'work' if you pull a tab. All these devices have been much appreciated by students and the children they have worked with.

Safety factors to do with using glue and scissors need to be made explicit to children. Younger children will need some help with the techniques of cutting, measuring, placing of illustrations and gluing. Children nearly always want a word-processed as well as a handwritten version of their book, and this is an excellent opportunity to teach about columns, font sizes and text size.

Making illustrations

Children enjoy making illustrations for their non-fiction books and for writing across the curriculum. They can be helped to make tables to accompany work in mathematics and science, timelines in history, and geographical diagrams summarising information about temperature and climate. Much of this will be done by hand – we know that concepts are often best grounded in action – but for some purposes children can be helped to use desk-top publishing to make tables and simple diagrams. Labelled cross-sections can be modelled on good examples in books. Children enjoy using photographs they have taken on outings and field trips to illustrate their writing.

Integrating reading and writing with other activities

The literacy hour is required to attend to specific objectives, but non-fiction reading and writing across the curriculum can be more flexible and benefits from being combined with other activities, for example watching slides or a video film related to the topic, going on a visit or outing, hearing a visitor's talk, or engaging in art or drama work that explores important issues.

Young researchers sharing all that has been learnt

Particularly when work on a topic or task has been sustained, it is satisfying to create a context for sharing the fruits of the children's work. Children enjoy making a display of objects and their own pictures and writing – this was one of the outcomes of the work on 'Snails' in case study 3.1 and in the 'Giant' work in case study 3.3. Showing another class or some of the parents their children's work and inviting their questions is another way of bringing things to a conclusion that reinforces the value of the work. Sometimes the class can be the audience, each saying what they enjoyed most and reading out loud from their work or an extract from a non-fiction book they found useful.

Some thoughts on supporting young bilingual readers and writers

Early years good practice suggests that young bilingual children can be helped by value being given to the spoken as well as the written language, respect being shown to the individual child, and by a positive attitude in the school towards linguistic diversity. Marian Whitehead sets out a coherent approach to supporting children learning to read and write in a second language. At the same time she shows how their special insight into language can enrich the linguistic environment for all the children (Whitehead, 1996: 15–28).

Parents can make a helpful contribution to informational kinds of reading and writing (as well as fiction) by translating recipes, messages, letters, labels, counting systems and information books for classroom use.

Dialogue journals can be used to help children of all ages and abilities: Redfern and Edwards (1997) suggest that they can take the form of interactive picture books in the case of children with little or no English. Children can provide the pictures and dictate the text. Teachers can encourage the extending of the written text orally by asking the children about what they have drawn and providing immediate response.

Eve Gregory suggests some ideas for classroom projects on 'Names', 'Food', 'Illness' in Appendix 3 of her book *Making Sense of a New World* for classes with a majority of emerging bilinguals. The approach includes both story and non-fiction (Gregory, 1996).

Word processing programs which offer a range of scripts and languages other than English are now available and offer children and parents the option of experimenting with multilingual word processing.[3]

The National Curriculum at key stage 1 (5–7)

Since the National Curriculum programmes first became statutory in Great Britain in 1990, revised versions of the English orders have increasingly brought non-fiction explicitly into the initial teaching of reading and writing. Advances in Information Communication Technology are reflected in the range of source materials we must now provide including software, CD-ROMs and the Internet as well as print resources including books, newspapers, charts and posters. We should expect future revisions of the National Curriculum and other official documents to reflect trends in a constantly changing world but some principles are likely to be enduring. Children need to be helped with information retrieval, organisation and presentation. Writing can be a powerful way of organising and developing ideas and information and successful work is to do with children having clear purposes and a strong sense of audience. The advice on the development of spelling, handwriting and punctuation abilities and on planning and reviewing writing applies to both fictional and factual writing. The same range of material can be used for phonics teaching and for grammar work. Primary practitioners strive to meet teaching and assessment requirements while presenting reading and writing not only as challenging activities but also as sources of pleasure. Exploring the world of information can be as enjoyable in its way as fiction.

The literacy hour at key stage 1

Much more specific requirements for reading and writing are set out in the National Literacy Strategy *Framework for Teaching*. The National Curriculum is the starting-point, of course, but objectives for each term of each year group are set out in some detail. This book consistently argues that non-fiction reading and writing need to take place in strong contexts that have social meaning. Furthermore, while there are a lot of skills and strategies that need to be taught about information retrieval, children have to have reasons for controlling these. We have to reinforce children's curiosity and sheer wonder at all the interesting and exciting things in our world. How can teachers implement the requirements of the National Literacy Project *and* be true to these overarching principles? I addressed this question in an article for *Books for Keeps* (Mallett, 1998) and now set out the main points here, particularly with five to seven year olds in mind.

1   Teachers can enjoy choosing a range of materials for their year group in collaboration with colleagues. A range of genres or kinds of writing and literacy objectives for each term are set out in *The Framework for Teaching*. (See 'Summary of the Range of Work for Each Term'.) All the kinds of non-fiction reading and writing required have been set out in this chapter together with some suggestions for materials of good quality to interest children at key stage 1.
2   There are important handwriting, spelling and punctuation skills but these, together with study and library skills, are best learnt 'within the framework of what it means to be a writer' (Redfern and Edwards, 1997: 3). I believe the key to success here lies in the links that can be made between the literacy hour and learning across the curriculum.
3   The value of these links is made explicit in *The Framework for Teaching*: 'Where appropriate, literacy teaching should be linked to other areas of the curriculum.' This means that the texts that are the basis of the literacy hour can be selected from the science, geography, art and history children are enjoying as part of a broad curriculum. Some schools are planning for the literacy hour alongside planning for all the subjects across the curriculum to take advantage of linkage. The labels, street and town names for a child's reception year can be made interesting and coherent by using or making a historical text (Bage, 1998; *Times Educational Supplement*, 4 Sept. 1998, p. 22). The recounts required in Year 1 can be linked to visitors' recounts of events within their lifetime – coronations, special visits to the area, sporting achievements and so on. Again this reinforces the idea of texts, both spoken

and written being embedded in the social world. One of the objectives for Year 2 is to do with non-narrative kinds of writing and this can be linked to work in geography and history. History work is very rich in texts: autobiographical kinds of reading and writing enliven history and can be a text for literacy hour study too.

4 Word-level objectives – phonics, spelling and vocabulary – can be carried with non-fiction texts that often involve a technical vocabulary.

5 Sentence-level objectives – grammar and punctuation – carried out with non-fiction will help explore the distinctive structure of the language of a non-narrative text. However, at this stage, many texts are transitional genres. The conventions of mature non-narrative are introduced gradually (see discussion of this in the 'Range issues' section of this chapter). Punctuation in the text of the week is often best tackled towards the end, when the children are more familiar with the meaning.

6 Text-level objectives are to do with the global structure of non-fiction texts, retrieval devices and the diagrams, charts and tables that complement the written text.

CASE STUDIES

All three case studies show non-fiction reading and writing taking place in broad contexts. The reception class investigating snails (case study 3.1) used the books to answer their own questions and became aware that sometimes what was in a book contradicted their first-hand observations. Then for case study 3.2 we join a Year 1 class in Hong Kong who are helped to use computers to make progress in their writing. Case study 3.3 shows how drama and fiction can be the starting-point for a range of writing, including informational kinds.

Case study 3.1: Snails

Children in a reception class integrate learning from experience and learning from books

The context of the work

Five year olds in a primary school in Greenwich were working with their teacher and a student teacher on a mini-beast topic. A selection of information books had been assembled for the children to browse through. Angela found a picture of a vivarium or home for small creatures. (This was in Caroline O'Hagan's *It's Easy to Have a Snail to Stay* – now out of print but similar diagrams can be found in other mini-beast books.) Using the instructions in the book, a group of the children were

Contents
Page

Figure 3.5 Contents page of book children made on 'Snails', structured around their questions.

helped to make a snail home. There was great excitement about the plan to find and care for some snails.

Observing the snails

The teacher suggested that the group make a book about the snails with their own pictures and writing. Before collecting the snails, the children needed to find out about the creature's habitat, life-cycle and feeding. They had a perfect context for using the books and CD-ROM encyclopaedias for a genuine purpose. Stones and some soil were brought in and some cabbage and lettuce for feeding the creatures.

Then there was an expedition to collect some snails from open land near the school. Back in the classroom, the children drew and coloured the snails from observation and were helped to write down annotations at the bottom of each page. In her lesson notes the student teacher, Ms H, pointed out that the combination of fieldwork, practical caring for and observation of the snails, discussion, drawing and writing helped the children to feel like young researchers. The first-hand activities were at the centre of the work rather than the secondary sources.

Children should always be encouraged to respect the needs and comfort of animals they study. The teacher checked that the snails were well cared for and they were returned to their original environment at the end of the project.

The place of books and resources

It was a picture of the vivarium in a book that inspired the work and helped the children make a suitable habitat for the creatures. After that there was an interplay between using the resources and observing and caring for the snails. The children had a powerful way of testing out what the books conveyed. For example, the food provided at first relied on what the books suggested. However, the children experimented with other foods and found that their snails particularly liked carrot. Thus they were able to write in their book original information not present in other books. While their writing was informed by what was read out from books by the teacher, the children were in control of what was included.

There were some things they needed to find out from secondary sources – not everything could be learnt first-hand. Just coming to appreciate this was important in their development as researchers. At one point when the children were watching the snails and making some sketches, they asked the teacher what the shells were made of. They all searched in the books to find some details about the snail's shell and the teacher read out that it was made of chalk and that the scientific name for this was 'calcium carbonate'.

Outcomes

Another class was invited to share all that had been found out during the project. The vivarium, the children's books and the diagram that had inspired the making of the home for the snails were all on display and the children answered questions from the visiting children.

Work like this can produce a range of reading and writing texts for use in the literacy hour, including procedural writing, recounts of the field trip and a consideration of labelled diagrams of snails and the vivarium.

Case study 3.2: The impact of the word processor on early writing

Year 1 children enjoy their first use of the computer as a writing tool alongside learning to handwrite

By the year 2000 the revised National Curriculum requires ICT skills to be integrated in every subject.[4] Early years teachers face the challenge of achieving this while staying true to important principles about writing development. In this case study the efforts of a teacher to make a beginning are shared.

The context of the work

Ms C, English co-ordinator at the international primary school in Hong Kong, wanted to bring computers into the school's already established writing programme. The teachers were committed to an 'emergent writing' approach and structured the writing programme using the material from the work of B. and M. Michael in *The Foundations of Writing Materials* (1987). The programme, which is in stages, stresses the social nature of written language and the need to write things that have meaning for others. It is a 'language experience' approach which uses the children's spoken language and drawing abilities and which recognizes what children have already learnt about the purposes of writing. The children 'compose' from the beginning using pockets of words in sentence makers on the lines of Mackay *et al.'s* (1970) *Breakthrough to Literacy*. They are taught to form letters systematically and only handwrite when they have reached a reasonable level of competence in forming the letters of the alphabet. Ms C and the other teachers wanted to discover the contribution the word processor might make to children's writing development.

Introducing J and T

Ms C spent three 30-minute sessions per week over a period of four months with the Year 1 teacher and her class of 30 six year olds. She worked mainly with two children from the middle of the ability range within their class: J, a British girl, and T, a boy, who is half British, half Chinese. Both children speak English as their first language and were beginner writers at the start of the work. Their handwritten work was phonetically spelt but the beginnings of words were mostly conventional. Punctuation was appearing, but not yet consistently. The children each had a 'personal' Acorn A4 laptop with Pendown word processing software and could see each other's screens and chat to each other and to Ms C. There were also two Acorn 5,000 machines set up in the shared area.

In line with the Michaels' approach, the children's first accounts both oral and in drawings and in writing were stories: non-fiction genres being added later. This short account of the work and main findings concentrates on the informational kinds of writing they attempted.

An integrated approach combining handwriting and word processing

There was no intention to replace handwriting by word processing. Indeed there are important reasons why the handwriting process must not be bypassed. Physically forming the letters by hand supports the whole process of becoming a writer, partly by helping children develop mental images of letters and words. We know that the roots of mental processes are often in action and that early mark-making and drawing are the forerunners of writing. Nevertheless there is considerable physical effort involved for a beginner writer. The movements of hand and eye have to be co-ordinated and there are both compositional and secretarial aspects to think about. The word processor can ease the burden of co-ordinating these elements. The children in this study used the Pendown word processing program, which included a dictionary, a range of fonts, a spell-check and cut and copy facilities.

Writing with the word processor

At first the children were encouraged to experiment on the computer, moving through the early stages of emergent writing from playing to attempts to convey meaning. At the same time, in class they were learning to handwrite the alphabet and to convey messages through their drawing and mark-making. Both children were familiar with the alphabet and with alphabetical order. They wrote their names and other words and got to know the keyboard. Their first sustained writing on the computer, in line with the Michaels' approach, was story but soon other genres were added. Informational kinds of writing often benefit from the fonts, print size variations and format made possible by word processing. For example, lists, labels and subheadings can all be made to look like a real book. Often writing tasks arose from the topics being covered by the class including 'picnics', 'pirates', 'the playground' and 'all about me'. Sometimes the children were helped to type news stories and simple recounts.

SUMMARY OF KINDS OF INFORMATIONAL WRITING ON THE
COMPUTER ATTEMPTED OVER THE FOUR MONTHS

- Lists (including new year's resolutions)
- Letters

- Labels and captions
- News items (baby Eleanor's visit to the classroom)
- Short recounts (including My Birthday Party, What I Did Yesterday and My Holiday)
- Procedural writing (how I made my caterpillar)

SCAFFOLDING CHILDREN'S ACCOUNTS

Three main kinds of support were given to the children in addition to help with the technical aspects of the computer – the teacher acted as scribe to their dictation, they were helped to edit and proof-read their work and occasionally provided with a writing frame.[5]

The news items below, about the visit a mother with her baby made to the classroom, were dictated by the children and copies were made to put in their folders and to take home.

News by J:
Eleanor, the baby came to visit us. Her mummy said I can play with Eleanor. She showed us things Eleanor liked to play with. We played with her toys. I liked Eleanor.

News by T:
Eleanor was a baby. She was very young. Her mummy showed us her plate and her food. Her food looked very smooth because she had no teeth.

How do we help children progress from brief recounts like these? Ms C helped J expand the following recount.

J's first draft of 'What I Did Yesterday':
I went to the swimming pool yesterday. I went to the playground and played with my sister we played clim the pol I played at home coloured a person in my colouring book

Ms C saw an opportunity to work with J on the computer to improve the composition of the piece and the secretarial aspects. After discussion J was able to make the time sequence clearer, pinpoint her achievements in the pool, and detail the events in the playground. They talked about where the pauses in the account should be.

J's second draft of 'What I Did Yesterday':
I went to the swimming pool yesterday. Now I can go under the water a little way and open my eyes under water. After that I went to the playground with my sister and we played climb the pole. She picked the flowers but we are not allowed so we picked the leaves

and gave them to my mummy. After that I played at home. I coloured a person in my colouring book.

Of course, J could have been helped to improve a handwritten account but it was much easier for her to amend her work, with teacher guidance, on the screen. The teacher's careful discussion and modelling of both composing and editing processes helped J improve her work and yet still feel it was her own account.

Occasionally children were offered a written framework for their writing. Particularly where children are exploring a new genre or kind of writing they may not control the organisational structure (Lewis and Wray, 1996). Writing frames can provide a structure of headings to help. Below is the writing frame which was put on the computer to help the children with their first attempts at procedural writing. The frame provided is in bold.

How I made my caterpillar by J:

First I cut out the circles.

Then I coloured all my circles.

After that I put my circles in order.

Then I carefully put the split pins into the circles and this joined my circles together.

Last of all I put on the chop-sticks.

What will my caterpillar eat?
My caterpillar will eat a leaf and some apples.

My caterpillar says Thank you for writing about me.

The frame has structured the writing task and, as Lewis and Wray constantly point out, the idea is for children to move on to their own accounts once the organisational and linguistic features of a particular kind of writing have been understood (Lewis and Wray, 1996: 5). Nevertheless there is a danger that young writers will not feel at the centre of their own writing and will lose spontaneity. Alternative kinds of support include the teacher talking through the stages of a procedural task before the young writer organises the piece, or helping them edit their first draft on the lines of the recount about activities above.

The class teacher knows best which strategies will help his or her pupils most. There is a place for teachers making their own DARTS (directed activities round texts) on the computer; cloze[6] procedures involve deleting words from a text and allowing the children to talk in a small group about how best to fill the gaps. This strategy is becoming more common in the UK as one of the group writing tasks in the literacy hour. At this time of prescribed programmes, teachers need more than ever to have their own reasons for all that they ask the children to do.

Advantages of the word processor as one of the tools of the writing programme

The computer can aid active thinking and concept formation if children are given the right kind of support. This includes careful checking that the particular writing task is best served by the computer, by supporting the skills of the young writer, and sometimes modifying software to make it serve the young writer's purposes. Ms C 's conclusions about the main advantages of using the word processor as part of an approach to writing are listed below, together with some other points to bear in mind.

ADVANTAGES

- The children were able to generate text before they were swift writers by hand. This stimulated their enthusiasm about writing on the computer.
- The playful experimental aspects of writing were reinforced as the children used the different fonts and type sizes.
- The computer made it easier to separate compositional and editing aspects of writing, freeing children to concentrate on composing before tidying up secretarial aspects. Both J and T developed a constructive approach to correcting errors.
- The use of the computer supported the kind of co-operatively achieved success important in Vygotsky's theory of learning and development (Vygotsky, 1986). This was linked with the teacher's emphasis on the social situations that give rise to particular kinds of talk and writing, for example, accounts of birthdays and outings. Collaboration with peers and interaction with the teacher were built into the work.
- Teacher modelling of the writing process was made easier and this led to children's reflection on what they had written.
- As the activities were on the screen, and therefore more public than handwriting, help from the teacher was easier and more immediate. Support could be given at the point at which the writing was done. Both children liked having their writing read back to them by the teacher. (Some computers have speech synthe-

sisers to provide this immediate feedback, thus linking all four language processes.)
- Saving writing on a floppy disk reinforced the children's understanding of the relative permanence of writing. Extra copies could be printed out to take home and thus the children's parents became involved with the work.
- It was satisfying for the children to see their work looking like the print of a real book.
- The children began to learn about how communication is influenced by layout and design.

THINGS TO BEAR IN MIND

- Care had to be taken that the computer did not take time needed for interaction with real objects.
- The computer is an essentially interactive device supporting active learning – too much individual work for long periods is best avoided.
- Teacher support is labour intensive. Ms C spent most time during her visits with only two children, mainly reading back their writing and helping them edit longer pieces of text.
- Some computer strategies, like moving text, are difficult for children. J had a setback which put her off moving text for some time. She was editing and adjusting paragraphs in one of her longer pieces when she lost the work!

Case study 3.3: Drama and writing

Seven year olds bring a new energy to a range of writing tasks in the context of role play and discussion

Drama is recognized as an important aspect of spoken and written English and has the potential to enrich every subject. It creates contexts beyond the bounds of the classroom. Role play and improvisation provide purposes and audiences for children's language in a range of genres, allowing statutory requirements to be fulfilled in an imaginative and enjoyable way. In this example Ms G, a final year mature student, aimed to energise children's writing by combining reading and writing with exciting drama work. In a most successful series of lessons, inspired by a picture book, *Giant*, by Julia and Charles Snape, she introduced both fiction and non-fiction at appropriate times to encourage the children's writing.

The context of the work

The children, 30 seven year olds, attended a West Kent primary school which draws its 250 pupils from both owner-occupier and local housing association homes. The classroom showed much evidence of the high value accorded to literacy – the book area was attractive, comfortable and well stocked, there was a well-resourced writing corner with a display board for children's self-directed work. Each child had an A5 sized, wide-lined personal jotter used for all manner of writing purposes in the classroom.

Introducing the Giant

The first part of session 1 took place in the classroom where Ms G had placed some resources: a flipchart, felt pens, a tape of country sounds (birdsong etc.) and two cassette players (one for playing and one for recording).

The teacher read out the first five pages of *Giant* and showed the pictures. The text reads as follows:

Lia and her family lived in a village at the foot of a mountain.

The villagers called their mountain 'Giant'. For many years they had used Giant.

Giant's plants gave them fruit. The village animals grazed on her slopes.

The villagers picnicked in shady places and played in the trees.

Lia and her brother, Felix, often spent whole days on the mountain. All the children played there.

The children were asked to say what they thought this particular giant was like and the sort of activities the children enjoyed. They took some cues from the fine illustrations but added their own ideas like flying a kite and making a tree house.

Beginning the role play

After moving into the school hall and enjoying some warm-up exercises based on getting up on a sunny morning, the children were divided into small groups. Each group was asked to improvise an activity on the mountain – building a house or camp, having a picnic, fishing and playing in a stream. The birdsong tape was played quietly in the background to add atmosphere. It was necessary for the children to experience through role play the enjoyment of the activities in the countryside so that they could understand what the village people were to lose when the Giant disappears. Each group presented part of their improvisation to the rest of the class.

Ms G read the next part of the story – the village children arrive the next morning to find a great hole in the earth where Giant had been: 'Gone were the lovely green meadows, gone were the trees and woods, gone were the streams and waterfalls – no birds were singing, no little animals were scampering through the grass. . .'

Writing letters in role

After considerable discussion the children decided to write a letter asking the Giant to come back. At this point there had to be a break in the work as it was time for the mid-morning assembly. Afterwards, back in the classroom, the letter writing began. Below is Louise's letter with invented address, postcode and a telephone number.

Huckleberry House
Green Village
Mountshire
TH6 LU5
0107322 34689

Dear Giant

The villagers and I certainly miss you and my sister is crying as she misses you such a lot. I miss you as well. I miss climbing on your stony rocks. You are so nice and peaceful but the children are not. I miss your bright green grass. I miss your browns, blacks and greens. I miss your lovely scents. When the rain falls on your silver rocks they glitter.

Love Louise

The Giant replies

For this session Ms G had prepared a letter from Giant to the children, written on a large piece of paper in a huge envelope with an outsize stamp.

Dear Children

Thank you for your letters. I am glad that you love my green fields and shady woods. I miss you. I have no children playing on me now. I would like to come back, but I'm afraid to.

Please come to Sandy Bay on Wednesday morning if you would like to help me.

Love from,

GIANT

Maurice indicated he was willing to 'suspend disbelief' and accept the Giant had sent the letter saying – 'I can't really believe it, but I can in my imagination.' The teacher took the chance to teach the children about some letter writing conventions – placing of address, postcode and telephone number – in supporting their letters to the Giant and helping them to read out loud the Giant's reply.

Ms G told the children that the Giant was staying in a nearby village by the sea. When the children entered the hall after reading the letter, Ms G signalled she was now in the role of the Giant by going out briefly and returning with some branches of leaves. A tape recording of seashore sounds was playing. The children ask why Giant left and the teacher, in role, explains that it was because the villagers were throwing rubbish in her streams and woods and litter in her fields. Flowers had been picked and some kinds were now rare.

An informational focus

This rich project included different kinds of reading and writing. The third session involved very successful poetry writing, celebrating all the beauties and fruits of the mountain Giant. One of the things to note is how children moved from fantasy to fact in learning about environmental issues. But of course the main interest here is in the informational focus. During Session 3 teacher and children, in role as Giant and village children, decided on some actions to persuade Giant to return to her place in the village. Asked how they could change people's behaviour in the countryside the children make suggestions as follows:

> 'Make signs!'
> 'And put them on trees.'
> 'With "do not leave rubbish around". . .'
> 'Put litter in bins.'
> 'Don't pick the flowers.'

Back in the classroom a non-fiction book *Conservation and Decay* by K. Gillett was introduced to take up some of the environmental issues explored in the role play. Ms G felt it was best to introduce the book after the children had already begun to think about the issues. The children were affected by the pictures showing the harm that had been caused to animals through thoughtless dropping of rubbish in the countryside: a porcupine is shown with its head stuck in a jagged tin can; a vole has become imprisoned in a bottle; and a small bird has become caught up in a discarded fishing line.

There was discussion about the poster genre and scrutiny of some examples the teacher had brought in. Together it was agreed that:

- writing needed to be large, clear and bold – to be read at a distance;
- the message was best simple and short – taking only a short time to read;
- positive messages – 'Do' rather than 'Don't' make the most impact;
- the illustrations not only look attractive but help reinforce the message and bring a touch of humour (one child also pointed out that pictures were crucial for those who could not read or who spoke another language);
- an exclamation mark can add extra effect;
- different techniques can be used, including stencilling, newspaper print collage and freehand bubble writing.

The children were given the option of working in pairs if they wished. All of them did a first draft in their jotters and sought advice on shortening their messages and checking spelling and punctuation. Ms G and the teacher made sure that a great variety of paper, card and writing implements was available. Ms G comments:

> I can honestly say that I have never seen a group of children so eager and enthusiastic about a writing activity as these children were during this session. They worked independently and with a strong sense of purpose throughout; children who had not finished asked to stay in at lunch time to complete their work.

Two boys who found sustained writing difficult worked very hard with the aid of stencils, and to produce posters this gave them a sense of satisfaction.

There is evidence the children were really thinking about their posters. Iain wrote 'PUT YOUR RUBBISH IN THE BIN' in his first draft in his jotter, but changed it to 'RUBBISH KILLS' on his actual poster, because he felt strongly about the pictures of damaged animals in the information book. He told Ms G that 'people might not know about the animals and why they should not throw their rubbish down'.

Many of the children chose to use newsprint letters on their posters. Ms G and the class teacher helped by cutting out in some cases whole words or parts of words likely to be appropriate. Some words were cut into separate syllables and letters. The children spoke among themselves about letter names, capital letters and small letters. There were also some punctuation marks cut out of newspapers and Ms G overheard the children discussing the use of full stops, commas, exclamation marks and question marks.

The task stretched the most and least able pupils. Jessie and Maurice, two able young writers, worked together and collaborated over drafting and made mature decisions about who was to be responsible for each part of the poster. 'Do not pick the flowers – Pollination in progress' was a caption chosen by Jessie and relates to some earlier science work. Maurice had the idea of illustrating the poster with speech bubbles coming out of animals' mouths. Ms G noticed that he put an exclamation mark after 'Help!' rather than at the end of the whole utterance 'Help us!'

He is clearly adhering to the rules he has created for himself at this stage, suggesting that children are active in their attempts to gain control over the writing system. The poster task involved children in deciding what they wanted to communicate and how this was best imparted. Deep reflection was encouraged. The social purposes of language were emphasised – this was certainly writing to inform and persuade. A meaningful context was created for learning about presentational aspects of this kind of communication and about the many choices a writer makes in bringing a piece to fruition. It differed from the letter writing in that it was for a wide and general audience. It also reinforced the relative permanence of writing. You can make verbal requests to people to stop doing things but you would have to expend a lot of energy keeping it up everyday. Posters can be pinned up and last some time.

This project was carried out just before schools were required to put the literacy hour in place, but Ms G would have had no difficulty in selecting texts to link with the Giant work. The information book used showed the kind of conventions – subheadings, index and contents page – that the NLP *Framework for Teaching* requires children to encounter in the last term of Year 2. Their understanding of the different features of fiction and non-fiction had been strengthened as well.

The work is within the framework of good early years principles and shows how informational reading and writing can benefit from embedding in the rich context drama work can provide.

Conclusion

Children in the early school years are interested in their world and eager to find out more. The best books and materials nourish children's sense of wonder and sheer need to find out. Children deserve resources of the highest quality, not least because attitudes are formed now towards this kind of literacy. Promising approaches to non-fiction reading and writing embed the learning of skills and retrieval strategies, including all the new resources of information communication technology, in children's wider interests. Collaboration with one another and with the teacher helps to create a community of young researchers with a positive and enquiring approach to the world and its phenomena. The case studies here show teachers working on sound early years principles and including all that children need to learn in interesting projects. Both Bruner (1986) and Egan (1992) reject the computer metaphor of learning. A lively mind constantly makes new combinations, sees new possibilities and includes how children feel about new information and ideas. In short – bring in the imagination and you bring in enjoyment.

Issues to discuss and reflect on

1   Make your own list of criteria for choosing the kind of materials that will help make non-fiction reading and writing a positive experience for all the children whatever their gender, community or ability. You may wish to think in particular about one kind of non-fiction.

2   What have you found to be some of the advantages of encouraging children to think of themselves as 'young researchers' working collaboratively?

3   How far does your own experience of children learning both to handwrite and to word-process confirm the teacher's experience in the case study?

4 What do you consider are some of the ways parents can support non-fiction kinds of literacy?

5 How might a primary team plan to make the literacy hour and work across the curriculum mutually supportive?

Notes

1 The well-established international definition of 'the early years' is 0–8. See Marian Whitehead's book (1996) *The Development of Language and Literacy in the Early Years*, Chapter 5, for a helpful literacy teacher's checklist for good practice.
2 Piaget's work has fallen out of favour recently, partly because of his relative undervaluing of the role of language in learning. However, his model of learning as adaptation, the accommodation of existing schemata of knowledge, and the assimilation of new information remain an illuminating explanation (see Wood, 1988: 38–9).
3 *Allwrite* – a multilingual word-processing program available in many languages including English, other European languages and Hindi, Punjabi, Tamil and Vietnamese – is increasingly used by parents to support minority languages in school.
4 NATE (National Association for the Teaching of English) has an expanding list of books to help teachers develop ICT at all levels. Available from NATE Office, 50 Broadfield Road, Sheffield S8 0XJ.
5 See Lewis, M. and Wray, D. (1996) *Writing Frames: Scaffolding Children's Non-fiction Writing in a Range of Genres*. Reading: Reading and Language Information Centre, University of Reading.
6 'Cloze' is short for 'closure' and refers to a reading task in which the children have to 'guess' how to fill the gaps deliberately left in the text. Thus it helps prediction.

Further reading

Calkins, L. (1986) *The Art of Teaching Writing*. Portsmouth, NH: Heinemann.
Compton, R. and Mann, R. (1996) *IT across the Primary Curriculum*. London: Cassell.
Egan, K. (1986) *Teaching as Story Telling*. London: Routledge.
Johnson, P. (1997) *Children Making Books*. Reading: Reading University, Reading and Language Information Centre.
Michael, B. and Michael, M. (1987) *The Foundations of Writing Materials*. Glasgow: Jordanhill College of Education.
Mr Togs the Tailor: A Context for Writing (1987) Scotland: The Scottish Consultative Council on the Curriculum.
Preston, C. (1995) *21st Century A–Z Literacy Handbook: Linking Literacy with Software*. Project Miranda. London: London Institute of Education.
Redfern, A. (1994) 'Introducing Owen, expert eggstraordinary: the launching of a young writer' in *TACTYC Early Years Journal*, Vol. 14, No. 2.

Redfern, A. and Edwards, V. (1997) *Practical Ways to Inspire Young Authors*. Reading: University of Reading, Reading and Language Information Centre.

Walker, S. (1993) *Desktop Publishing for Teachers*. Reading: Reading University, Reading and Language Information Centre.

Walker, S., Edwards, V. and Leonard, H. (1998) *Write around the World*. Reading: Reading University, Reading and Language Information Centre.

Whitehead, M. (1996) *The Development of Language and Literacy*. London: Hodder & Stoughton.

Woolland, B. (1993) *The Teaching of Drama in the Primary School*. London: Longman.

Children's books and resources mentioned

Arnold, N. and Lewis, J. (illus.) (1997) *Sticky Maps*. London: Scholastic Books.

Asher, J. (1997) *Round the World Cookbook*. London: Dorling Kindersley.

Beasant, P. and Smith, A. (1993) *How to Draw Maps and Charts*. London: Usborne.

Big Book of Mapwork 1 and *Big Book of Mapwork 2* (1998). Hove: Wayland.

Bryant Mole, K. (1995) *Is It Shiny?*, *Does It Bounce?* and *Is It Heavy?* Buzzwords Series. London: A & C Black.

Carlisle, R. and Wendon, L. (1998) *Letterland ABC* and *First Alphabetic Frieze*. London: HarperCollins Educational.

Cave, K. (1998) *W is for World*. London: Frances Lincoln with Oxfam.

Coltman, P. and Sparks-Linfield, R. (1998) *The Human Body*. Pelican Big Books. London: Longman.

Crewe, S. (1996) *Step-by-Step: Maps and Globes*. London: Franklin Watts.

Davies, N. and Maland, N. (illus.) (1997) *Big Blue Whale*. London: Walker Books.

Dewan, T. (1992) *Inside the Whale and Other Animals*. London: Dorling Kindersley.

Dorling Kindersley Children's Illustrated Encyclopedia (1997). Ed. A. Kramer. London: Dorling Kindersley.

Dorling Kindersley Children's Picture Encylopedia (1997). Ed. C. Llewellyn. London: Dorling Kindersley.

French, V. and Wisenfield, A. (1994) *Spider Watching*. Read and Wonder series. London: Walker Books.

Gillett, K. (1994) *Conservation and Decay*. Oxford Primary series. Oxford: Oxford University Press.

Godwin, S. and Abel, S. (1998) *The Drop Goes Plop: A Seed in Need*. London: Macdonald Young Books.

Hooper, M. and Kitchen, B. (illus.) (1996) *Dinosaur*. Cambridge: Cambridge University Press.

Hughes, S. (1998) *Make Hay while the Sun Shines: A Book of Proverbs*. London: Faber & Faber.

Johnson, P. (1998) *You Can Make Your Own Book!* Harlow: Addison Wesley (in big and small book format).

Llewellyn, C. (1993) *My First Book of Time*. London: Dorling Kindersley.

Longman Keystart First Atlas (1997) Ed. S. Scoffham. London: Longman.

MacCarthay, P. (1990) *Herds of Words*, London: Macmillan.

Manning, M. and Granström, B. (1997) *Splish, Splash, Splosh* and *What's under the Bed?* Wonderwise series. London: Franklin Watts (in big and small book format).

Manning, M. and Granström, B. (1998) *Wild and Free* and *Out There Somewhere It's Time To . . .* London: Frances Lincoln.
My First Oxford Dictionary (1997). Ed. E. Goldsmith. Oxford: Oxford University Press.
Onyefulu, I. (1997) *A is for Africa*. London: Frances Lincoln.
Oxford Children's Encyclopedia (1998). 9 vols. Oxford: Oxford University Press.
Oxford First Encyclopedia (1998). Ed. E. Langley. Oxford: Oxford University Press.
Parsons, A. and Young, J. (photographer) (1990) *Amazing Spiders*. London: Dorling Kindersley.
Petty, K. (1993) *Roundabouts: Maps and Journeys*. London: A. & C. Black.
Pienkowski, J. (1998) *1001 Words*. London: Heinemann.
Pipe, J. (1998) *The Giant Book of Bugs*. London: Dorling Kindersley.
Purkis, S. (1998) *Looking at Teddy Bears*. Pelican Big Books. London: Longman.
Ransford, S. and Kitchen, B. (illus.) (1999) *The Otter*; *The Barn Owl*. Animal Lives series. London: Kingfisher.
Selway, M. (1998) *What Can I Write? Rosie Writes Again*. London: Red Fox Books.
Snape, J. and Snape, C. (1990) *Giant*. London: Walker Books.
Taylor, B; illustrated by Richardson-Jones, T. and Cox, S. (1995) *Going Places: Finding the Way*. London: A. & C. Black.
Wallace, K. (1993) *Think of an Eel*. Read and Wonder series. London: Walker Books.
Wayland's First Picture Atlas (1992) Hove: Wayland.
Witherington, A. and Neate, B. (1998) *What Babies Used to Wear*. Pelican Big Books. London: Longman.
Yildirim, E. (1997) *Aunty Dot's Incredible Adventure Atlas*. London: Collins Children's Books.

Reading schemes

Cambridge Reading, Becoming a Reader. Cambridge: Cambridge University Press. (Includes *Dinosaur* and *Coral Reef*.)
Discovery World, the non-fiction aspect of Heinemann's Evaluation Pack. The core of the progamme is 42 good quality children's books with a suggested sequence but also includes three big books, two large-format Literacy Lesson books, and a teacher's *Skills and Assessment Guide*.
Ginn Science. *Year 1 Information Books* (sets 1 & 2).
Longman Book Project, non-fiction 1 (*Toys*, *Babies*, *Food*, and *Home*). London: Longman.
Oxford Reading Tree, *Fact Finders* (Unit A). Oxford: Oxford University Press.
Progress with Meaning Library has a non-fiction component in seven levels. Andover: Nelson. £11.95 to £14.95 per pack.
Story Chest (Stage 2 non-fiction small and big books). London: Kingscourt.
Sunshine History KS1 (Packs 1–4). Sunshine Books. London: Heinemann.
Wonder World. London: Badger Publishing Packs 1–4. Compiled by Wendy Body. (Tel. 01438 356907). (Also of interest from Badger Publishing are the *Infant Curriculum Related Non-Fiction sets*, also compiled by Wendy Body (1998). Similar sets for 7–11 year olds are likely to appear in 1999/2000.)

Software

Allwrite LETSS (0181 850 0100).

Concept keyboard overlays in English and other languages available from Hounslow Language Support Service, Hounslow Education Centre, Martindale Road, Hounslow (0181 570 4186).

EasyPage (1998, Windows 95 version). Porters Primary Software. Recommended for five year olds because it is easy to use. Illustrations can be drawn, a text written and read out, and then combined with the pictures. Desk-top publishing for the very young. (0114 258 2878).

EasyWorks Aztec (01274 596716).

Expression TAG (01474 357350).

HyperStudio TAG (01474 357350).

Kid Works 2 TAG (01474 357350).

Look! Here! Talking Topics Sherston (01666 8404330).

My First Incredible, Amazing Dictionary Dorling Kindersley (0171 836 5411).

Picture Dictionary TAG (01474 357350).

Smudge and Spaniel software, Storm Educational Software with uncluttered graphics and interactive activities linked to National Curriculum English, Maths, Science and Geography, suitable for children of differing abilities and offering project suggestions (01935 817699).

Through My Window Triple unit CD-ROM. Anglia Multimedia (0160 361 5151).

Write with Me Novell WordPerfect (01344 724000).

Star books: nourishing wonder and curiosity

Davies, N. and Maland, N. (1997) *Big Blue Whale*. London: Walker Books. One of the few books for young children that goes into detail about the questions children ask about the whale's young.

Kirkwood, J. (1997) *Firefighters*; *Trucks*. Cutaway. The lively cutaway drawings are detailed and well researched. *The School Librarian*, Summer 1998, describes the books as 'bright, informative and oozing with excitement'.

Macquitty, M. (1998) *Ocean*. London: Dorling Kindersley. Inside Guides. Even the lice on the barnacles of the grey whale are shown, together with many other fascinating facts about ocean creatures from jellyfish to sharks.

Manning, M. and Granström, B. (1998) *How Did I Begin?* London: Franklin Watts. Clear text and attractive pictures to explain the facts of life to young children.

Powell, J. (1998) *Wind and Us*; and *Sun and Us*. London: Belitha Press. An inviting series showing how the weather affects our daily lives.

Stewart, D. (1997) *From Tadpole to Frog* and *From Seed to Sunflower*. London: Franklin Watts. The life-cycle approach gives a natural narrative structure helpful to younger key stage 1 children.

The Usborne Animated Children's Encyclopedia (1998). Ed. J. Elliott and C. King. London: Usborne. This fact book is good browsing material for beginner readers and in CD-ROM form has interesting animations and sound effects.

Wildsmith, B. (1997) *Joseph*. Oxford: Oxford University Press. This beautifully illustrated version of the Bible story shows the hard life of the tent dwellers in contrast to the richness of Pharaonic Egypt. Children will learn much about the clothes, animals and landscapes of this period.

4 Informational reading and writing at key stage 2 (7–9)

Making progress in satisfying and pleasurable contexts

> And so the lesson continues: the children using the book to enrich their observation, and their observation to elucidate the text of the book. . . . direct observation and consultation of reference material are complementary ways of obtaining information, each illuminating the other.
>
> (Wells, 1986: 115)

Introduction

By the time they reach the middle years of the primary school, most children are settled and enjoying their growing competence in a range of physical and intellectual activities. The teacher's approval is important to them and they need the respect and friendship of their peers. Teachers of Year 3 and Year 4 classes often remark that they appreciate the sheer enthusiasm and liveliness of many children at this stage. In a broad and balanced curriculum, literacy develops alongside other ways of representing experience: mathematical and musical symbols; achievements in art and design; and expression through movement and mime. Children's reading and writing develop through their encounters with texts across the curriculum – in geography, science, history, art and religious studies at least as importantly as in the literacy hour. Often, as in the epigraph that heads this chapter, reading integrates with and extends practical observation.

Parents and families continue to be a crucial background to all that children do, and co-operation and communication between parents and school remain important. Children have special home-based interests and hobbies from the earliest years, but it is in these middle primary years in particular that they enjoy making labelled and annotated collections of stamps, wild pressed flowers, shells, fossils and stones. Often parents and friends buy books and CD-ROMs as gifts to develop children's hobbies. Sometimes hobbies and interests start at home and can be celebrated and shared in the classroom; alternatively, interests can be sparked in school and continue at home.

Children are essentially social beings and need help in developing good relationships with the teacher and other adults in the school. They need also to be able to make friendships and to work and play well with their peers. Success here, and indeed in all aspects of life at home and school, contributes to children's emotional well-being and, in turn, to children's ability to learn and enjoy school life. The ability to collaborate and co-operate with other children is a very important factor in the success of work across the curriculum and in the reading and writing activities that are part of it.

As children journey through the stages of schooling, they become increasingly aware of the requirements of the society in which they live. Great demands on teachers in Great Britain are now made to plan, teach and assess a prescribed curriculum. All this has a considerable effect on how we set up and carry out a programme of reading and writing.

This book has consistently argued that non-fiction reading and writing gains its point and vitality from being embedded in contexts that provide purposes and audiences for children's work. The direct teaching of library and study skills required by the National Literacy Strategy Group, and set out in lists in the *Framework for Teaching* (DfEE, 1998), is best achieved by linking children's work across the curriculum to the literacy strategy objectives. While good fiction creates its own context, the settings in which informational kinds of literacy are placed is of great importance. It cannot be said too often that lists of objectives, however sensible and desirable, can only be achieved by practitioners of professional skill and imagination.

The quality of the different materials and resources provided also has a major effect on children's attitudes towards reading for finding out, and this chapter begins with a discussion of the range of quality books and resources, including multimedia, that are appropriate at this stage. The account continues by suggesting some strategies for using the materials to develop children's abilities as readers and writers of non-fiction. Finally case studies of promising practice are shared. In case study 4.1 we join Sarah as she creates an information book about making pizza and learns about how procedures and illustrations of the stages in a process are best set out. In case study 4.2 we join a class using both fiction and non-fiction to explore a theme and see their progress in assessing the distinctive contributions of different kinds of material. This promising practice shows children as young researchers who are acquiring knowledge about particular kinds of reading and writing as well as about the topics across the curriculum.

Range issues: choosing texts to inform and to feed the imagination

There is a huge amount of informational material for children in the mid-primary years in book and software form. As we would expect, it varies in quality. It is best for schools not to get locked into one publisher's programme as, however generally good, not every title will be of equal merit. Choosing resources for a class or year group is one of the pleasures of teaching, and the reflective practitioner remains in control of how the money is spent.

Teachers know that seven to nine year olds vary greatly in their reading interests and abilities: the reader may thus find it helpful to look at the lists in both Chapter 3 for five to seven year olds and Chapter 5 for nine to eleven year olds. The following suggestions are offered for consideration. I have tried to keep to materials that are likely still to be in print, that are good of their kind, and which help children find enjoyment in this aspect of their developing literacy. I have also had an eye on the genres which teachers are required to include in their programmes (objectives listed in the NLS *Framework for Teaching*).

In Year 3 the main kinds of materials are: information texts on topics of interest; texts including instructions; reference texts (dictionaries, thesauruses and encyclopaedias); and letters.

In Year 4 the following text types are added: articles from newspapers and magazines; information texts on the same themes (for comparison); explanations; persuasive writing including adverts and flyers; discussion texts to stimulate debates; and information texts (linked to other curriculum areas).

Chronological non-fiction

Here we include procedural kinds of writing: instructions for using machinery like the classroom computer or tape recorder; science experiments; cooking instructions; and instructions for making things. Accessible books which could serve as models for children's own writing include Helen Drew's *My First Baking Book*, Angela Wilkes's *My First Science Book* and Dave King's *Photography*.

Non-fiction in story form can have a special power. A good series to introduce this way of organising material is the Walker Books' Animals at Risk series. *Whale*, for example, by Judy Allen and illustrated beautifully by Tudor Humphries, tells the story of a humpback whale in danger. The fact sheet at the end is generally welcomed by young readers who are moved by the cruel fate of many whales. This book lends itself to being read out loud by the teacher and discussed.

The 'fact through story' approach is most successful in Jane Goodall's book *With Love: Stories of Chimpanzees in the Wild*. The tales and anecdotes of chimpanzees overcoming danger and caring for their offspring are likely to make young readers more understanding of efforts to protect species under threat. The fact pages at the end show a different way of presenting information, and this could be a good discussion point in or out of the literacy hour. Like the previous example, this would be an excellent book to read out loud to the class. Able readers in Year 4 would be able to read it for themselves.

History gives rise to a particularly rich variety of texts: some show that a time sequence organization can be combined with analysis and evaluation. Dorling Kindersley's Discoveries series combines telling the story of an exciting event, for example the destruction of Pompeii, with an analysis of its significance. Only the ablest readers in the middle primary years would be able to manage this on their own. For the seven year age range, Ginn's History stories (such as Joan Blyth's *Tudor and Stuart Times*) or Black's *History Mysteries* are more accessible. Sherston's *Time Detectives . . . The Victorians* software helps children to learn about the period while following the adventures of three lost children. Life-cycles of creatures move naturally through time: Karen Wallace's *Think of an Eel* and French and Milne's *The Apple Tree* – titles from Walker Books Read and Wonder series are original and interesting examples.

Non-narrative texts

In the middle primary years children increasingly use texts that are organized according to the needs of the subject rather than chronologically. The authorial voice needs to be inviting to match children's interest and curiosity, but we would expect them to be able to manage more demanding written text and illustrations. Watts, Wayland, A. & C. Black and Dorling Kindersley are among a number of publishers producing books with well set-out retrieval devices.

If you want to combine looking at nature study with helping children with retrieval devices like contents page, index and glossary (perhaps to reinforce literacy hour demonstration with big books), children around seven years would enjoy the wonderful pictures of creatures in their environments in Dorling Kindersley's Look Closer series. Greenaway and Taylor's *Pond Life*, for instance, shows startling pictures of the faces of a frog and a snail.

There is a welcome trend towards inviting experts on a topic to write information books for children, often in collaboration with teachers and children. Children of about seven or eight enjoy Patrick Moore's robust little books on aspects of Space. Paul Doherty's pictures look striking on a black background; the picture of the exploding star (a supernova) is stunning, and the explanations never patronise. The tone is that of 'I find this interesting and I think you will too'. I particularly liked the information on how stars are born out of patches of dust and gas called nebulae, and how they die – they become 'heavy, cold and dark' and even the large star that we call the sun cannot live forever. For Year 3 one of these books would make a good literacy hour text of the week; it shows information book conventions and introduces a new and exciting vocabulary in context.

Towards the age of nine, the Dorling Kindersley 3D series (*Insect*; *Microlife*; *Plant*; *Reptile*) will appeal. Research into 3D imaging and display is exploited in these books which provide the young reader with a 'mirror viewer' to see objects usually invisible to the human eye. Dorling Kindersley's

Discoveries series, covering historical events like the volcanic eruption at Pompeii and the life and death of Tutankhamun, is intended for this age group. Another Dorling Kindersley series, the Eyewitness Guides, can be useful to readers of any age. The materials cover every possible topic: nature study, history, geography and indeed all the subjects of the primary curriculum and beyond. The hundredth title, *Future*, is about to be published at the time of writing. Some nine year olds, perhaps those with a particular hobby or interest, will manage particular titles with some adult help. Teachers of much younger children often use these books for their own reference purposes and are often able to bring the pictures into the children's work (see the 'Journeys' case study 2.1).

It is impossible not to mention Dorling Kindersley quite a lot if you are investigating the information books and computer software on the market for the primary years. Their achievements are considerable. They have incorporated new technology in the production of excellent photographs and diagrams, and have brought retrieval devices and structural guiders to a new level of clarity. However, teachers still need to look at individual titles in a series to check whether they match their children's needs. Without detracting from DK's achievements, I think a classroom or school too dominated by their titles would give the impression that all knowledge on every topic can be reduced to a series of double spreads! There is room for the quirky and unusual- for a book whose vitality and originality make its lack of conventional retrieval devices forgivable. *If I Didn't Have Elbows: The Alternative Body Book* by Sandi Toksvig manages to be delightfully subversive – 'if you haven't got £4.99 you could get someone else to buy you this book' – and yet it covers a lot of interesting information and makes us think deeply about the functions of different parts of the body. If we had no skin, 'we would have to wear Band Aids all over' is accompanied by a humorous drawing. But it does remind us that this largest organ of the body has a crucial job to do in protecting all our body parts.

The titles in the Dorling Kindersley Why Do We? series are entertaining and enlightening. *Why Do We Laugh?*, for example, explains well the mechanisms that come into play when we laugh. I like the humour in Kingfisher's I Wonder Why? series, which provides the answers as to why camels have humps, why soap has bubbles, and why castles had moats. In Anita Ganon's *I Wonder Why the Wind Blows and Other Questions about Our Planet* there is a splendid picture and explanation with the advice 'Don't sit and watch a stalactite grow. It can take 1,000 years to get a centimetre longer.' The books in these two series show how children might take some related questions as a theme for their writing.

Big books

These have been used by teachers to model aspects of reading both fiction and non-fiction for some time. The non-fiction kind in particular has been brought into greater prominence by the emphasis in the literacy hour on demonstrating flexible reading strategies. They vary in quality and some criteria for choosing them are set out under 'Big Books' in Chapter 3.

Some big books used at key stage 1 will also be helpful to many children in Year 3. Several titles in the Wayland/Macdonald Big Book series fit into this category. Indeed, Kath Cox and Pat Hughes's *History from Photographs*, which is built around beautifully produced photographs comparing schools now with those at the turn of the century, would interest readers of any age. There are scholarly details about the sources of each photograph at the end to help the adult answer children's questions. There are two text levels and excellent retrieval devices.

An increasing number of publishers are producing reading programmes that include big and matching small books to suit each reading stage. Cambridge Reading have excellent books in the Information Books Strand of 'Towards Independence: C' for this age range – for example, *Coral Reef*, *Desert* and *Rainforest*, all by Meredith Hooper. Longman's Book Project also provides big and small books of quality.

Reading schemes and programmes

Teachers often use a mix of books and resources and nearly always include some from reading schemes. In his regularly updated book *Twenty-five Years of Individualised Reading*, Cliff Moon presents lists of quality books arranged in readability levels for children from five to eleven years. The following selections for Year 3 and Year 4 draw on the non-fiction recommendations in Moon's lists.

For seven year olds working at and within level 2 of the 1995 National Curriculum (Moon's stages 8 and 9), the following schemes and series include good non-fiction books: *All Aboard* (Ginn, stages 7 and 8); *Ginn Science* (Information books, sets 1 and 2); *Ginn History* (topic books A); *Cambridge Reading* (Towards Independence: A); *Oxford Reading Tree* (Fact finders, Unit B); *Wonder World* (Badger Publishing Ltd, Pack 3); *Wellington Square*, *Nelson* (non-fiction books, level 3); *Sunshine Books* (Heinemann, Early Fluency non-fiction, level 2 and 3); *Picture Puffin Fact Books*; *People Who Help Us*; *Favourite Foods* (Wayland); *First Discovery* (Moonlight Publishing); *Find Out About* (Watts); *English through Topics* (Oliver and Boyd); *Collins Educational Book Bus* (non-fiction titles from B1, Independent packs); *History from Objects* and *History from Photographs* (Wayland); *Kaleidoscope Reading Sets* (shared reading and non-fiction).

The non-fiction schemes and series recommended for eight to nine year olds working within level 2 include: *All Aboard* (Ginn, stage 2); *Book Bus* (Collins Educational, non-fiction titles from Independent packs B1–B4); *Cambridge Reading* (Towards Independence: C); *Famous People*; *Famous Lives* (Watts); *Ladybird Books* (Young Discovery); *Fact Finders* (Oxford Reading Tree, units D and E); *Young Scientists Investigate* (Evans); *Victorian*

Times; *People through Time*; *Take It Apart* (all from Wayland); *Reading 2,000* (Longman, level 1, topic readers); *Book Project* (Longman, non-fiction 2); *Ecology Story Books* (Frances Lincoln/Windward); *First Countries*; *First Nature*; *First History* (All from Wayland).

Reference material

Dictionaries and thesauruses

A good dictionary introduces children not only to alphabetic order but also to the use of phrases to explain meanings and to the notion that context helps us know the sense in which a word with more than one meaning is being used. The inclusion of parts of speech other than the stem word are helpful. *The Usborne First Dictionary* (2,500 words) for children up to eight has all these features and also tries to make browsing through a dictionary fun by including word games and spelling tips. 'Some words with "r" sound are written with a "w", e.g. wrist, wrestle and write'.

Children are required by Year 3, Term 2 to use dictionaries 'without illustrations' according to the NLS Summary of the Range of Work for Each Term (for some reason, this is not mentioned in Section 2, 'The Termly Objectives'). Presumably this objective implies that these dictionaries should be used *for some of the time*, since there are splendid illustrated dictionaries for children at least to the end of the primary years. I believe *The Oxford Young Reader's Dictionary* (6,000 entries) to be an excellent, non-illustrated dictionary for children from about seven years upwards. Most children's dictionaries have bold print headwords, phrases and parts of speech but this one is particularly clear with dark print on creamy coloured paper. The 'using this dictionary page' is both lucid and inviting.

The publishers who produce children's dictionaries usually also offer thesauruses of antonyms and synonyms. In his introduction to the very good *Oxford Children's Thesaurus*, Alan Spooner (1991) expresses the hope that it 'includes a wide enough vocabulary to make it interesting and thought provoking'. This is the point – a good thesaurus reinforces the idea that language is essentially creative and exciting, and offers us a range of options to express our meaning.

There are many software dictionaries and thesauruses and word processing for children brings the benefits of spell-checks and a built-in thesaurus.

Encyclopaedias

What do children want from a one-volume encyclopaedia when they are aged around eight? All the usual criteria of a clear and accessible text, technical language well contextualised and up-to-date information apply. But above all we seek easy retrieval of information, plus illustrations that are not only attractive but which also show clear structures and processes. Dorling

Kindersley's *Children's Illustrated Encyclopedia* has 450 main entries cover- ing what children are likely to need to look up in the middle primary years. The visual images are useful and vibrant and the retrieval devices, including the comprehensive index and 22 page fact-finder, make this a good book for demonstration. A very important criterion for choosing encyclopaedias and other materials is that they are up to date, not only in terms of the accuracy of the information, but that they also reflect changing perceptions and attitudes towards 'the facts'. It is good, therefore, to note that under 'Explorers' the encyclopaedia just described recognises that 'people already lived in most of these "newly discovered" lands. And all too often the new arrivals exploited the native peoples, destroying their cultures.'

Generally, my own preference is for alphabetically organised encyclopae- dias for this age range and above, but I do like the organisation of the 1998 *The Oxford First Encyclopedia*: it starts from the child's body, then moves to other people, the earth and then science and technology. Many seven to eight year olds would enjoy this in school or at home. Clear contents pages and index and very useful and attractive illustrations make this a particu- larly inviting reference book. *Collin's Children's Encyclopedia* adopts a similar principle, beginning with the familiar and extending to space and time. This would be useful throughout the middle and upper primary years and a good family resource. The *Dorling Kindersley Children's Picture Encyclopedia* is organised alphabetically and has good 'about using this book' pages and helpful 'find out more' advice at the end of each double spread. The labelled diagrams are particularly good, for example the bold flower diagram. A large, single-volume encyclopaedia that would be useful from about age seven upwards is the *Kingfisher Children's Encyclopedia* which has 3,500 entries and 2,000 illustrations. The diagrams are well labelled and include cross-sections, like that of a frog, and diagrams with a key, like that showing different kinds of fish. I enjoyed a browse through this and found the content of the entries went beyond the basic. For example, under the 'medicine' entry, alternative as well as conventional approaches are included.

For general reference at home or school during the primary years there are a number of multi-volume encyclopaedias. Amongst these are the nine-volume *Oxford Children's Encyclopedia* and the *Millennium Family Encyclopedia* (available exclusively through DKFL advisers). Children would need much adult mediation to use these resources, but children's questions often require the depth and detail these books provide.

Reference books with a difference include those in the Usborne Facts and Lists series. Not only are some of the ways of presenting information mentioned in the NLS *Framework for Teaching* (use of bullet points, infor- mation boxes, etc.) but in addition the facts and figures – on cities and pop- ulations in, for example, *Earth Facts* – will intrigue some young learners.

There are a large number of specialist encyclopaedias on science, mathematics, space, natural history and so on. The *Ladybird Discovery*

Encyclopaedia of the Natural World is arranged in 15 topics. I learnt a lot during my browse through it – how earthquakes can be predicted and prevented, and that volcanoes are not a phenomenon peculiar to planet earth: Mount Olympus on Mars, for example, is a volcano.

Longman Book Project has an introductory encyclopaedia of Wild Animals in four volumes. The *New Lion Encyclopedia of the Bible*, edited by John Drane, is an excellent resource for the primary school library, providing interesting and comprehensive coverage of Bible history, the life and teachings of Jesus, and all the books of the Bible. In the review section of the *Times Educational Supplement* (4 Dec. 1998, page 24), Jack Priestley suggests that this encyclopaedia would be a good companion to the *Lion Graphic Bible*, which tells the Bible stories in a robust manner which might appeal to reluctant readers, especially boys from about age nine.

Atlases

Maps communicate information visually. Very young children begin by being helped to make their own simple maps of the classroom perhaps or a room at home. Wayland's *Big Book of Mapwork 1*, recommended for children at key stage 1, will still be helpful for younger Year 3 children who need concepts of compass directions and using grid references reinforced, and *Big Book of Mapwork 2* will take mapping skills further. The next stage is often for children to study maps of one country – Longman (Book Project) have an *Atlas of the British Isles* suitable for this age range. *Collins Ultimate Atlas of Almost Everything*, which features good maps and tables with clearly written and useful annotations, is nicely presented under headings like 'Planet Earth', 'Wildlife', 'People and Places' and 'Atlas of the World'. As well as being useful to support children's work, I think this would make a nice present for a seven to nine year old to enjoy browsing through at home.

Also worth considering is David Green's *The Eyewitness Atlas of the World* (Dorling Kindersley) which is an easy to use picture atlas packed with information. Although intended for older primary and secondary aged children, the *Oxford School Atlas* would be useful in the school library for reference by teachers and children (highly recommended by the Schools Library Service in their publication *Going Places*).

Software

By the age of about eight, children have become aware of some of the features and qualities of ICT texts as compared with books and magazines. They are ready to work with and reflect on texts that are scrolled and non-linear in structure, which incorporate sound or still and moving images, which can be changed and which have a spatial dimension (see Year 4, Term 1, NLS *Framework for Teaching* [DfEE 1998]). All this informs what we select in the way of software, CD-ROMs and so on.

A regularly updated resource which helps teachers keep up with the latest developments in literacy, language and communications is the *21st Century A–Z Literacy Handbook: Linking Literacy with Software* by Christine Preston of Project Miranda. The list in this book, entitled 'Literacy software for key stage 2', sets out some of the main products used in school at the time of writing.

In the middle primary years the presentational aspects of writing are important – *ClarisWorks Primary Templates*, *EasyWorks*, *Write with Me*, *Writer's Toolkit* and *First Page* all help.

Landmarks Microworlds from Longman Logotron allows children to enter an animated virtual world in which lifestyles of the past can be explored. *Time Detectives . . . The Victorians* also supports history work by following the adventures of three children. Two other user-friendly CD-ROMs are *Ancient Lands* from Microsoft and *Eyewitness History of the World* from Dorling Kindersley. You enter the first mentioned by way of a map on which the three ancient civilisations are shown: Egypt, Rome and Greece. Both use animated sequences – the *Eyewitness History* includes music and the writing of Pliny the Younger to bring alive the eruption of Vesuvius.

The *Mapper Series: Body, Weather, Home* introduces vocabulary reinforced by pictures. Young researchers can find materials to support their writing and reporting back to the class on *Microsoft Reference CDs*.

A number of dictionaries and encyclopaedias are now on disk, including Dorling Kindersley's *My First Incredible, Amazing Dictionary* which has 1,000 words and offers games and puzzles to practise dictionary and alphabet skills. *Word Bank* and *Crossword Creator* both make possible the creation of a pupil's own personal dictionary.

Letters, flyers, newspaper articles and advertisements

All of the above have a place in the resource collection for this age range. Teachers and children often make their own folders of items- collections of different kinds of letters from personal to formal, and newspaper articles or adverts round a particular theme or aimed at a particular audience (e.g. children). Letters and newspaper articles are also primary source material for history.

We can regard letters from real life and letters from fiction flexibly with good results. *Dear Greenpeace* by Simon James is structured round five letters from Emily, who is convinced she has a whale in her pond and five responses from Greenpeace. The Ahlbergs' *The Jolly Postman* is well established as a starting-point for writing letters to fictional characters.

As well as advertisements from magazines and articles, the collection can usefully include radio and television advertisements on cassette tape or video-film. There are excellent software packages to help with newspaper reporting. *EasyWorks* from Aztec for example, and both *Banner* and

BannerMania (from TAG) can help children make professional-looking posters in any size. The next main section in this chapter indicates how advertisements can be used to persuade, manipulate and influence readers.

Illustrations to invite young readers in

The illustrations in books and software for seven to nine year olds increase in complexity to match the more challenging concepts explained in writing. The different kinds of information texts (e.g. those setting out instructions or procedures, non-chronological writing in information books and articles in encyclopaedias and text, to accompany advertisements and newspaper articles) are all mentioned in the NLS objectives for Years 3 and 4 and have distinctive visual aids.

The quality of the illustrations is an important contribution to the worth of a resource and is frequently commented on in the book recommendations above. Visual aids also vary according to the area of the curriculum to which a text relates. We look for various things: in mathematics and science materials we need well-labelled, clear diagrams showing structures and processes; in history the focus is on time-lines, photographs, portraits and artistic reconstructions; in geography, the requirement is for maps, tables, charts showing population or temperature variations and photographs. In each case we need to ask what the purpose of the visual aid is, how well it integrates with the written text, and if it is a good model for the young learner to use in their own work.

CD-ROMs can show developing diagrams of a human or animal body structures – the system of muscles or bones for example, or processes like the blood or digestive system.

Important as diagrammatically represented structures and functions and summarising tables are, we must remember that drawings, portraits and photographs can impart extremely important information and can make a strong emotional impact. In some advertising material, drawings and photographs can be used to manipulate and deceive but in good materials for children they usually aim to enlighten and interest. The portraits shown and explained in Joy Richardson's excellent book *Making Faces* show how these images can communicate human feelings and invite us to empathise. It is pointed out that in Picasso's *Weeping Woman*, the subject 'has smart hair and a bright hat but she is feeling very sad'. Feeling is shown by the tears and jagged lines round her crying mouth, her fingers gripping a handkerchief and the colours used. Illustrations can also be a bridge between fact and fiction (Graham, 1996). The wonderful photographs in Waylands' History from Photographs series shows us how things were. Cox and Hughes's *School*, for example, fires our imagination by making us think about the lives of the individual children shown in their Edwardian classroom. I think writers and publishers of children's books should not be afraid to show the harsher, more distressing side of life in the illustrations used. Too much of the bland and the cosy dilutes our feelings of involvement.

Strategies to help children make progress

There are some challenging concepts and ideas and some demanding new study skills to acquire during the middle primary years. Children should be encouraged and stretched and often a particular technique, like note-taking for example, needs careful teaching. However, pupils of any age are more likely to put in the hard work if they have a broader purpose and if they can see the point of their efforts.

The National Literacy Strategy *Framework for Teaching* lists reading and writing objectives for each term of each year group. Only teachers and children can infuse these with life and meaning. Three things will help:

1   We need to take up the invitation to link the literacy hour objectives with lessons across the curriculum. History, geography, science, art and mathematics all provide excellent contexts for reading and writing texts.
2   We need to keep reading and writing together as two sides of the same literacy coin. There are links between NLP objectives for non-fiction reading and writing. For example, in Year 3, Term 1, looking at chapters, headings and information boxes – both in books and on the screen – informs children's own non-chronological writing.
3   We need to base, as far as possible, these literacy experiences in a motivating setting. Of course I do not mean that we can never teach a particular point except in these contexts. But if teachers were to interpret the NLS objectives narrowly and to organize non-fiction reading and writing in the form of exercises, children would be likely to lose out in a number of ways. They would not be supported to become self-motivated and assured readers and writers. Active readers transform new information and ideas to become part of their way of thinking and imagining – this would be difficult to achieve through worksheet-organized tasks. A mechanistic approach also fails to help children appreciate that kinds of reading and writing are culturally and socially situated and have become valued because they serve social needs. This is the strength of the functional model of kinds of texts set out in Chapter 1.

A framework of strategies to help children make progress in reading and writing non-fiction, used by good practitioners for some time and shown to be helpful in classroom-based research, is set out in Chapter 1. Below these strategies have been adapted to the interest and needs of seven to nine year olds. As in the chapters on other age groups, for reasons of convenience, reading strategies will be discussed first, followed by writing activities while keeping in mind the fundamental links.

Supporting children's non-fiction reading

The reading corner or area

In the middle primary years the contents of a good reading corner, which is likely to extend into a writing space (see under 'writing corner' below), will reflect the new reading materials with which the children will be working. In addition to books, encyclopaedias and software, folders of newspaper articles and advertisements will provide models of the persuasive kinds of writing children will be using, particularly in Year 4. A range of letters of varying degrees of formality will also support work during these two years.

It is important that children have an attractive area in the classroom in which to read informally and to browse, even though they will be making increasing use of the central library.

The library environment and library skills

The central library should be an accessible and inviting part of the school for children of all age groups. Attention should be given to clear labelling, illustrated sign-posting, a library notice board, a display area and large, clear, alphabetically arranged charts that indicate where resources on every topic can be found. Children start to acquire library skills from the beginning of their school life. They need to know that the central books and resources will be catalogued by author's name, title and subject in a card index or computer system. Both the catalogue system and the borrowing rules need to be made clear and perhaps reinforced by an encouragingly worded chart. Most school libraries use an abridged Dewey system, with a subject index and fiction catalogue. Some flexibility is desirable; for instance, books on a particular topic or a series of books could be grouped together as a collection. All this needs to be explained.

By the middle primary years, work is becoming more text based and use of the library will intensify. National Curriculum requirements have brought new areas of study into the primary years and this has been reflected in central library collections. In addition to books, resources are likely to include most of the following: computer software, CD-ROMs, the Internet, teletext/oracle, video-film, slides, cassette tapes, magazines, articles from newspapers, photographs, records and wall charts. Decisions will need to be made about storage and cataloguing based on the needs and preferences of the children and teachers in a particular school. Systems will need to be demonstrated to the children.

The English co-ordinator, and indeed all the staff, need to know what the library contains in order to direct and support the children's work. The demands of the literacy hour will have some impact on which books particular year groups will need at particular times of the year. The borrowing system needs to yield information about most and least used books, as this not only informs future orders but also helps the staff to evaluate the provision and its use.

Pre-reading activities

By the middle primary years, children's learning is more secondary source based than in the early years. To keep learning involved and active, the way in which we set up the context for teaching a new topic is important. I find that something as simple as saying 'We are going to be learning about . . . so if anyone finds a book or picture about this please bring it in' encourages a culture of co-operation. Even a modest start to a developing display of artefacts, books and materials can help spark interest at the beginning of the work. organization of prior knowledge through class discussion can involve joint note-taking on the board or flipchart. Making notes and summaries is a main theme through the NLS Objectives for Teaching. Opportunities for modelling this come up all the time and do not need to be contrived.

Children like to hear at the beginning of a series of lessons what they will be learning about and the tasks they will be carrying out. Even at this time of a more prescribed curriculum, I find there is room for some choice. Asking the children for suggestions as to what else might be included is often very rewarding. If what is suggested cannot be accommodated in the mainstream work, a child can be asked to do his or her own research at home and to share the fruits of it in the classroom.

Although we do not want to get into an inflexible pattern of pre-reading activities, it is nearly always helpful to ask the children what they think they need to find out. Sometimes the questions can be shared in discussion, sometimes written down in a jotter. Some teachers use the EXEL Writing Frame, which has spaces for children to write what they know and what they want to find out. No resource should be used mechanistically though, as Lewis and Wray (1996) make clear.

Modelling skimming, scanning and use of retrieval devices

The teacher will have prepared a mix of resources to support children's learning in the lesson or series of lessons. It is a good idea too for the teacher to say something about the resources – how they are to be used and to comment on any new features of the books. The non-narrative information books the children are now using will have more detailed retrieval devices which need to be explained. Increasing use of encyclopaedias and dictionaries in book and software form can be supported by the teacher demonstrating how information to answer one the children's questions might be found.

It is in this context that the flexible kind of reading strategies can be shown. Lunzer and Gardner identify different kinds of reading from scanning for a name or date, skimming through to get the gist of a passage, section or chapter to the reflective kind of reading needed when we evaluate a set of facts or ideas (Lunzer and Gardner, 1979). Reading information text out loud helps children become more familiar with the kind of vocabulary and syntax used. Teachers also make evaluative comments like 'this book has no glossary, but I've included it because of the very good photographs of. . .' Children can also be asked to prepare readings from a book they have been using. I find children like to be invited to evaluate the books at the end of a series of lessons or a project, particularly if they are asked to keep this in mind from the start. As well as the text, the illustrations need some com- ment – how easy or difficult are the diagrams to understand and how help- ful are the photographs in creating an environment or showing a close-up of a phenomenon? Teacher and children are both researching a topic and find- ing out about the resources.

Sharing the fruits of research

In a world that overwhelms us with information, time for reflection on facts and ideas needs to be preserved. One of the best features of the literacy hour is the plenary session during which teacher and children reflect on things of note and resavour what has been achieved. We need to make time in every lesson for children's feedback on their research. Again, it is possible to settle into too predictable a pattern and we need to ring the changes. Sometimes one member of each group might share the findings with the class or present them to another group. On other occasions another class can be invited to watch a short presentation on a project. School assemblies and open days are other contexts for sharing what has been achieved in a special project. The children in the case study who researched animals and ethical issues greatly enjoyed presenting the debates to other classes.

Supporting children's non-fiction writing

Good practitioners have their own views about what writing development is and how it can be supported in the middle primary years. These views are informed by teaching experience and by the findings of research studies and investigations like those for *The National Writing Project* (Czerniewska, 1992). This project worked at the grass roots and encouraged teachers to carry out their own research and evaluation of the writing programmes in their schools. It is worth thinking about our aims and priorities before get- ting locked into the National Literary Strategy objectives. We certainly want children to control an increasing number of the writing genres valued in our society. Long ago in 1970 James Britton, in one of the wisest books ever written on language development, *Language and Learning*, made this point. Linked to this is the need for children to understand the purposes and audiences for all the different kinds of writing. Clearly children need to be helped to control their writing – both its compositional and transcriptional aspects – so that it communicates what they want it to. But writing is also a powerful means of organizing thinking, of making sense of experience. It is this function of language in general and writing in particular which seems to me to be lacking in the National Literacy Strategy framework. In Chapter 1 it was suggested we see writing as serving different functions – literary, referential, persuasive and expressive. It is the last one – 'expressive' writing to give voice to children's more explorative thinking and feeling about a range of topics, as a tool for organising thinking – which seems relatively lacking. There is every reason why teachers should allow opportunities for this kind of writing. Learning to write goes alongside writing to learn in every lesson. The recounts children write of experiences in and out of the classroom often have an expressive flavour which suggests the writing task is helping to organise their thoughts. How children feel about experiences and issues is also often evident in this kind of writing. We would expect expressive touches also in early attempts at writing with a persuasive purpose.

This section starts with the kind of environment the good literacy teacher creates in the middle primary years. Next, some of the ways in which we teach and support non-fiction writing are considered, including help with note-taking and summarising. The increasingly important role of the computer in expanding what children can achieve at every stage of the writing process is emphasized.

Children are becoming able by the middle primary years to understand the status of different kinds of writing – which kinds are to do with fact and which express an opinion about those facts. Ways of supporting these developing abilities are suggested. Finally we look at outcomes for children's written work.

The writing environment

The literacy corners or areas that are such a strong feature of early years classrooms also have an important place in the junior years. In the middle primary years a good writing area, usually an extension of the reading corner, has lively displays of children's work with clear labels and annotations, a range of different kinds and sizes of paper and card, hard covers, book spines, glue and so on for book-making, and a selection of writing implements. At least one of the class computers will be placed here.

We would expect a Year 3 writing corner to provide examples of some of the new kinds of writing introduced at this stage: examples of notes on a topic of interest; non-fiction relevant to work in a curriculum area set out in different formats using headings and bullet points; examples of alphabetically ordered lists and leaflets; examples of desktop publishing; letters of different kinds; and perhaps a folder with the same information produced as a story, letter or news report. Some charts, possibly made by teacher and children, setting out key points to bear in mind when making notes, writing instructions and the principles on which writing is divided into paragraphs would also be helpful.

Much of all this would also be found in a good Year 4 literacy area with the addition of examples of some of the writing forms introduced at this stage. These include newspaper-type reports, charts and diagrams using information from different sources, explanations of processes, advertisements and other persuasive kinds of writing. Non-fiction book reviews on display could usefully include children's evaluations of two books on the same topic.

Of course the good writing area or corner must go beyond just looking impressive. When you go into a classroom it is soon evident if the writing corner is at the heart of everyday work. The work and displays are referred to constantly during the day and children have fair access to the relative privacy of the area as individuals or in groups. The displays are likely to be used and learnt from if they are genuine outcomes of the writing activities of each week. A developing display, one that is constantly modified and extended, reflects the dynamic nature of good practice.

Above all, a good writing corner conveys a sense of children feeling able to experiment, take initiative and enjoy becoming writers.

Supporting writing at 7–9 years

In the middle primary years children meet new kinds of material which demand particular skills and strategies in reading and in writing. More of children's learning across the curriculum is text mediated. A long-term issue of continuing importance is children's tendency to copy or closely paraphrase from the more challenging non-chronological texts which they need to control as they journey through the primary school (Mallett, 1992; Neate, 1992; Wray and Lewis, 1992). Making notes and summaries has considerable emphasis in the National Literacy Strategy objectives for the middle primary years. In my view there is no need to contrive exercises using random text when the children are using books and resources across the whole curriculum. It is far better to take a close look at a relevant text in the literacy hour and then exploit this in history, science or geography. There is a welcome linkage in the objectives of the National Literacy Strategy between reading and writing. The information books and instructions they read provide models for their writing.

THE RESEARCHER'S TOOLS: HELP WITH FORMAT AND PRESENTATION, NOTE-TAKING AND SUMMARIES

We need to convince children that becoming able to carry out the above strategies will help them research and present better all those things they want to find out about. 'Format' is to do with the global structure of a writing task and shows at a glance the scope and emphasis of the work.

Desk-top publishing packages like TAG's *First Page* are making a considerable contribution to children's understanding of the choices available. Children can use the new technology to achieve satisfying and professional-looking presentation of the different kinds of writing they encounter in their reading material. Use of headings, bullet points for lists, and information boxes can be modelled by the teacher and then applied when the children write their own informational accounts.

Learning to make notes and summaries is an intellectually challenging and important part of becoming a researcher. Making notes from reading, for example, helps children compose their own writing rather than to closely paraphrase what an author has already organised. How then do we help children learn to take notes? I have observed several Year 3 teachers involve a whole class in note-taking. In one case, notes were made from a book they had been using during work on the planets and stars. The teacher showed a page on the overhead projector and read out loud. The children were invited to say which bit could be underlined as the most important point or points and then these were written in bullet points on a flipchart. Children's accounts were written using the notes. As we would expect, there was differentiation by outcome. All the children included the main points while the more forward writers enriched their work with subsidiary information.

Another promising strategy is to read a section from an information book that is being currently used for work in any lesson or the literacy hour, and to ask the children to listen and write down five key points – about 'the Diet of the Ancient Greeks' or about 'Young and Old Rivers'. Children love reading out their lists and these can be discussed in a constructive way. Was there a main point missed out, for example? This helps children to begin to reflect on the status of particular pieces of information. From skeleton notes summaries can be written on parts of books.

Photocopies of a page of text can be used in group activities which involve children in highlighting the key vocabulary on a page and then discussing it or marking key information to be used in their own summary. These directed activities round texts (DARTS) have been used in classrooms for a long time. They have come to new prominence as part of work at sentence and word level in the literacy hour. Skilled practitioners are able to indicate how note-taking skills can help children go about their research in every lesson. Talking about the reasons why some points are more central than others energises the learning. In one classroom this could be a dreary exercise while in another the children are clearly being encouraged to see the activities as steps towards controlling texts and engaging more powerfully with the ideas.

These activities are best grounded in work across the curriculum and reinforced and linked with a close look at text in the literacy hour. I have found that making notes from pictures and diagrams rather than from text can be helpful in the early stages of note-making.

TEACHER SUPPORT FOR ORGANIZING WRITING AND ILLUSTRATING

Children can be helped to reflect on the structure of a particular piece of writing by thinking it through with the teacher or a child partner. The talk, or in Graves' term 'conference', with its stress on collaboration at each stage of the writing process, is probably the finest support that can be given. There is immediate feedback on the young writer's ideas. Writing is hard and the thought of sharing the processes is appealing. The difficulty is over-allocation of time and not every child can have a detailed set of conferences for each writing task. Informational writing can be planned under headings, for example like Sarah's instruction book on making pizza in the first case study at the end of this chapter. This approach to planning a booklet was used in Mallett's work with children learning about grey squirrels and how their structure affected function. The children made a working contents page to organize their work and modified it later in the light of what they had actually done (Mallett, 1992).

Another approach is to provide a framework of headings with spaces for children to write. The EXEL team at Exeter University have carried out considerable classroom based work to produce a collection of writing frames to help structure children's writing in a variety of genres (Lewis and Wray, 1996). Teachers have found these helpful, particularly where young learners have great difficulty in managing writing tasks. The researchers consider that when it comes to a new or difficult genre, having a skeleton structure, often with a vocabulary that drives the writing on, leaves the children free to concentrate on the content. Of course, the aim is to provide a prop until children can write independently. Some teachers report that children who rarely manage more than a few lines have managed to write much more using the framework. Others feel it can deprive a child of an important part of the writing process – the organization of the piece. Writing frames are mentioned as a possible way of making progress in instructional kinds of writing in the NLS objectives for Year 3, Term 1. The main thing is that, as Lewis and Wray would wish, teachers are aware of the frames as a tool to use if and when they seem helpful.

LETTERS

Children will have some knowledge of the social purposes of letters and with some help will be able to make some categories: personal letters to friends and relatives; more formal letters to known people like the teacher explaining absence from school; formal business letters; and letters as primary sources in history.

Drama and role play can provide a helpful context for writing all sorts of letters as the 'Giant' case study 3.3 shows. An issue taken up through drama – for example an environmental problem – could be a setting for the children writing in role to a newspaper expressing different viewpoints about animals in danger or plans to build on a children's park. This could provide a writing activity for the literacy hour and would include the conventions of writing formal letters. One class I visited was asked to write to invite parents and friends of their school to a special open day and to make the letter interesting enough to make the people want to attend. Several children designed a tear-off slip for recipients to return. Writing this sort of letter was one of the writing task choices for the 1998 English tests for Year 6.

A very interesting aspect is letters used as a literary device in fiction. Books that teachers might like to consider are *Dear Greenpeace* by Simon James, *Chips and Jessie* by Shirley Hughes, *Dear Mr Henshaw* by Beverley Cleary, *Boy: Tales of Childhood* by Roald Dahl and *The Last Polar Bears* by Harry Horse. Children might be asked what the audience and purpose is of the letters, and to try to write some of their own in role. This is an example of how fiction can often be the starting-point for learning.

FACT AND OPINION: WRITING TO PERSUADE – FLYERS AND ADVERTISEMENTS

Very young children can understand that people have different viewpoints about important issues. Five year olds listening to Sheldon and Blythe's *The Whales' Song* recognised that the hard-boiled utilitarian views of Uncle Fred were challenged by the feelings of Lucy and her grandmother that whales were beautiful creatures who should not be allowed to die out. The children in case study 4.2 felt a similar concern about the fate of laboratory animals and, interestingly, this concern was awakened by a work of fiction.

Children who have been encouraged to think about different perspectives in this sympathetic kind of way are more likely to benefit from work around the persuasive kinds of texts like advertisements, flyers and circulars, which are an NLS objective in the final term of Year 4. A series of advertisements about one product or all aimed at a particular audience could be the literacy hour texts for a week and children could scrutinise them to find what was evidence and what conjecture. Language is used to create an image for a product and analysis of this can help children on the journey to becoming critical readers.

Children enjoy making their own flyers and posters (perhaps for a school event) and several software programs (e.g. *Banner* and *BannerMania*) make their efforts look professional. However, while these tools can and should be brought into the literacy programme, children also like to design their posters using stencils and felt tips. Making a poster on the floor in this way is a different but equally valuable experience as using the computer.

Learning from fiction and non-fiction

By the middle primary years children recognise some of the features that identify a text with a particular genre. They appreciate that stories and poems are read or listened to in their entirety while referential books and materials are turned to when specific information is sought. Using the terms 'fiction' and 'non-fiction' appropriately is a formal requirement of the National Literacy Strategy (Year 3, Term 1). But in the classroom case studies in this book, we find teachers and children often using fiction and non-fiction flexibly to learn about the world and human experience within it. This links with the recognition that a story, a letter or a news account are different ways of recounting an event (NLS FFT Year 3, Term 3). One of the case studies in this chapter shows children enjoying Robert O'Brien's novel, *Mrs Frisby and the Rats of Nimh*, and then turning to an information book to find out more about how we treat animals.

Novels, short stories and poetry all teach us about real life, often powerfully creating environments across the world and over time. Historical novels and stories about time slippage – one of the most acclaimed being Philippa Pearce's *Tom's Midnight Garden*, in which a child finds the past at night in the Victorian garden of the house in which he is staying – share with children the writer's imaginative reconstruction of the past. The texture of urban childhood experience is explored in Michael Rosen's poetry, which interestingly draws on a range of different kinds of utterance including science reports, lists and news items.

Walker's Read and Wonder series recognises people's feelings about issues and phenomena as a part of knowing the truth; in French and Wisenfield's *Spider Watching*, attitudes towards spiders are part of the picture. Feelings and factual information are wonderfully combined in E.B. White's *Charlotte's Web*, which explains so carefully the life-cycle of a spider.

Illustrations can provide a useful link between fact and fiction. Graham shows how meticulously the best creators of picture books research environments, costumes and artefacts to inform both text and illustration (Graham, 1996). Charles Keeping's picture books show the changing landscape of the streets of East London in *Railway Passage* and *Sammy Streetsinger*. All this can be discussed by teacher and children as part of 'noticing the differences in the style and structure of fiction and non-fiction writing' (Year 3, Term 1).

Perhaps the most important contribution that quality fiction makes is to remind us of the wholeness of learning. Feelings, atmospheres and moods are all part of a sense of place or an understanding of an issue, and these are often well captured in story or poem. In each chapter we find teachers sometimes using story and informational text as mutually enriching in taking on the complexity of issues.

One important issue is to do with the reading preferences of girls and boys – it is often thought that girls generally prefer fiction and boys feel more comfortable with non-fiction, reflecting perhaps the emphasis in their parents' reading. However, recent studies show a more complex picture and suggest how we can help all children appreciate what different kinds of text offer (Mallett, 1997; Millard, 1997).

The National Curriculum at key stage 2: non-fiction reading

Societal changes in technological cultures are relentless, and statutory documentation, like the National Curriculum in the UK, is modified and reshaped to keep pace. Schools now frequently have web sites on the Internet and children's computer skills are used to further their progress in all aspects of their education at school and often at home too.

The scale and scope of informational reading and writing will continue to change, but the key skills in reading such as posing questions, identifying information, considering an argument critically, distinguishing between fact and opinion, representing information in different forms, using library and classification systems, catalogues and indexes, are likely to remain central. Similarly, the emphasis on writing for different purposes and audiences, and the plan, draft, revise, proof-read and present stages is likely to endure.

There is a non-fiction element in the SATs at the end of key stage 1 and key stage 2 – see Chapter 7. Teachers constantly observe and monitor children's reading and writing strategies and collect samples of work for reading and writing records and folders. Children's current achievement is assessed partly by looking at their work alongside the National Curriculum level descriptions for reading and writing. The descriptions include both fiction and non-fiction reading and writing.

Non-fiction in the literacy hour, Years 3 and 4

This book is informed by the National Curriculum requirements summarised above and by the more detailed National Literacy Strategy 1998 objectives. Official requirements change constantly and this is one of the reasons why I have chosen not to start each chapter by recounting them. Instead, I have tried to set out what is likely always to be true about supporting children's learning from non-fiction. Nevertheless the suggested strategies above cover the following major areas to do with non-fiction reading and writing listed in the *Framework for Teaching*.

Year 3 non-fiction programme

Children should be conversant with the following:

- use of retrieval devices, presentation of information in books and ICT sources, making and using notes (Term 1);
- evaluation of different texts, organisation of instructional texts, note making and using, writing for a particular audience (Term 2);
- placing letters on a continuum from formal to informal, acquiring library skills, using ICT to bring writing to a published form, developing work on note-taking and learning to summarise (Term 3).

Year 4 non-fiction programme

Children should learn to:

- identify features of non-fiction text, read newspaper reports and write their own using ICT and appropriate format, understand reading strategies for ICT texts, achieve cohesion in writing instructional text and develop writing of non-chronological report (Term 1);
- develop scanning and skimming skills, identify key features of explanatory text and to link what is learnt through reading to their own writing (Term 2);
- understand how arguments are presented in texts like advertisements with supporting diagrams, develop summarising ability and to carry out their own persuasive writing (Term 3).

CASE STUDIES

The classroom examples take up two areas important in the middle years of the primary school. First, with an eye on what is involved in learning to read and write procedural text, we follow eight year old Sarah's progress through the stages of writing out instructions for a recipe and illustrating the work. Second, we join a Year 4 class who, inspired by a novel, become clearer about the different kinds of learning achievable from fiction and non-fiction texts.

Case study 4.1: Making pizza

An eight year old is helped to write and illustrate a book about making pizza

The context of the work

This example concentrates on detailed book-making work carried out with one child by a mature student teacher, Carol Eagleton, over a number of weeks in a south east London C. of E. school. The intention was to help eight year old Sarah to develop her literacy in the context of an enjoyable task. Each stage of the book-making was discussed and the purpose (to make it possible for someone to create a pizza from the instructions) and intended audience of the book (the other children in the class) focused the discussions. There was considerable adult intervention and the reflection through talk about the writing task was a most important element in the work.

Choosing the topic and planning the global structure of the book

Sarah wanted to make an information book about how to make pizza and said her mother had a very good recipe. This project linked school and home in a very fruitful way as Sarah's mother agreed to allow Sarah to make the pizza at home. The writing and assembling of the book was carried out at school.

First Ms E asked Sarah to think of some headings to organise the book and these became the contents page and the global structure of the book.

Contents

What kind of illustrations?

Mrs E brought in some examples of books with a procedural text – Dorling Kindersley cookery books with photographs to accompany the different stages and books with drawings to demonstrate procedures. (Since this work was carried out, some very good cookbooks for children have been produced, for example Jane Asher's *Round the World Cookbook*, which is in big and small book form and can be used for class-based work on procedural kinds of writing.) Sarah thought photographs of herself making the pizza would make it a personal account. Her mother offered to be the photographer.

Kinds of writing

After looking through some good cookery books, Sarah and Ms E decided there were two main kinds of writing involved – lists and a step-by-step account of the procedures.

To add a playful touch Sarah invented the name of an Italian chef –

Signor Mozzerelli – and said she was making Signor Mozzerelli's pizza recipe.

To break up the list, some of the ingredients were indented using the computer. Presentation helps identify text with a genre and lists can be made using bullet points. Using desktop publishing, children can box instructions in a number of different ways that make them look professional.

Writing the instructions

Instructions for older children and adults are sometimes written in the passive tense. Recipes, however, are usually written in the second person. In spite of reading second-person task instructions in books, Sarah wanted to write her instructions as a first-person narrative. She felt her audience, the other children in the class, would prefer this, particularly as she was using photographs of herself at work in the kitchen. She was meticulous in describing each stage of her preparation and cooking and one had the impression she has heard her mother talking through the procedures.

She showed considerable awareness of the needs of her audience, giving reasons for the things she was doing – 'I stir the mixture to help the yeast and sugar to dissolve' and 'I have to put the flour in a sieve to shake out any lumps.' Asked by Ms E how she could make sure none of the other children came to any harm if they tried to make the pizza, Sarah wrote: 'My mother helped me to take the pizza out of the oven when it was ready.'

The photographs were an excellent aide-mémoire. Sarah and Ms E did the editing together, deciding on the sequence of photographs and creating an explanatory text round them. Sarah showed good control over the terminology of cooking in her use of process words like weighing, dissolving, mixing, shaking, kneading, heating, stirring, thickening, slicing, arranging and rolling, like 'a sprinkling of oregano', 'a drizzle of olive oil'. She also looked with Ms E at the pattern of words like 'first', 'then', 'next', 'when' and 'after', which give instructional text cohesion.

Ms E pointed out that books often have an 'about the author' section. Using a book featuring this as a model, Sarah wrote a short piece giving her age, family details and hobbies and arranged this round a recent photograph of herself. Sarah was very aware that her peers were the main audience for the book and was delighted with Ms E's final suggestion for making the book fun as well as useful. Together they created a wonderful novelty feature on the back page; Sarah's drawing of a large pizza was cut out and made into portions which came together and separated as a tag of attached cardboard was pulled. On the central disc were the words 'I love pizza'. Underneath Sarah had typed

'Here is Signor Mozzerelli's Pizza. Now you see it, now you don't.' Knowing her classmates well, Sarah was anxious that the novelty was not swiftly broken and she printed 'Very fragile – Please handle with care' at the bottom of the page.

Outcomes

Several copies of the text were printed out so that the class could have one in their library, Ms E could submit a copy with her college English assignment, and Sarah and her mother could have a copy at home. Each copy was carefully paginated and laminated.

Finally Sarah was asked to tell her class about the book-making experience and to read out her lists and some of the instructions and show the photographs.

Making such a successful book with the help of both Ms E and her mother was clearly a rewarding experience for Sarah and contributed greatly to her developing literacy. She is ready now to go on to second-person accounts as part of her developing control over instructional writing. Talking about the stages of the task, examining other books of the same genre, and experiencing direct teaching about reading and writing all made this a rich experience. The interplay between text, action and observation was similar in some respects to the example of the children learning about trees in the quotation that begins this chapter. The social purposes of writing were particularly apparent and Sarah constantly had the readers of her recipe in mind as she created the book. She learnt about the global features and the conventional language of instructional text. The way in which illustrations contribute was central in the task. Unlike many authors, she had the pleasure of sharing her book with her intended audience and seeing their very positive response. (No teacher or parent will be surprised to learn that the moving pizza picture made of cardboard was liked and remembered most.)

While it is helpful and interesting to reflect on teacher-intensive work like this, we have to consider what is practical and possible for teachers working with the whole class and within the constraints of the literacy hour.

Work on instructional texts is located in Year 3, Term 2 of the National Literacy Strategy objectives, where children are required to 'write instructions or rules for playing games or recipes using a range of organisational devices'. Another of the objectives is to do with 'identifying the intended audience' for writing. All this and much more was achieved in this example. How could it be adapted for whole-class and group literacy hour work?

There is no reason why a recipe, or series of recipes, should not be the text or texts of the week. A parent, a child or the teacher could write out their favourite recipe on an overhead projector for the class-based work. The linguistic and presentational aspects would be considered before group work on children's own lists, instructions and illustrations of the processes. This could lead to a class book of favourite recipes or a display of mounted recipes and instructions in the writing corner.

Case study 4.2: Animals in danger

Year 4: Animals and ethics – from fiction to fact

Children's involvement with their learning intensifies when they use information to reflect on issues of real concern; indeed, one of the objectives for Year 4, Term 3, in the NLS *Framework for Teaching* is to do with evaluating arguments and viewpoints from books and other materials. This builds on Year 4, Term 1 work on learning to distinguish between fact and opinion and is the forerunner of more advanced work on reading and writing with a persuasive function in the later primary years. This example, based on work first described in Mallett (1992) is from a Croydon junior school.

Starting with fiction

The teacher and children had shared a reading over a number of weeks of *Mrs Frisby and the Rats of Nimh* by Robert O'Brien. The story begins with Mrs Frisby, a field mouse, requesting that some rats help her move her home away from the threat of a farmer's tractor. She soon finds that in return for their favour she is helping them. The teacher told me that the children were very affected by the passages in the book about the catching of the rats and the locking of them into laboratory cages. Asked how the author had made this aspect of the story so vivid, one of the children thought the first-person 'voice' made it seem as if Nicodemus was talking – it made the danger seem more immediate:

> That cage was my home for a long time. It was not uncomfortable; it had a floor of some kind of plastic, medium soft and warm to the touch; with wire walls and ceiling, it was airy enough. Yet just the fact that it was a cage made it horrible. I, who had always run where I wanted, could go three hops forward, three hops back again, and that was all. But worse was the dreadful feeling – I know we all had it – that we were completely at the mercy of someone we knew not at all, for some purpose we could not guess. What were their plans for us?
>
> (O'Brien, 1972: 92)

In one sense this tells us more about what it is like for human beings to be kept captive. It is people and not animals who have the ability to reflect on events and therefore to experience fear on a different plane. Nevertheless, it does raise issues about keeping animals in laboratories and subjecting them to injections and experiments that will not benefit them or their species. These children who were described as 'normally rather reserved' asked many questions about how true the account was and, if so, why animals were experimented on.

Turning to non-fiction for specific information

The children appreciated that a different sort of text was needed to answer these more precise questions. The teacher brought in Miles Barton's *Why Do People Harm Animals?* to help structure the discussion. She remarked to me that she had never known an information book make such an impact on a whole class. It was read out aloud and then the children borrowed it in turn. When I visited the class one of the children drew my attention to the front cover picture showing a monkey hideously made up and dressed in clothes. It brought home to the children how unnatural it was to take animals away from their natural surroundings and to force them to endure lotions and makeup on their skins. The teacher felt the monkey picture became an important image of animals' exploitation in the work that followed the reading of the novels.

Miles Barton's book takes on the complexity of the issues and is the sort of text we should seek out to support children's discussion. Talking points inspired by the book included the following:

• As far as we know, animals only have a present (except in fiction like *Mrs Frisby*), but should this mean we can do whatever we like to them?
• Should we make a division between experiments for medical purposes and experiments for yet more cosmetics?
• Are there alternative ways of finding cures for human ailments?

Although it did not happen in this case, the discussions could have led to a range of written work – taking up a viewpoint in a letter, writing a newspaper report or a day in the life of a laboratory animal.

Animal charities and research laboratories sometimes have educational materials for children on request. A similar case study arising out of a reading of Dick King Smith's *The Sheep-pig* led to reading materials sent by a charity called Compassion in World Farming (Mallett, 1992).

Returning to this case study, the teacher considered that the work had helped the children understand more clearly what fiction and non-fiction can contribute to learning about the world. Moreover, on reading the information book, they were helped to see that people arrive at different viewpoints on the same evidence, helping them to differentiate fact from opinion.

Conclusion

Quality books and resources and interesting tasks are the key to making reading and writing to learn worthwhile in the important middle primary years. Young researchers need to acquire new tools – some direct teaching of note-taking strategies and summarising is necessary. The computer is a powerful tool for developing some kinds of reading and writing and greatly facilitates presentational considerations like choosing appropriate formats for particular writing tasks and learning about paragraphing. Work across the curriculum and in the literacy hour is becoming more text based and children need to control a number of non-fiction genres as readers and writers. We must not allow new requirements to make us lose sight of children's need to bring their imagination and feelings to their work as well as their intellects. As Egan reminds us, the human mind is not like a computer, not least because we can transform all the knowledge that we encounter and see possibilities as well as actualities (Egan, 1992).

Children need help in identifying the genre features of particular kinds of texts and these features are very often linked to social purposes and intended audiences. Illustrations help link a text with a particular kind of writing and can have a humanising effect, as we see in the case study on animals at risk. Fiction is a powerful vehicle for many kinds of learning and often creates an interest in issues which can be explored later through informational sources.

Collaboration over projects energises children's learning. Working with others and reflecting jointly, paradoxically often supports our development as independent readers. We must remember the power of spoken language to explore ideas from books and resources and to plan and reflect on writing.

Issues to discuss and reflect on

1   What do you consider is the potential of computers to accelerate children's progress as readers and writers of non-fiction from seven to nine years?

2 Examine some dictionaries and thesauruses on the market, both books and software, for this age range and note their relative merits.

3 With reference to some encyclopaedias or non-narrative information books, consider what the advantages are of 'browsing time'.

4 What do you consider are some of the advantages and disadvantages of using writing frames to structure children's writing in the middle primary years? Would a writing frame, for instance, have helped Sarah (pizza case study) with the global structure of her task?

5 List some interesting and helpful ways of helping children make notes and summaries (a) from practical activities like science or cooking and /or (b) from their reading.

6 Some research suggests that in general boys prefer non-fiction and girls prefer fiction. How can we encourage all the children to enjoy all kinds of reading and writing? In reflecting on this you may like to consider the possible role of the same-gender parent in children's reading preferences.

7 With reference to your own practice, discuss how you have used or might use texts of different kinds, fiction and non-fiction, to support children's learning about a topic.

Note

Myra Barr's (1997) *The Core Booklist* from the Centre for Language for Language in Primary Education (CLPE) includes a collection of 30 information books for key stage 2 to provide the 'voices' of different kinds of information books, each good of its kind.

Further reading

BECTA *(The British Educational and Communications Technology Agency)* has a site on the Internet, <http://www.becta.org.uk>. This is a huge database which can be searched by subject or key stage and which includes reviews on resources by teachers, advisers and librarians. This links with the National Grid for Learning/Virtual Teacher Centre which provides other resources and links to other teachers.

Czerniewska, P. (1992) *Learning About Writing*. Oxford: Blackwell.

Egan, K. (1992) *Imagination in Teaching and Learning: The Middle School Years*. Chicago: University of Chicago Press.

Mallett, M. (1992) *Making Facts Matter: Reading Non-fiction 5–11*. London: Paul Chapman.

Millard, E. (1997) *Differently Literate: Boys, Girls and the Schooling of Literacy*. London: Falmer.

Moon, C. (1998) *Twenty-five Years of Individualised Reading*. Reading: Reading and Language Information Centre, Reading University.

Preston, C. (first edition 1995, regularly updated) *21st Century A–Z Literacy Handbook: Linking Literacy with Software*. Available from Project Miranda, Institute of Education, 20 Bedford Way, London WC1H OAL. (0181 686 8769).

School Library Services. *Going Places* (Oct. 1997) (Guide to atlases and map books).

Children's books and resources mentioned

(NB: Reading scheme books and some series are set out under 'Range' in this chapter.)

Ahlberg, J. and Ahlberg, A. (1990) *The Jolly Postman*. London: Heinemann.

Allen, J. and Humphries, T. (1998) *Whale*. Animals at Risk series. London: Walker Books.

Ardley, N. (1998) *Sound; Water*. Make Science Fun series. London: Dorling Kindersley.

Asher, J. (1998) *Round the World Cookbook*. London: Longman Book Project.

Atlas of the British Isles (1994). Ed. S. Palmer. London: Longman Book Project, non-fiction 1, tier 2 text.

Barton, M. (1988) *Why Do People Harm Animals?* London: Aladdin Books.

Big Book of Mapwork 1 and *Big Book of Mapwork 2* (1998). Hove: Wayland Publishers.

Blyth, J. (1993) *Tudor and Stuart Times*. History Stories series. London: Ginn and Company.

Bresler, L. (1998) *Earth Facts*. Facts and Lists series. London: Usborne.

Cleary, B. (1983) *Dear Mr. Henshaw*. Harmondsworth: Penguin/Puffin.

Coiley, J. (1992) *Trains*. Eyewitness Guides. London: Dorling Kindersley.

Collins Children's Encyclopedia (1998). Ed. J. Farndon. London: HarperCollins.

Collins Ultimate Atlas of Almost Everything (1998). Ed. S. Parker, S. Morgan and P. Steele. London: HarperCollins.

Cox, K. and Hughes, P. (1995) *School*. History From Photographs series. London: Wayland/Macdonald.

Dahl, R. (1984) *Boy: Tales of Childhood*. Harmondsworth: Penguin/Puffin.

Dorling Kindersley Children's Illustrated Encyclopedia (1997). Ed. A. Kramer. London: Dorling Kindersley.

Dorling Kindersley Children's Picture Encyclopedia (1997). Ed. C. Llewellyn. London: Dorling Kindersley.

Dorling Kindersley's Discoveries series (1998) includes: *Pompeii: The Day a City Was Buried* and *Tutankhamun: The Life and Death of a Pharaoh*. London: Dorling Kindersley.

Dorling Kindersley's 3D series (1998) includes: *Insect*; *Microfile*; *Plant*; *Reptile* with mirror viewer. London: Dorling Kindersley.

Dorling Kindersley's Why Do We? series (1996) includes: *Why Do We Laugh?* Ed. H. Ziefert and E. Boon. London: Dorling Kindersley.

Drew, H. (1996) *My First Baking Book* (also *Cook* in the same series) London: Dorling Kindersley.

Eyewitness Atlas of the World (1996). Ed. D. Green. London: Dorling Kindersley.

Farmer, A. (1991) *Invaders and Settlers*. History Stories series. London: Ginn and Company.

French, V. and Milne, T. (1994) *The Apple Tree*. Read and Wonder series. London: Walker Books.

French, V. and Wisenfield, A. (1994) *Spider Watching*. Read and Wonder series. London: Walker Books.

Ganon, A. (1994) *I Wonder Why the Wind Blows and Other Questions about Our Planet*. London: Kingfisher.

Goodall, J. (1994) *With Love, Stories of Chimpanzees in the Wild*. London: North South Books.

Greenaway, F. and Taylor, B. (1998) *Rock Pool*; *Pondlife*; *Desert Life*; *Rain Forest*. Look Closer series. London: Dorling Kindersley.

Hooper, M. (1997) *Coral Reef*, *Desert*, and *Rain Forest*. Cambridge Reading Scheme. Cambridge: Cambridge University Press.

Horse, H. (1993) *The Last Polar Bears*. Harmondsworth: Penguin/Viking.

Hughes, S. (1987) *Chips and Jessie*. Young Lions. London: Collins.

James, S. (1991) *Dear Greenpeace*. London: Walker Books

Keeping, C. (1974) *Railway Passage*. Oxford: Oxford University Press.

Keeping, C. (1989) *Sammy Streetsinger*. Oxford: Oxford University Press.

King, D. (1994) *Photography*. My First series. London: Dorling Kindersley.

King-Smith, D. (1983) *The Sheep-pig*. Harmondsworth: Penguin.

Kingfisher Children's Encyclopedia (1998). Ed. S. Milan. London: Kingfisher/ Larousse.

Ladybird Discovery Encyclopedia of the Natural World (1998). Comp. R. C. Dungworth. London: Ladybird Books.

Lion Graphic Bible (1998). Ed. J. Anderson and M. Maddox. Oxford: Lion.

Longman Book Project Wild Animal Encyclopedia (1994) 4 vols. London: Longman.

Millennium Family Encyclopedia (1998) London: Dorling Kindersley. Available through Dorling Kindersley Family Learning (01403 833200).

Moore, P. and Doherty, P. (illus.)(1994) *The Stars*; *Comets and Shooting Stars*. London: Riverswift Books.

New Lion Encyclopedia of the Bible (1998). Ed. J. Drane. Oxford: Lion.

O'Brien, R. (1972) *Mrs Frisby and the Rats of Nimh*. London: Victor Gollancz.

Oxford Children's Encyclopedia (1998). Ed. B. Dupre. 9 vols. Oxford: Oxford University Press.

Oxford Children's Thesaurus (1991). Comp. A. Spooner. London: Oxford University Press.

Oxford First Encyclopedia (1998). Ed. A. Langley. Oxford: Oxford University Press.

Oxford School Atlas (1997). Ed. P. Wiegand. Oxford: Oxford University Press.

Oxford Young Reader's Dictionary (1997). Ed. R. Sansome, D. Reid and A. Spooner. Oxford: Oxford University Press.

Pearce, P. (1958) *Tom's Midnight Garden*. Oxford: Oxford University Press.

Richardson, J. (1997) *Making Faces*. Looking at Pictures series. London: Franklin Watts.

Sheldon, D. and Blythe, G. (1990) *The Whales' Song*. London: Hutchinson.

Sirett, D. (1994) *Painting*. My First series. London: Dorling Kindersley.

Toksvig, S. (1997) *If I Didn't Have Elbows: The Alternative Body Book*. London: Zero to Ten.

Usborne First Dictionary (1995). Ed. R. Wardley and J. Bingham. London: Usborne.

Wallace, K. (1993) *Think of an Eel*. Read and Wonder series. London: Walker Books.

White, E. B. (1952) *Charlotte's Web*. Harmondsworth: Penguin.

Wilkes, A. (1994) *My First Science Book*. My First series. London; Dorling Kindersley.

Yildirim, E. (1997) *Aunty Dot's Incredible Adventure Atlas*. London: Collins Children's Books.

Software

Ancient Lands CD-ROM Microsoft 1994/1955.

Banner (posters which can be printed in any size). TAG (01474 357350).

BannerMania (posters made from favourite pictures or from scratch).TAG (01474 357350).

ClarisWorks Primary Templates (story starters, diary, etc.). TAG (01474 357350).

Crossword Creator (helps children create their own puzzles and includes Roget's Thesaurus. Aids newspaper-making). MacLine/WindowsLine (0181 1111/1177).

EasyWorks (aids newspaper reports and surveys). Aztec (01274 596716).

Eyewitness History of the World CD-ROM Dorling Kindersley (0171 836 5411).

First Page (desk-top publishing package for the primary classroom). TAG (01474 357350).

Landmarks Microworlds Longman Logotron (01223 425558).

Mapper Series: Body, Weather, Home (aids vocabulary development through illustration). TAG (01474 357350).

Microsoft Reference CDs (Research materials to give authenticity to reporting to the class) Kim Tec (01202 888873).

My First Incredible, Amazing Dictionary (1,000 word dictionary with word games and puzzles to reinforce alphabet and dictionary skills). Dorling Kindersley (0171 836 5411).

Time Detectives . . . The Victorians (history through story) Sherston (01666 840433).

Word Bank (a dictionary of words can be created for a particular class or pupil). TAG (01474 357350).

Write with Me (helps create cards and signs) Novell WordPerfect (01344 724000).

Writer's Toolkit (allows experimentation with different writing styles including journalism) SCET (0141 334 9314).

Star books for the mid-primary years

Alderton, D. (1997) *Stick Insect*. Your First series. TFH/Kingdom Books. These small books on a huge range of mammals, fish and reptiles are recommended for any age from age five upwards. Seven to nine year olds will like the detailed information and the practical advice about collecting and housing.

Binch, C. (1998) *Since Dad Left*. London: Frances Lincoln. Seven to eight year olds will find this story about Sid who lives with his mother and many pets informative about parental separation and the traveller lifestyle.

Deary, T. (1997) *The Prince of Rags and Patches; The King in Blood Red and Gold*. London: Dolphin. Like the book above this is a story. Although the Marsden family are fictional, the meticulous research carried out by the author means children would learn much about life between 1483 and 1603. There are helpful dates and facts at the end of the story.

Janulewicz, M. (1997) *Yikes!* London: Collins Children's Books. While adults' stomachs may churn a bit at the magnified bits of the human body under the flaps, children will love seeing the cracks and crevices in skin and into the depths of the mouth and stomach.

Kellerhals-Stewart, H. and Zwolak, P. (1997) *My Brother's Train*. London: Groundwood. Seven to eight year olds will learn about the 1930s steam train, with a cow catcher on the front and an open platform at the rear, on which a brother and sister journey to what seems to be Canada. This, like Caroline Binch's book on parental separation, is included because it helps children learn about things less likely to be sympathetically communicated through an informational approach.

Manning, M. and Granström, B. (1998) *Yum-Yum!* London: Franklin Watts. A clear and entertaining account of the food chain- who hunts and who eats what.

Royston, A. (1997) *Weather Around You; Where People Live*. London: Wayland. Children will like the light touch here and the themes link helpfully with key stage 2 geography.

Treays, R. (1998) *Understanding Your Muscles and Bones*. London: Usborne. Shortlisted for the 1998 Rhône-Poulenc junior science prize, this book invites the young reader in with diagrams and comic strips and lots of fascinating information about how bones heal and how muscles make the eyes able to see.

5 Informational reading and writing at key stage 2 (9–11)

Meeting new challenges creatively

> With older children, what we want from information texts are those
> qualities that entice a reader in, support reading for meaning, encourage
> interest and stimulate a desire to know more . . . they should be beautiful,
> well written and organized and *exciting* . . . lending themselves to enquiry
> and discussion and therefore research.
>
> (Nicholson, 1996/7: 34)

Introduction

At this age children are expected to deal with increasingly complex materials both as readers and as writers. More of their learning, in all parts of the curriculum, is from secondary sources. They have to grapple with books, computer software and CD-ROMs and the Internet, newspapers and journals, instructions and diagrams of many kinds. This should both increase their knowledge of the world and help them grow intellectually – to become able to define and understand a task and to find ways of dealing with it. So, while the work done in these years will be worthwhile in itself, it will also prepare children for the challenges of the secondary years.

By the later primary years children better understand the different ways in which people interact and communicate and that there are different kinds of language forms, spoken and written, to serve different purposes. In other words they come to understand that language is socially situated and that some forms enjoy a high status and therefore are included in the school programme.

These years provide a critical opportunity to help children consolidate the skill of being able to transform what they read. The good teacher helps them bring to their writing the answers to their own questions, to synthesise what they know and to build their defences against the danger of taking over mechanically what any one source has to offer. Above all, it is critically important to inspire, interest and foster that sense of wonder in the world and its phenomena that very young children bring naturally to their learning.

This chapter looks first at the range of written material appropriate at this stage. Children need books and software that is 'educationally alive' and which raises important issues as well as transmitting information (Egan, 1992). A mechanistic interpretation of the National Literacy Strategy objectives could encourage publishers to produce material full of unchallenged fact and miscellaneous information – the world 'in bits' as Meek describes it (Meek, 1996).

The analysis then moves to strategies to support children's development as readers and writers. While children have to be taught the conventions, they also need to think for themselves if learning is to become part of their way of approaching the world for the rest of their lives. Development in controlling genres already encountered is discussed as well as approaches to newer forms – persuasive and journalistic writing.

Finally, vignettes of promising classroom practice are offered for consideration. These include glimpses of children responding to a powerful photograph of a drowned sailor's shoe, preparing material for a radio programme advertising their school and, inspired by an Indian chief's speech, constructing a letter about environmental issues.

Range issues: existing and new genres

This section considers all the kinds of reading and writing children have developed throughout the primary years and some new forms – presenting an argument and certain kinds of journalistic writing – which become important at this stage. I have spent a lot of time in book-shops carrying out research during the writing of this book. While the content and layout of books for younger age groups have improved over the last ten years, I find some of the books for older children rather cluttered and uninviting. I agree with those teachers who find that many of the books recommended for Years 5 and 6 are only easily managed without support by the abler readers. Therefore quite a lot of the books recommended in the previous chapter will still be helpful to some older children. In line with my policy throughout, I shall only give examples of books I consider to be good of their kind.

In Chapter 1 a model was set out showing kinds of written material in terms of functions or aims. These functions are: expressive, persuasive, literary and referential. This emphasises the dynamic nature of writing and its relationship with purpose and audience. While the familiar subheadings of reference books, non-narrative information books are still included, they are subsumed under their main functional categories now that the children's books are becoming more like the adult versions. The term 'expressive' is not mentioned in the National Curriculum or National Literary Strategy's *Framework for Teaching* in relation to a kind of writing. Nevertheless it is a useful term to describe the news reports, anecdotes children use in all kinds of writing, and writing to get thinking straight. First drafts of referential kinds of writing may have an expressive flavour.

As teachers know, the National Curriculum lists the *range* of genres of fiction and non-fiction for key stage 1 and key stage 2. It is helpful to take stock of the range of genres as children move towards the end of the primary years.

Range of non-fiction genres in the National Curriculum and literacy hour

The *Framework for Teaching* brings this to a much more detailed and systematic level, listing the kinds of reading and writing to be covered in the literacy hour for each term of each year group. This brings requirements to a degree of prescriptiveness never before experienced in the British education system.

The framework objectives look rather daunting at first sight and it is true that many teachers managed to produce sound and comprehensive programmes working from the National Curriculum and their own knowledge of the reading and writing processes gleaned from their wider reading of research and thinking and their experience of children's development and progress. However, two points are worth making. First, creative teachers are fortunately difficult to suppress and only they can bring these lists to life through imaginative work with a particular class of children – in other words it is still possible to teach creatively within this framework. Second, close scrutiny shows that it does make a spiral curriculum approach possible. There is recognition that we return to the main kinds of reading and writing at different levels as the children weave upwards through the educational process. Thus in the first term of Year 5 recount is revisited (it appears first in Year 1, Term 3) and the discussion texts first mentioned in Year 4, Term 3 are revisited in Year 6, Term 2. The details are easily available

Table 5.1 Range of non-fiction reading and writing in the 1995 National Curriculum, English, key stage 2

Writing	Reading
Writing for a range of audiences; teachers, peers, adults known and imagined	Sources of information not just for children
Argument	ICT-based reference material
Commentary	Reference sources including newspapers, dictionaries, thesauruses, encyclopaedias
Layout of different kinds of letters, reports, notices, explanations and instructions	Texts on screen or books that feature challenging subject matter
	A variety of structural and presentational features

in the school's copy of the 1998 framework or whatever may have replaced it in the future. Here is only necessary to comment on the main trends in each year group.

The National Literacy Strategy objectives: Year 5

The year begins with a return to the recount and to instructional texts, moving to non-chronological kinds of writing in Term 2 with advice to link this to subjects across the curriculum. In Term 3 the focus is on persuasive writing and reference materials, including ICT.

The National Literacy Strategy objectives: Year 6

Autobiography and biography are mentioned for the first time but children will already have experience of reading and writing letters, news and journal entries and anecdotes to draw on in looking at and writing longer works. The journalistic kinds of writing mentioned are an opportunity for understanding the social situation of language and the importance of audience. The middle term is devoted to discussion texts and formal writing of notices and public documents. This is a chance to practise using the impersonal tone and the passive voice. There is recognition that the explanatory and non-chronological reports mentioned need to be linked to work across the curriculum.

Developing children's understanding of genres already encountered

Writing with expressive aims

Throughout the primary years children write accounts that include their own thoughts and feelings about a range of things. Writing with expressive aims is valid in its own right and has a development. By the later primary years children's writing in news diaries and journals, in letters and personal accounts of museum visits and field trips becomes more mature, and can be the forerunner of autobiography and travel accounts, although of course few go on to become adult authors. Writing their own ideas, thoughts and feelings in journals helps children read the work of others more perceptively. Mallett, for example, combined journal writing for a Year 6 class with reading *Anne Frank's Diary* and Roald Dahl's *Boy: Tales of Childhood* and found the reading and writing mutually supportive, the links being clinched by talk (Mallett, 1997: 10–14).

Some of the factual kinds of writing children do will still include anecdotes and small asides which show that, as well as communicating information, the young learner is using the act of writing to get their thinking clear. This transitional kind of writing has an 'expressive' purpose and it would be unfortunate if the genre-based approach now in place pressed upon young writers too soon adult modes, like those using the passive tense. No one has written more perceptively than James Britton about the role of writing in organizing thinking. He believes writing with 'expressive' aims helps children reflect on what they are learning (Britton, 1970: 178–79).

Reading and writing with referential aims

Referential kinds of writing continue to be important in the later primary years: recount, instruction, information, explanation, discussion and reference.

RECOUNT

Recount – of events, activities and visits – is one of the earliest kinds of reading and writing we need to control. Young children enjoy reading about the activities of other children in non-fiction picture books like Fiona Pragoff's. Their early writing often describes visits to the park, or to relatives, or other outings. While the recounts of the very young are expressive in function, those of older children have come some way towards referential aims. Recounts older primary children read include newspaper reports and contemporary accounts of historical events. Of course, these detailed narratives evaluate what happens; and when it comes to their own writing, we would expect older children's accounts – of, for example, a museum visit in connection with work in history or geography – to include some analysis of the experience as well as description. Much more research is needed into how we can support children's learning from CD-ROM, and not least how rich resources like *How We Used to Live: 1936–1953* might nourish children's writing. This CD-ROM follows the fortunes of one family in the period leading up to the Second World War, during it and after it and is intended to support the history unit 'Britain since 1930'.

Observational records in science will be longer, more detailed and where appropriate children will show some control over the passive tense as readers and writers.

INSTRUCTIONAL TEXTS (PROCEDURAL)

Instructional texts are another genre children encounter early on as readers and writers. By the later primary years we would expect the children to move up a gear and to take on reading and writing instructions for using computers, CD-ROMs and the Internet. A recent series by Watts provides good examples of this kind of writing, for example Chris Oxlade's *Electronic Communication* and Catherine Chamber's *All about Maps*. The latter explains clearly how both to read a map and to construct your own.

INFORMATION TEXTS (REPORT)

Non-chronological reports to describe and classify phenomena and explanations of processes feature greatly in what children both read and write across the curriculum: in science how the digestive system works or how to understand the rain cycle; in history how new technologies this century have brought about change or how the Ancient Greek culture, or other non-European culture, has affected our life today; in geography how people affect the environment or the main physical and human features of phenomena like cliffs, valleys, housing estates and water pollution.

Is there still a place for big books in the later primary years? Children might well feel they have had enough of these during the hundreds of literacy hours they will have had! However, occasional use to explain a concept to the class or group seems reasonable. For example, Brian Moses' *An Encyclopedia of Greek and Roman Gods and Heroes* and Sue Palmer's *Words Borrowed from Other Languages,* both from Pelican Big Books, can be used to show how this kind of reference material works. There could also be imaginative work developed round Longman's imaginative big book *World War II Anthology,* which combines fiction and poems with non-fiction forms like telegrams.

We need to select strong non-narrative texts to support learning across the curriculum at this stage – texts that encourage children to speculate on issues and ideas. The dramatic illustrations in Bonson and Platt's book *Disaster! Catastrophes that Shook the World* would invite young readers in. It distinguishes helpfully between disasters that came about through nature and those that occurred because of human error. This provides a good browse but also links well with several National Curriculum themes in geography and history. Another well-illustrated series is that of the Restless Earth by the publisher Belitha, for example Terry Jennings' *Mountains and Rivers.*

When it comes to writing, children will need to set out more mature notes both from what people say and from books (see Chapter 4 for a discussion of note-taking and summarising). Some CD-ROMs have a notepad to help here – for example Ransom Publishing's *Rivers.* Children will enjoy designing information sheets for a range of purposes and constructing questionnaires to collect information.

Sally Hewitt's science books, for example *Full of Energy*, explain scientific concepts in clear everyday language.

If you dislike series of books cloned to the same format, you might like Wayland's 'Technology in the Time of . . .' series. These useful resource books on *Vikings, The Aztecs, Ancient Egypt* and a number of other cultures are each presented differently, although the same categories are covered – food, clothing, industry and so on.

EXPLANATION TEXTS

These are a particular kind of information text, mentioned in the *Framework for Teaching*, which explain a structure or process. Two imaginative works appropriate for older primary children are David Macaulay's *The New Way Things Work* and Stephen Biesty's *Incredible Cross Sections* (in both book and CD-ROM formats).

DISCUSSION TEXTS

Discussion texts, spoken or written, present different viewpoints on a subject with supporting evidence; the text may end by favouring one viewpoint or invite the reader or listener to choose. The problem with a prescriptive list like the Summary of Range in the *Framework for Teaching* is that it does not allow for special opportunities in a particular school or class to debate an issue that may not conveniently occur in Term 3 of Year 4 or Term 2 of Year 5 – the times where discussion texts are mentioned. In my experience, and as many of the classroom examples in this book show, children of any age can be helped to consider an issue if it is presented in a way that makes sense to them.

By Years 5 and 6 children can enjoy and benefit from informed discussion of a range of issues that come up across the curriculum. Their greater experience of the world makes it increasingly possible to think and share their ideas on controversial issues of our times- environmental, social and cultural. We must remember that children have literacy experience outside school and this can be drawn on to enhance learning in school. For example, children would with some encouragement bring in reports from newspapers and magazines to serve as discussion texts.

The first case study at the end of this chapter shows how an illustration can serve as a discussion text. The second reveals children reflecting on their own spoken and written texts, which raised issues of cultural diversity and social attitudes towards different languages in their community. A picture book becomes the discussion text in the final case study.

REFERENCE BOOKS AND RESOURCES

Older primary children move towards more mature text in their reference materials, but there is still a strong role for illustrations, obviously in atlases and encyclopaedias and sometimes in dictionaries and thesauruses. Reference material is constantly updated but basic criteria for quality texts and CD-ROMs remain the same:

- interesting, accurate and relevant content;
- clear writing which indicates the meaning of new vocabulary and concepts through context and which invites the young reader into the topic;
- good format and design so that the source is easy to use;

- useful retrieval devices – including differentiated indexes for these older junior readers. A clear indication of how children can access information from an information-packed CD-ROM or from the web sites on the Internet is needed;
- clear diagrams, charts and tables and helpful drawings and photographs which complement and extend the text and invite speculation;
- absence of unwelcome stereotyping and bias;
- avoidance of the impression that information is best communicated in separate bundles – by showing how different subjects link with and enrich each other;
- achievement of just the right authorial 'voice'.

Below are lists of suggested reference material suitable for older primary children to give a flavour of what is available. All lists reflect the views and preferences of the compiler and there are no doubt many other dictionaries, thesauruses, encyclopaedias and atlases of equal merit. Readers may also wish to look at the lists in the previous chapter for reference material for nine year olds and older children with special literacy needs.

Dictionaries
Older juniors will understand some of the genre features of dictionaries, including the use of phrases as well as sentences, the provision of several meanings and the abbreviations used by the compiler. More mature dictionaries with more text and fewer illustrations can now be used. Most publishing houses specialising in children's books have a selection of dictionaries and other reference books for different age groups and will send their catalogue. Older juniors would find *Usborne Illustrated Dictionary* inviting; it provides a particularly helpful user's guide to parts of speech, and hints and guidelines on forming plurals and using apostrophes. *Crossword Creator* enables children to build their own dictionaries to make crosswords and also provides practice with *Roget's Thesaurus*. I particularly like *Collins School Dictionary* for abler Year 6 children. It is easy to use – each sense is given on a new line and there is guidance on grammar and pronunciation. Another good dictionary for older juniors is the *Oxford School Dictionary* which is recommended for age eleven years upwards, and has 40,000 headwords, with plurals, tenses, nouns as appropriate. New words like 'Internet' and 'virtual reality' are included. The format is plain but very clear.

There are a number of good specialist dictionaries, including Dorling Kindersley's *Dictionary of Science*. It is an interesting browse for older primary children but the lack of an A–Z organization makes it seem like an encyclopaedia.

Thesauruses
Thesauruses of antonyms and synonyms become increasingly important as children get older and there are several good ones for the upper junior age range. A welcome feature of this resource is that it reinforces the notion of

language as essentially creative and varied with a range of options for the speaker or writer to express their meaning. Most publishers of dictionaries also publish thesauruses. Children of ten and over will like the format of the *Usborne Illustrated Thesaurus*. This has 60,000 words and many helpfully labelled illustrations which make it a good browse. The introduction explains how a thesaurus helps you to 'choose the best word'. The cover has a pirate theme and includes shipwreck words (after a shipwreck you may be 'marooned, sole survivor, encounter sharks') and wanted posters and reinforces the idea that a thesaurus can be fun.

Alan Spooner has compiled a number of thesauruses for different age groups, including the *Oxford Junior Thesaurus*, a useful resource suitable for the whole key stage 2 phase. Big concepts – measurement and entertainment for example- are placed on a blue background and annotated more fully. The *Oxford Mini Thesaurus* (1991) and the *Oxford Pocket Thesaurus* (1996), also compiled by Alan Spooner, are for the ablest readers in Year 6 and above. (See also *Crossword Creator* detailed above which includes *Roget's Thesaurus*).

Encyclopaedias

New technology has made it possible to make interactive CD-ROM versions of encyclopaedias with video extracts and music. But rather than replacing book formats all this has led to a general improvement in design and illustration. Computer technology is used in updating, indexing and generally speeding up the production of books. As with other age groups, in Britain, a helpful encyclopaedia needs to include something on the subjects covered by the National Curriculum programmes of study. However, there is something attractive about an internationalist approach, particularly when it is combined with some special coverage of Britain. By this stage encyclopaedias are often in several volumes and expensive enough to make careful research of the market necessary before making a selection.

As well as meeting the general criteria for reference books suggested above, we want encyclopaedias to inspire and interest – to develop new enthusiasms rather than just set out chunks of information. Although older children need to control more difficult kinds of reading and writing and can cope with longer sentences and more technical vocabulary, they can still find long dreary passages off-putting (Littlefair, 1991: 38). Encyclopaedias often give the first summary of a topic that children need, providing a framework for further research in other books. It is thus important that the introduction is inviting.

There are advantages in a thematic approach to the entries but publishers' surveys find that children, teachers and parents seem to prefer the simplicity of an alphabetical organization.

By this stage children will have become used to the signs, symbols and cross-referencing systems usually explained at the beginning of an encyclopaedia. They also now need to know how to elicit relevant information from CD-ROMs and the Internet. Children with special educational needs can find all this overwhelming and will still need careful support.

One useful CD-ROM is Anglia Multimedia's *Eureka! Encyclopaedia of Discovery and Invention*. I prefer the simplicity of an alphabetical organization, but there is a case for placing the items in sub-categories, as this resource does – under food, transport, etc. Another good resource is *Dorling Kindersley Children's Illustrated Encyclopedia*. This is frequently updated to keep up with a changing world and with 450 entries organized alphabetically, it is visually exciting and good to browse through as well as for looking things up. The nine-volume (including seven volumes A–Z with 192 pages, a biography volume and an index volume) *Oxford Children's Encyclopedia* covers a vast range of information in an interesting way. We can take all the usual requirements of retrieval devices and good illustrations and clear text for granted in a major initiative like this. It would be particularly useful as an upper primary school resource because of the up-to-date articles on science, technology, history, geography, sport, music and the arts.

Atlases
As with other age groups, when choosing an atlas for older primary children we seek merit in the cartography, the design and the supporting materials. CD-ROM atlases enable children to explore the world using multimedia strategies like interactive maps and video-clips. The new technology motivates children but they do need to be taught how to get the most out of the disks. For many purposes an ordinary atlas of good quality will serve just as well.

Atlases at key stage 2 (Years 5 and 6)
Dorling Kindersley's CD-ROM package *My First Amazing World Explorer* is often bought for children between six and nine. However, this package, which includes an interactive picture atlas, games and activities to teach about map skills and some enjoyable extras like a sticker map and a jigsaw, is also recommended for older juniors with special literacy needs.

Much information, some of it in the form of detailed statistics, is included in Dorling Kindersley's *World Reference Atlas*, updated 1998, also in 1995 PC and Apple versions. *Encarta 97 World Atlas* (1996) Microsoft (PC version – Windows 95), is a comprehensive resource providing vast amounts of information in the maps and satellite views of major cities. There are sound-clips, music, an illustrated glossary and articles on the history, customs and culture of each country. Relevant web sites can be accessed. Children would need help to move around the maps. Support would also be necessary for children using David Flint's *Satellite Atlas*, probably in combination with a conventional atlas. There are satellite images of towns, rivers and whole continents.

Dorling Kindersley's *Eyewitness Atlas of the World* has attractive illustrations as well as clear information. *Philip's Junior Atlas* has clear physical and political maps. There is good introductory material on atlas skills and 'skill quest' boxes with activities to practise skills. Location is aided by an index using alphanumeric co-ordinates and latitude/longitude. It benefits from clear cartography and good thematic maps in addition to a substantial coverage of British Isles and carefully chosen supporting material. *Philips Foundation Atlas* follows on from the Philips atlas above and includes good thematic maps and some cross-sections. *The Oxford Practical Atlas* is aimed at children aged eleven and above, this would be excellent reference material for the abler Year 6 age range. Grid co-ordinates and latitude/longitude feature in the index. Further good advice on choosing atlases is available in the Schools' Library Service publication entitled *Going Places: Resources for Geography*.

New genres for Years 5 and 6

Teachers of older primary children have always included work based on reading and writing with a persuasive aim. Autobiography and biography, examples of non-fiction writing with a literary aim, have also traditionally taken a stronger place in the reading collection. The National Curriculum and the National Literacy Strategy *Framework for Teaching* recognises the place of these forms in the programme for Years 5 and 6.

Written material with a persuasive aim

Persuasive kinds of writing are first mentioned in the final term of Year 4 in the *Framework for Teaching*. Much younger children can understand that people have different viewpoints about issues. *The Whales' Song* by Diana Sheldon contrasts the view of Uncle Fred, that whales are for blubber and oil, with that of Lucy and her grandmother who regard whales as beautiful and interesting creatures. But it is usually not until the last two years of primary schooling that children learn to control more difficult arguments as both readers and writers.

The case study, towards the end of this chapter, describing the work of Year 6 children developing viewpoints on conservation of the environment, shows it is a challenging kind of genre even where the teacher has embedded the reading and writing tasks in an interesting context. Constructing an argument involves holding in your mind different viewpoints and presenting one of these systematically, giving reasons for your opinion.

Looking at advertisements, public notices and texts in different media draws children's attention to language as a social phenomenon. Teachers need to provide examples of these and of journalistic kinds of writing – newspaper and magazine articles. Michael Foreman's *War Games* is a story about four friends who journey to France when they are called up to serve in the First World War. Although a narrative about fictional characters, it includes posters and letters which make it one of those texts which

Dogs were sometimes used as sentries in some sections, particularly by the French. Some dogs also searched for wounded men and others were messenger dogs.

EVEN A DOG ENLISTS WHY NOT YOU?

Figure 5.1 Dutiful dog from Michael Foreman's *War Games* (1989). This shows children the persuasive power of the visual, especially when reinforced by language. The picture of the dutiful dog, combined with the caption, makes a strong emotional appeal.

transcends the simple fact/fiction divide. The war posters would make an interesting study of how the media can manipulate and persuade.

Reading and writing with literary aims

While younger children enjoy autobiographical and biographical reading and writing, by the later primary years children are able to read texts more like their adult forms. This kind of reading can be a highly enjoyable way of learning about history and learning about the experience of other people.

AUTOBIOGRAPHY

An autobiography is a individual's life story written in the first person. Children's experience of reading and writing letters and making diary entries prepares them for reading full-length autobiographies. This kind of writing provides an insight into people's lives, experiences, feelings and motivations. The versions children write, first-person narratives with anecdotes, have expressive aims but the mature form, autobiographies by mature writers, have a literary aim.

First-person reading and writing have an important role across the curriculum: letters, diaries and other first-person accounts provide important sources for history, while in geography there is a long tradition of travel writing in the first person where personal response and evaluation of all that is encountered is of relevance and value.

Autobiographical writing is different from other kinds of writing normally placed under the informational umbrella. McArthur comments that, 'Some autobiographies come near to being works of fiction and many works of fiction have autobiographical aspects' (McArthur, 1992: 98). Writing one's autobiography involves weaving our own story round a skeleton of incontrovertible facts. Perhaps the line between fact and fiction blurs most in this kind of writing, which suggests that we should regard texts more flexibly.

One of the most interesting aspects of autobiography are the letters people write in different circumstances. Children encounter letters in both fiction and informational writing. I worked with some Year 6 children who very much enjoyed Roald Dahl's *Boy: Tales of Childhood*. They were impressed to read that over the 20 years from 1925–45, Dahl wrote 600 letters to his mother. He had got into the habit of writing to her once a week because he was obliged to do so at the schools he attended. In the chapter entitled 'Writing Home' Dahl remarks:

> Letter-writing was a serious business at St. Peter's. It was as much a lesson in spelling and punctuation as anything else because the Headmaster would patrol the classroom all through the sessions, peering over our shoulders to read what we were writing and to point out our mistakes. But that, I am quite sure, was not the main reason for his interest. He was there to make sure that we said nothing horrid about his school.
>
> (Dahl, 1984: 82)

He goes on to list some of the things he and the other boys would have liked to have mentioned – that the food was horrible, or a teacher had been unkind, or that undeserved punishments had been carried out. The whole book is sprinkled with letters and postcards written at various times in Dahl's life. His very first letter from St Peter's is bland and children enjoy writing an alternative one not to be seen by the headteacher.

Dear Mama

I am having a lovely time here. We play football every day here. The beds have no springs. Will you send my stamp album and quite a lot of stamps.

The masters are very nice. I've got all my clothes now, and a belt and ties and a school jumper.

Love from

Boy

(Dahl, 1984: 80)

Children need help with the format for different kinds of letter. Teachers try to embed letter-writing in sensible contexts: to thank personnel at museums and zoos after class outings; to give information to parents or to invite them and other visitors who have given talks or made special contributions; to ask organizations or individuals for help and to give opinions. When the letter is formal, children can be shown the conventions of address, date, degrees of formality at the end of the letter and so on.

Sometimes special opportunities arise where there is a genuine need to write a letter. There might be a local issue that the children feel strongly about which may generate correspondence they can contribute to in the local paper.

In the later primary years children can be helped to make explicit their developing realization that a letter's audience and purpose affect its level of formality. If an opportunity for genuine letters does not arise, interesting contexts can be contrived. One teacher organized role-play around a summer holiday camp with her Year 5 class. After improvising some incidents, the children were invited to write letters to different people, varying the tone and choice of incident in the letter as well as the degree of formality according to the intended recipient. The children greatly enjoyed reading their range of letters out loud and explaining why they had included things in their letter to a friend which did not appear in their letter to their grandparents.

There is an account of Year 6 children reading *Anne Frank's Diary* alongside writing their own diary-type entries in *First Person Reading and Writing in the Primary Years* by Mallett (1997a). This publication also includes lists of books written in the first person. This kind of reading and writing causes a blurring of the divisions between fact and fiction since some books of fiction use the first person as a literary device. *Amazon Diary: the Jungle Adventures of Alex Winters* by Hudson Talbot and Mark Greenaway is written as if we are reading the diary of a ten year old.

BIOGRAPHY

Biographies are life-stories of an individual by another person written in the third person. Children read short examples of biographical writing in early history books and can enjoy longer works by the upper primary years. There are some recently published historical biographies for older juniors. Leon Ashworth's *Queen Victoria* helps young readers visualise the queen herself and the personalities and events of her time. *The School Librarian,* Summer 1998 praises the choice and quality of the illustrations, which include a time-line and contemporary photographs.

Josephine Poole's *Joan of Arc* combines a poetic text with beautifully detailed illustrations by Angela Barrett. Older primary children can enjoy and be inspired by picture books of this subtlety and quality. The Watts Expedition series includes *Marco Polo* and *Magellan,* both by Fiona MacDonald, and introduces young readers to the features of mature biography. The biography of Roald Dahl (Evans's Tell Me about Writing series) would furnish material for an interesting comparison with Dahl's *Boy.* There is a lot of detailed information which some children will need help with. *My Life with the Indians* by Robin Moore tells the dramatic story of Mary Jemison's capture by the Shawnee Indians. She was adopted by the Seneca tribe and raised a large family during the time when Indian lifestyles were under threat. The genuine letters of Sara Wheeler to her godson are used to structure the experiences in Antarctica in *Dear Daniel: Letters from Antarctica.* This helps children reflect more generally on the role of letters and diaries in both autobiographies and biographies.

Software and the Internet

Some older primary children are impressively computer literate; others need help to keep pace with rapidly changing technology. Three books would be helpful to teachers wishing to keep ahead. Christina Preston's (1995) *21st Century A–Z Literacy Handbook* sets out an annotated list of literacy software. Chris Oxlade's (1998) book on *Virtual Reality* and Herbie Brennan's (1998) on *The Internet* provide good introductions to the topics.

Much of the software recommended in the previous chapter for seven to nine year olds continues to be useful and appropriate in the later primary years. TAG's *Banner, BannerMania* and *First Page* are useful tools in making the posters and public notices that are part of the work on persuasive and journalistic kinds of reading and writing at this stage. TAG has also produced a multimedia authoring tool called *HyperStudio.* Where children need to present their work in different writing styles – reporting experiments and journalistic writing, for example – *Writer's Toolkit* from SCET is helpful.

Longman Logotron's *Landmarks Microworlds* is one of a number of packages that enable children to examine historical periods through an animated virtual world. A good geography resource for key stage 2 is Ransome's *Rivers,* which shows the stages in a river's development. *How We Used to Live: 1936–53* (CD-ROM) is an exciting support for the history unit 'Britain since 1930' which reveals how events in the years before, during and after the Second World War affect one family.

ThinkSheet from TAG creates cards of information to help children plan their writing. Also useful for presenting research reports is *Microsoft Reference CDs* from KimTec.

Illustrations – a neglected element of non-fiction books and resources

In Chapter 1 the main kinds of visual aid are discussed. Just as we expect children to cope with more difficult text by the upper primary years, they also 'read' more challenging diagrams and pictures. They need to illustrate and extend their own written accounts and they model these on what they see in their reading materials. Thus the quality of the illustrations is a major factor in choosing informational and reference material. Margaret Meek, in a powerful argument in *Information and Book Learning* (1996), regrets that many superficially bright and colourful books have failed to choose illustrations which, on scrutiny, illuminate the written information and encourage speculation. While we want to celebrate the beauty of all the things in the human and natural world, we should not avoid the raw and sometimes disturbing.

Diagrams

New technology has transformed the way illustrations are set out and multimedia has brought interactive, moving pictures so that children can see, for example, how the blood system in the body works and how the parts of a machine move. In the *21st Century A–Z Literacy Handbook*, Christina Preston remarks that the wide availability of multimedia is causing us to reflect more deeply on how meaning is created (Preston, 1995).

Rather than replacing books, new technology has helped make diagrams in all kinds of media. Carefully labelled and annotated diagrams are a strong feature of Dorling Kindersley's books, for example the Eyewitness series. Even for older primary children over-detailed diagrams can confuse. Sometimes a series of diagrams, helpfully labelled and annotated, are needed to explain something complicated. For example, in his book and CD-ROM *The New Way Things Work*, David Macaulay provides many clear diagrams to show how different kinds of lever work. The mechanics of movement differ in first-class, second-class, third-class and multiple levers.

The use of pie charts, graphs and histograms is shown in Alison Hodge's book *The Caribbean*. This is a book to stretch the abler readers and it does offer good models of how diagrams can extend and complement written text.

Drawings and pictures

There are a number of reasons why drawings are sometimes preferred to photographs. Sometimes phenomena are not easily photographed: for example, in spite of amazing new technology, what goes on under the sea and in space is still relatively inaccessible. A drawing based on what is known at the present time provides an alternative visual aid. Even where photographs are possible, it may take a drawing to show something clearly. For example, it may be helpful to simplify parts of a creature's body structure to help young learners understand. Photographs and drawings can work alongside, as in the Eagle Books Life Story Series, for example Michael Chinery's *Frog* and *Butterfly*. Above all, drawings and pictures can sometimes communicate a sense of atmosphere in a special way. In Karen Wallace's *Think of an Eel*, beautiful water-colour paintings are used to create the creature's watery environment. (The last three books mentioned include mature concepts explained clearly enough for less forward older readers.)

Some of the most imaginative books are illustrated with pictures, for example Charles Keeping's *Railway Passage*. The exciting complexity of Stephen Biesty's cross-section books, including *Incredible Cross Sections* and *Castle*, is appreciated by children in the later primary years. The books can now be enjoyed on CD-ROM by children and adults. Enormous research has gone into tools, buildings and clothes of different historical periods and a great deal of information is communicated through drawing and writing. The humorous touches (including in *Castle* part of a fifteenth-century manuscript about table manners, an anecdote about a dog trained to turn the spit-roasted meat, and the visual joke of the guard who had lost all his clothes in a game of dice) make these books favourites.

Perhaps we tend to associate pop-up books with younger children, but Robert Crowther's five intriguing double spreads showing the world of mining, tunnelling, underwater exploring, caving and interlarding in *Deep Down Underground* would interest older pupils and adults. The facts and humorous asides of the people involved in the activities remind me of the illustrations some children enjoy creating. I remember a nine year old at an inner London school showing a mature comic ability in making an illustrated book on 'Absurd Inventions'.

Photographs

We have seen in previous chapters the impact photographs can have on younger age groups. It has been suggested that photographs can complement and extend the written text in a unique way. They have an important role in books and resources in every subject. New technology has made exciting things possible. Photographs can be taken in almost every situation and atlases and geography books now feature fascinating satellite pictures. By Year 5 children's reading in history, geography and science is much more challenging and photographs can often illuminate a new idea.

Photographs can show scientific and geographical phenomena, while in history and religious studies they can illuminate aspects of social history. For example, in the Waylands Migrations series, photographs are used to show environments and people from the past. In chapter 4 of Hakim Adi's *African Migrations* there are family photographs showing ten year old Yemisi in Nigeria and then, after 1967, in London the capital of her new country. The photographs show the contrasts between the two environments in a way that even a huge amount of writing could not. This series links well with the key stage 2 history unit on 'Britain since 1930' and the social changes that have taken place, and it is the photographs in the book that show the human issues involved. Brian Moses uses photographs well to show how British civilians fared in the Second World War in *The War Years: The Home Front*. These help children to feel empathy for those who were separated from their loved ones.

Photographs can have an emotional impact which stimulates questions and further research. We must remember that they can sometimes be used as propaganda to manipulate and deceive, and we must be as critical of them as we are of written text. More often, however, they can appeal to the feelings as well as to the intellect in a positive way. Case study 5.1 at the end of this chapter shows how photographs of the artefacts found in the wreck of the *Mary Rose* had an emotional impact on the children which brought home to them that history is about real people living real and often difficult lives.

Strategies to support reading and writing across the curriculum

Reading and writing areas, which are such a strong feature in the early and middle primary years, are just as important for older children. The class library will be augmented by books from the main library to match both the requirements for lessons across the curriculum and the needs of the literacy hour. Reference materials in book form and in software packages and CD-ROM need to be easily available.

At least one computer and if possible the Internet as well will have an important place in the up-to-date literacy area. Displays of the kinds of reading and writing the children have been doing, and the range of formats and presentations they might try for the journalistic and persuasive kinds of material that will be part of the programme, all add interest. The children will enjoy being part of a rota of helpers, keeping a check on books lent out and on developing displays.

Non-fiction in the literacy hour: reading at text, sentence and word level

The literacy hour, devised by the National Literacy Strategy team, is likely to be constantly changed and adjusted – hopefully in the light of informed comments from teachers. At present, work is required to follow the text, sentence and word level structure set out in the *Framework for Teaching* published by the DfEE and distributed to schools in March 1998.

The range of texts to be covered is considered in the previous section. During the first 15 minutes of the class-based part of the literacy hour the organisation of the different texts, their distinctive global structure and their meaning will be discussed. Sometimes the teacher and class will read together and on other occasions they may carry out a shared writing task.

The second 15 minutes of the class-based work is for analysis at word and sentence level. The distinctive vocabulary used in particular information books will be pointed out. The syntax of the different kinds of non-fiction reflects its purpose and audience. Conventions like lists in bullet points and annotations and labels on diagrams can be demonstrated. Another area of study is how punctuation and paragraphing are used to link prose with informational genres.

The next part of the hour, 20 minutes, is for group work. Guided text work, either reading or writing, will take place in two groups. Children might try making their own word lists or glossaries of new technical vocabulary or write summaries of the information they have heard in the class-based part of the hour. Children have to be helped to tune in quickly to the reading and writing tasks because of the time pressure. This is, of course good practice for the SATs at the end of key stage 2.

The other three groups will be set independent work related to the text of the day. It is important that these children have clearly set tasks, including extension tasks, and all the resources they are likely to need to hand. Children not used to working in this way will need some training and support until they understand what is required. Talk about the texts and the tasks will be an important part of the learning in groups. It also features in the final 10 minutes, the plenary session when the teacher invites the children to share what they consider they have achieved.

The literacy hour encourages very focused tasks with clear purposes because of the time restraint. Particularly in the case of these older children, opportunities for extended reading and writing will need to be built into the rest of the programme outside of the literacy hour. Teachers are already planning so that work across the curriculum links with the literacy hour. On page 13 of the NLS *Framework for Teaching* it is suggested that during the literacy hour 'pupils might be searching and retrieving from information texts used in science, writing instructions linked to a technology project, studying myths, autobiographies or stories linked to a study unit in history'. Similarly, something that has awakened interest in the literacy hour might be developed as a sustained reading or writing task in another lesson.

It would be unfortunate if time for lessons across the curriculum was so reduced that opportunities for longer writing episodes was put at risk. History, geography and religious studies provide excellent contexts for interesting writing tasks which engage children's interest. Informational writing, as much as fictional kinds, greatly benefits from being embedded in larger projects, as the case studies in this book have consistently shown.

Scaffolding reading

By age nine or ten, children have had considerable experience of working with books and materials across the curriculum and of producing their own written accounts. However, for quite a number of children the books available for their age range are difficult, and they will need teacher mediation. Of continuing importance in scaffolding both reading and writing is spoken language. In his book *Common Knowledge*, Neil Mercer (1981) considers that one of the teacher's key roles is to provide interactive contexts rather than too much concentration on worksheets or lonely hours on the computer.

When it comes to reading, children will have been encouraged to take their own questions to the resources, so that they are in the driving seat of their own learning as readers and when they organize their written work. This makes it less likely that they will closely paraphrase authors in their own written work. In Mallett's study of using non-fiction, nine year olds learn about squirrels – how their physical structure relates to function (for example the tail makes possible an arboreal lifestyle) – by formulating questions to take to the books and resources. These were questions which the children were helped to group according to subject – food, lifestyle, physical attributes and so on – not only to focus their reading but also to provide a framework for their writing (Mallett, 1992: 95–196).

Teacher and children reading information texts out loud and group reading and discussion remain important ways of helping older children assimilate and reflect on new ideas and information. We must not forget that the diagrams and photographs benefit from discussion as well.

Supporting non-fiction writing

Two important aspects any writer has to contend with are the content (the communication of the facts and ideas) and the form or genre required for a particular kind of writing. Talk, between teacher and pupils and between pupil and pupil, plays a powerful part in illuminating content and clarifying purposes and audiences for writing. It is quite a lot to expect, even of older primary children, that in addition to wrestling with new hierarchies of facts and ideas they also have to fit all this into a particular format. We are reminded by Myra Barrs that, in addition to communication, an important function of writing is to aid learning. Of course, teachers have to carry out the genre-based requirements of the National Curriculum, and now too the range of reading and writing types set out in the National Literacy Strategy's Framework. We can help by encouraging what Barrs calls 'provisional and informal genres'; by this she means lists, memos, logs and journals which are often a useful preliminary to more formal writing. Adults find such strategies useful and anything that helps young learners use language as a tool to thinking is worthwhile (Barrs, 1997: ii).

A useful strategy for encouraging children to use rather than just copy information from secondary sources is to set a task in another genre. We might ask children to write information in the form of a letter, diary entry or news report, using facts from a non-narrative information book. Lewis and Wray call this 'genre exchange' and there are useful examples of this in their book, including an advertisement for scribes written by children who have researched the jobs people did in Ancient Egypt (Lewis and Wray, 1996). A good model for this kind of approach is Andrew Langley and Philip de Souza's *The Roman News* – a delightfully anachronistic Roman newspaper! Children are encouraged to make notes and base their writing on these. For a discussion of note-taking and making summaries, see Chapter 4.

Writing frames

These are frameworks provided by the teacher to structure the writing process. Children work their own ideas into the sentence starts and connectives provided. The work of Lewis and Wray in the 1990s on the EXEL Extending Reading project provided a set of writing frames to get children started on writing with different aims – expressive, persuasive, literary and referential. This kind of scaffolding may help some children, particularly the less confident writers (case study 6.5). However, we would want children to learn to organise their own written accounts and Wray and Lewis would be the first to say that the frames are a temporary aid and not to be used too long or too mechanistically. Part of becoming a competent writer is being able to structure your own global framework. Mallett (1992) shows how children used their own questions to structure books on squirrels.

Older primary children might be helped with the demanding persuasive kinds of writing where an argument has to be constructed by the following frame, adapted from Lewis and Wray (1996). There are different views about how often to use the frames or even whether to use them at all. You need to read their book entitled *Writing Frames* (1996) to come to your own view about this kind of scaffolding.

Books can provide a good starting-point for taking up a viewpoint on environmental issues – David Bellamy's *How Green Are You?* is full of interesting facts to make children think. Newspaper and magazine articles can also be the starting-point for discussing interesting issues.

Book-making is still important

Children continue to enjoy making their own non-fiction books either individually or in groups. These can be made for different audiences – personal dictionaries and language books for their own use, simple non-fiction books for younger children in the school, and books of instructions for

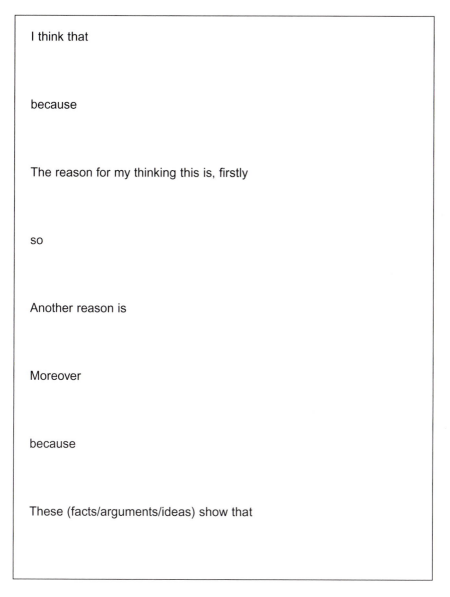

I think that

because

The reason for my thinking this is, firstly

so

Another reason is

Moreover

because

These (facts/arguments/ideas) show that

Figure 5.2 Persuasive writing frame adapted from Maureen Lewis and David Wray's
    Writing Frames (1996).

using classroom equipment for their peers. It is to be hoped that the reduced
time for history and geography will still allow for the satisfying books children have often made individually or as a group as an excellent outcome of
their research.

The SATs at the end of key stage 2

Informational kinds of reading and writing are well represented in the test booklets. All the kinds of material likely to be included are covered in this chapter including recounts, instructional kinds of reading and writing and autobiographical accounts. For some children, those who are less forward in their literacy progress and for children whose first language is not English, the time constraint will be difficult.

Teachers will be wise to give some timed reading and writing practice in the formats that appear in the booklets. The SATs are likely to change to link more closely with the objectives of the National Literacy Strategy. There is a more detailed account of non-fiction in the SATs in Chapters 1 and 7.

CASE STUDIES

There follow three examples of promising practice. The first presents a vignette in which children respond to a photograph of a Tudor sailor's shoe found when the *Mary Rose* wreck was raised. The other two are in the area of persuasive writing so important at this stage: one involves writing with journalistic aims; the other is about writing also with persuasive aims, but of an almost political nature to press home a viewpoint with considerable passion.

Case study 5.1: Learning from illustrations

How Year 6 children were affected by a photograph of a sailor's shoe found on the Mary Rose[1]

I have often found that a particular visual image assumes great signifi-cance for children working in a sustained way on a project. For Michael, the plague doctor became the symbol of Tudor times (see case 6.6). For another group in Michael's class a photograph of the shoe of a Tudor sailor was remembered long after the work was completed. Joanna had been finding out about the raising of the *Mary Rose* wreck and what the artefacts found told us about the lives of Tudor sailors. The picture she chose to share with her group of six showed a worn leather shoe. The text below the photograph included the macabre detail that foot bones were found in some of the shoes recovered. There were other photographs on the same double spread of leather buckets, wooden combs and a medicine flask, syringe, bowls and jars (pages 13 and 14 in J. Shuter's *Tudor Times*). Joanne was asked why it was the shoe out of all these items that she had chosen to discuss. She replied: 'Because you can see where a real foot has stretched the leather at particular places – the little toe might have had a corn that pushed the leather out of shape. A real sailor wore that shoe.'

A leather
shoe. Some
shoes were found
with foot bones in them.

Figure 5.3 Sailor's shoe found in the wreck of the *Mary Rose*, which led to much children's discussion in case study 5.1.

In fact it was seeing this photograph that had helped Joanne to decide to find out more about the raising of the Mary Rose. She was intrigued by a modern painting of life aboard a Tudor ship in the same book, and pointed out to the group that shoes, similar in every detail to the one in the photograph, were worn by the sailors. As one of the children in the group remarked, looking at clothes, utensils and games from a wreck could inform children's own illustrations.

Many teachers encourage children to build up their own composi-
tions by including contemporary items either seen directly in museums or in book photographs. This encourages an informed kind of
imagining using the fruits of genuine research and evidence to
support children's own creative achievements.

(Mallett, 1996/7)

Joanne told me she had found the written text in some of the books about the original sinking of the ship and the raising of the wreck this century 'very difficult'. Another member of the group, Christina, was researching Tudor food and was able to help Joanne build up an idea of what the sailors would have eaten and drunk. But it was the emotional power of the shoe photograph which sustained her in her preparation for her presentation to the group. The other children were moved by the photograph too. After listening to Joanne's account, the talk turned to what we learn from illustrations and what we learn from writing. Adam remarked:

The picture of the shoe and the other things found make you realise real sailors were drowned . . . people that were using everyday
things and living their lives on the ship – but you need the writing as
well to know more about why the ship sank and how many people
were drowned and what happened after that.

In the course of the history project the children had all looked at a
range of illustrations – at cross-sections of Tudor buildings and ships, at
time-lines and plans of Tudor gardens. All of these had a contribution to
make to developing knowledge and insight and served a clear purpose
in the work. However, the quality of response to a photograph of the
emotional power of a drowned sailor's shoe reminds us that even these
older primary children need learning to be humanised.

Case study 5.2: Journalistic kinds of writing

Example of children's work on 'Advertising our school'[2]

A class of Year 5 and 6 children was divided into groups for work on a
project on their school. Each group chose to work on a text in a different medium and for a different audience, ranging from a script for a talk
to parents to an advertisement for a television programme. One group
produced a radio advertisement to persuade local parents to choose
this school for their children.

The importance of a sense of audience

A very interesting aspect of this work was the decision, reached collaboratively, to present the script in Urdu as well as in English. The children
showed a good understanding of language variety and the linguistic
needs of some of the local mothers. They wanted to include the sentence, 'The behaviour at this school is superb' and discovered that
translation from one language to another is far from mechanistic. The
problem was to find an Urdu word or phrase for 'behaviour': to substi-
tute the word 'work' would alter the meaning. They knew from talking
with parents that standards of behaviour were thought just as important
as academic achievements. They went to much trouble to find a fluent
Urdu speaker to help them. The teacher had created a context that
motivated these children to care about getting even the smallest details
of their work right. Sealey comments that it was the specified audience
'which provided the context for such a detailed exploration of lexis and
semantics'.

Understanding linguistic diversity and social attitudes

There was an interesting extension to this group's work. With the teacher's agreement, they contacted a local radio producer and asked if he would record their advertisement for transmission over the air. He came to the school to work with the children on the script and he recorded the full dual-language presentation. The children were disappointed when they listened to the magazine programme to discover that only the English version of their tape had been used. The teacher made this issue the subject of a class discussion in which different views were expressed. Some children thought that if space on the programme was limited, the producer might have felt very few listeners would be Urdu-only speakers and justified the omission on those grounds. Others felt Urdu speakers were being marginalised.

This project generated much interest and helped the children to refine their ability to see both sides of an argument as well as learning about language and texts. Members of the group each kept a diary during the making of the programme and included their thoughts and feelings about all that happened. They also made a tape recording for other children who might want to make a radio broadcast; it set out procedures and gave helpful advice in language adjusted for child listeners.

Literacy hour focus

Part of the children's text either of the original broadcast or the advice tape could be shown on a screen and scrutinised by the whole class for words and phrases to inform, persuade and influence. Group writing tasks might include children constructing and refining an argument round a computer.

Case study 5.3: Learning to express a viewpoint

Example of children being helped to enjoy and respond to a distinctive kind of persuasive writing and then to write their own piece in the genre

A strong context helps children gather enough momentum and interest to grapple with the more difficult kinds of writing. A text in the form of a book, poster, letter or pamphlet can provide this context. A final practice student teacher, Bennett Sills, had been working with a Year 6 class on environmental issues and wanted them to attempt a piece of writing expressing a coherent view about an issue.

The power of a quality text as starting-point

He read out loud from Barbara Jeffers' retelling of *Brother Eagle, Sister Sky*, a picture book based on the powerful message of Chief Seattle 150 years ago to the government in Washington who wanted to buy the land of his defeated people. The text is a most eloquent, poetic and moving plea for the preservation of the environment. It is also a time-less warning that by harming the natural world human beings risk bringing about their own destruction. The children were particularly impressed by the wonderful metaphor of the world as a huge web of which human beings are a small part.

> This we know: All things are connected like the blood that unites us.
> We did not weave the web of life,
> We are merely a strand in it.
> Whatever we do to the web, we do to ourselves.

The drawings create the land of the Indian people with great care. We learn about the landscape, hills, plains, streams, rivers, trees, plants, birds and animals and about the lifestyle of the Indian people who are shown riding and canoeing. The text is haunting, both celebrating the beauty of the wilderness land of the native Americans and lamenting its imminent destruction.

> How can you buy the sky? Chief Seattle began.
> How can you own the rain and wind?
> My mother told me,
> Every part of this earth is sacred to our people.
> Every pine needle. Every sandy shore.
> Every mist in dark woods.
> Every meadow and humming insect.
> All are holy in the memory of our people.

If we need convincing, this book shows that picture books need not just be for the very young. This one is highly sophisticated and likely to make an impact on people of any age. The children talked about the speech, quoting their favourite passages and discussing the issues. We owe authors the courtesy of reading and reflecting their work for its own sake as well as the other purposes we may have in mind.

The invitation to the writing task

The teacher asked the children to think about what they would like to say to Chief Seattle about our environmental problems today if they could. They noted down their main points in a jotter. The next stage was to compose a letter setting out a view. Robert's response is shown below. While he is not fully in control of this genre as writer, finding it difficult to reconcile good and less good aspects of progress, he writes personally and sincerely and does make some good points. Above all he has been encouraged to try and his efforts help the teacher to see how to help further.

Robert's letter

Dear Chief Seattle

I am writing to tell you about the things that are happening now (1996). There have been many changes in the world since you were alive, most of them as you predicted. People today are set on making things for their convenience, not for their needs.

For a very long time people were chopping down trees to build places to live and new places to build machines (Moving Metal Monsters), but in the last few years things have got a little better. Every week there are new things being made such as medicine to help human health, I believe that is good. But some things people make nowadays are not needed. Some of them damage the air we breathe and bring us bad health.

My opinion is for every good thing people make there is a bad thing. I believe the people that make these machines should think about the people who suffer because they breathe air. I for one am a sufferer.

You were right.

Yours sincerely

Robert M.
Age 10

Literacy hour focus

Part of Chief Seattle's speech could be put up on the screen for the class text-based work – perhaps the part where there is the metaphor of the earth as spider's web. Children could be helped to see how poetic writing with powerful imagery can sometimes make an argument particularly clearly.

Conclusion

This book has argued that even the youngest children can have viewpoints and evaluate what they read or have read to them. By the later primary years we hope that children will be critical readers in two respects. First they will be able to judge the content of the books – the accuracy, depth and interest of the information. Second, they will have views on the format, illustrations, retrieval devices and the quality of the written text of different books on the same topics.

Critical readers reflect on what they read and have an affective as well as an intellectual response. They can, in Bruner's terms, imagine the possible as well as the actual (Bruner, 1986). Children are more likely to become successful readers and writers of non-fiction if they have become convinced that it can be satisfying and enjoyable. The children in the case studies throughout the book were helped to harness study skills and reading strategies to their bigger intentions and purposes. They were also helped to increase their knowledge about both spoken and written language, not least its relationship to the social world we all inhabit. Nowhere is this more striking than in case study 5.2, which joins the children in their committed efforts to produce a radio programme that will truly communicate to the intended audience.

Issues to discuss and reflect on

1   How far do you agree that children's reading preferences become more gender related as they move towards the end of the primary school years? Suggest how you would ensure that all the children are given the opportunity to enjoy a range of reading of both fiction and non-fiction.

2   We have seen how important spoken language is in promoting younger children's progress in reading and writing. What do you consider to be the role of speaking and listening in developing the literacy of nine to eleven year olds? You may like to think about this with reference to the case studies.

3   Writing to set out an argument is one of the greatest challenges to young writers. Describe some of the contexts you have created, or intend to create, for children's writing to persuade.

4   Look at the section on writing frames as a way of scaffolding children's writing, then jot down some of the advantages and disadvantages of using this kind of support. Your notes could be the basis of a group discussion making the case for your view.

5   There is not time within the structure of the literacy hour for older primary children to carry out sustained writing tasks. How would you provide opportunities across the curriculum for these longer informational accounts?

6   Elaine Millard in her book Differently Literate (Millard 1997) assumes, with many others, that narrative is the major tool for literacy development. What do you consider might be the contribution of non-narrative texts to children's progress in becoming readers and writers?

Notes

1 This case study draws on an analysis in 'Engaging heart and mind in reading to learn', *Language Matters*, 1996/7.
2 Based on Alison Sealey's case study (Sealey 1996: 30–31).

Further reading

Brennan, H. (1998) *The Internet*. 'Talking Point'. London: Scholastic Books.
Bruner, J. (1986) *Actual Minds, Possible Worlds*. Cambridge MA: Harvard University Press.
Egan, K. (1992) *Imagination in Teaching and Learning: The Middle School Years*. Chicago: University of Chicago Press.
Going Places: Library Resource for Geography (1997). Schools Libarary Service.
Mallett, M. (1997) 'Gender and genre: reading and writing choices of older juniors' in *Reading* UKRA, Vol. 31, No. 2.
Mallett, M. (1998) *First Person Reading and Writing in the Primary Years: Enjoying and Reflecting on Diaries, Letters, Autobiographies and First Person Writing*. Sheffield: National Association for the Teaching of English. (Contains a case study based on a series of lessons with Year 6 and practical suggestions for work with other age groups).
Meek, M. (1996) *Information and Book Learning*. Stroud: The Thimble Press.
Mercer, N. (1981) *Common Knowledge*. London: Edward Arnold.
Minns, H. (1991) *Language, Literacy and Gender*. London: Hodder & Stoughton. (See case study of children writing to a newspaper to express a strongly felt viewpoint.)
Oxlade, C. (1998) *Virtual Reality: What's the Big Idea?* London: Hodder & Stoughton.
Wray, D. (1995) *English 7–11: Developing Primary Teaching Skills*. London: Routledge. (See page 92 for an nine year old's writing about changing our attitudes and behaviour if we do not want some species of plants and animals to become extinct.)
Wray, D. and Lewis, M. (1997) *Practical Ways to Teach Reading for Information*. Reading: University of Reading, Reading and Language Information Centre.

Children's books and resources mentioned

Adi, H. (1994) *African Migrations*. Hove: Wayland.
Anne Frank's Diary (1960). Ed. G. Jameson. London: Unicorn Books, Hutchinson Educational.
Ashworth, L. (1997) *Queen Victoria*. London: Cherrytree Books.

Bardi, P. (1997) *The Atlas of Ancient Greece and Ancient Rome*. London: Macdonald Young Books.

Bellamy, D. (1998, pbk) *How Green Are You?* London: Frances Lincoln.

Biesty, S. (1994) *Incredible Cross Sections: Castles*. London: Dorling Kindersley.

Biesty, S. (1998) *Incredible Everything*. London: Dorling Kindersley.

Chambers, C. (1997) *All About Maps*. London: Franklin Watts.

Chinery, M. (1992) *Frog*; *Butterfly*. Life Story series London: Eagle Books.

Collin's School Dictionary (1996). Comp. P. Hanks. London and Glasgow: Collins.

Crowther, R. (1998) *Deep Down Underground*. London: Walker Books.

Dahl, R. (1984) *Boy: Tales of Childhood*. Harmondsworth: Penguin/Puffin.

Dictionary of Science (1994). Comp. N. Ardley. London: Dorling Kindersley.

Eyewitness Atlas of the World (1996). Comp. D. Green. London: Dorling Kindersley.

Flint, D. (1997) *The Satellite Atlas*. London: Belitha Press.

Foreman, M. (1993) *War Games*. London: Pavilion.

Hewitt, S. (1997) *Full of Energy*; *Forces Around Me*; *Solid, Liquid or Gas*; *Machines We Use*. It's Science series. London: Franklin Watts

Hodge, A. (1998) *The Caribbean*. Macdonald World Fact Files. London: MacDonald.

Hudson, T. and Greenaway, M. (1997) *Amazon Diary: The Jungle Adventures of Alex Winters*. London: Orchard Books.

Jeffers, B. (1992) *Brother Eagle, Sister Sky*. London: Penguin/Puffin.

Jennings, T. (1997) *Mountains*; *Rivers*. Restless Earth series. London: Belitha Press.

Keeping, C. (1994) *Railway Passage*. Oxford: Oxford University Press.

Langley, A. and de Souza, P. (1997) *The Roman News*. London: Walker Books.

Macaulay, D. (1988) *The Way Things Work*. London: Dorling Kindersley.

Macaulay, D. (1998) *The New Way Things Work*. London: Dorling Kindersley.

Macdonald, F. (1997) *Marco Polo*. Expedition Series. London: Franklin Watts.

Macdonald, F. (1997) *Magellan*. Expedition Series. London: Franklin Watts.

Moore, R. (1997) *My Life with the Indians*. London: Orchard Books.

Morgan, N. (1997) *Technology in the Time of the Aztecs*. London: Wayland.

Moses, B. (1997) *An Encyclopedia of Greek and Roman Gods and Heroes*. London: Pelican Big Books.

Moses, B. (1998) *The War Years: The Home Front*. London: Wayland.

Oxford Children's Encyclopedia (1998). Ed. B. Dupre. 9 vols. Oxford: Oxford University Press.

Oxford Junior Thesaurus (1995). Comp. A. Spooner. Oxford: Oxford University Press.

Oxford Mini Thesaurus (1991). Comp. A. Spooner. Oxford: Oxford University Press.

Oxford Pocket Thesaurus (1991). Comp. A. Spooner. Oxford: Oxford University Press.

Oxford Practical Atlas (1997). Comp. P. Wiegand. Oxford: Oxford University Press.

Oxford School Dictionary (1996). Comp. J. Hawkins. Oxford: Oxford University Press.

Oxlade, C. (1997) *Electronic Communication*. London: Franklin Watts.

Palmer, S. (1997) *Words Borrowed from Other Languages*. London: Pelican Big Books (also small book versions).

Philip's Foundation Atlas (1997). Comp. G. Philip. London: Ginn & Co.

Philip's Junior Atlas (1997). Comp. G. Philip. London: Ginn & Co.

Poole, J. (1998) (illus. A. Barrett) *Joan of Arc*. London: Hutchinson.

Schools Library Service (1997) *Going Places: Resources for Geography*. Hertfordshire: Schools Library Service.

Shuter, J. *et al.* (1995) *Tudor Times.* London: Heinemann.
Usborne Illustrated Dictionary (1996). Ed. J. Bingham. London: Usborne.
Usborne Illustrated Thesaurus (1996). Ed. J. Bingham and F. Chandler. London: Usborne.
Wallace, K. (1993) *Think of an Eel.* London: Walker Books.
Warner, R. (1994) *Indian Migrations.* Migrations series. Hove: Wayland.
Wheeler, S. (1997) *Dear Daniel: Letters from Antarctica.* London: Macdonald Young Books.
Woodruff, J. (1997) *Energy.* London: Wayland Science.
World War II Anthology (1998) Comp. W. Body. London: Pelican Big Books.

Software

Banner and *BannerMania.* TAG (01474 357350)
Crossword Creator. MacLine/WindowLine (0181 401 1111/1177)
Encarta 97 World Atlas Microsoft. KimTec (01202 888873).
Eureka! An Encyclopaedia of Discoveries and Inventions. Anglia Multimedia (Fax no. 01268 755811). Website <http://www.anglia.co.uk> Inventions and inventors are divided into themes: Food, Energy, Transport, etc.
First Page TAG (01474 357350).
How We Used to Live: 1936–53. PC and Acorn 1998 (YITM, Television Centre, Kirkstall Road, Leeds LS3 IJS).
HyperStudio TAG (01474 357350).
Landmarks Microworlds Longman Logotron (01223 425558).
Microsoft Reference CDs KimTec (01202 888873)
My First Amazing World Explorer Dorling Kindersley (0171 836 5411).
Rivers Ransom Publishing (01491 613711).
The Way Things Work Dorling Kindersley (0171 836 5411).
Writer's Toolkit SCET (0141 334 9314).

Star books for older juniors

Bonson, R. and Platt, R. (1997) *Disaster! Catastrophes that Shook the World.* London: Dorling Kindersley.
Couper, H. and Henbest, N. (1998) *The Big Bang: The Story of the Universe.* London: Dorling Kindesley. An exciting account of the beginning of the universe with its old age in the future. (Shortlisted for the Rhône-Poulenc science prize, 1998.)
Ford, H. (1998) *The Young Astronomer.* London: Dorling Kindersley. This practical book would reinforce the idea that non-fiction can be read for enjoyment and to develop a hobby – investigating the skies.
Kindersley, B. and Kindersley, A. (1997) *Celebration! Children Just Like Me.* London: Dorling Kindersley. The authors describe 25 festivals celebrated across the world and provide beautiful photographs of the countries they visited.
Lambert, D. (1997) *The Kingfisher Book of Oceans.* London: Kingfisher. Myths and legends are covered as well as marine animals and plants. (Shortlisted for the 1998 Rhône-Poulenc prize for junior science books that entertain as well as inform).
Macaulay, D. (1991) *Ship.* London: Dorling Kindersley. This is about a search for a sixteenth-century caravel ship in the reefs of the Caribbean. The story is told using pictures of documents, maps and diagrams and includes how a ship is made.

6 Young researchers with special literacy needs

The writers here . . . highlight the importance of ICT and emphasise the importance of the creation of learning paths for individual children rather than the use of pre-determined programmes.

(O'Sullivan and Barrs, 1998)

Introduction

How do teachers respond to what can be a considerable range of ability in their class? This of course raises a set of issues that need to be tackled at school level: good communication between the special educational needs co-ordinator, the English co-ordinator, the class teachers and the parents is essential. There are many new requirements and the complexity of the challenge to help all children achieve as much as possible is increasingly recognised.

In this chapter special literacy needs are considered as they affect children's ability to use reading and writing to learn. Children whose special needs are to do with slower language development cause teachers most concern, but the needs of children who are forward readers and writers for challenging work and more demanding materials are also important.

First we look at materials that teachers find particularly suitable for these young learners, who may need help in becoming interested enough to make the effort required. Then promising strategies to support progress in informational kinds of reading and writing are considered. Teachers need to provide differentiated tasks and materials for every lesson, ensuring that enough support is provided for those children with difficulties and that extension tasks are varied and challenging enough for the abler pupils. The chapter ends with a number of classroom vignettes of teachers working with young learners who, for one reason or another, have a special need. These suggest that wanting to know and feeling an interest in a topic has great power to awaken a will to read.

Range of resources

Many of the books recommended for all children in an age range are suitable for young learners at extreme ends of the ability range. However, it is worth drawing attention to books and software that seem particularly appropriate for them.

Choosing books and resources for struggling young readers

Books

A very good aid to matching books to children's reading level is Cliff Moon's 'Individualised Reading' system which is updated each year and contains both fiction and informational kinds of reading. This book, *25 Years of Individualised Reading 1973–98*, is an approximate guide to what children of average reading ability for their chronological age will manage to read. Kaleidoscope have now added some new non-fiction titles to their reading sets which are boxed sets of books organised into Cliff Moon's individualized reading stages. This helps teachers to scrutinise the selections for books which are of mature content but at the right level for young learners reading below the average for their chronological age. Each stage in Moon's system has a colour code: below stage 1 is red; stage 1 is yellow; stage 2 is white and so on. Teachers could add a symbol to indicate which books at the easier reading levels have content of likely interest to less forward readers.

In general, clearly written text and pages without too much clutter are best. Children who find reading challenging will respond positively to bold headings and attractive illustrations. Case study 6.6 on 'the Plague Doctor' shows how it can be the illustrations that invite a young reader into a book. Good retrieval devices help, but these are best dealt with gradually. Cambridge Reading is one of a number of reading programmes which begin with books showing a few features of an informational text and gradually adding more for older readers. Although teachers always need to check individual titles in a generally good series, some of the other publishers normally providing some of the features mentioned above include Dorling Kindersley, Kingfisher and Longman (Book Project), Collins and Nelson.

Books with two levels of text in different print sizes are flexible and helpful, for example the books from the Longman Book Project, Cambridge Reading and Walker Books Read and Wonder series.

However, we must remember that these young readers with some difficulties are, like the rest of us, more likely to be interested by the unusual, the fascinating and even the disturbing. We only have to see how Andrew was intrigued by the diseased squirrel in a photograph in case study 6.4 to understand this. Children might therefore like Jim Pipe's series of *My Giant*

Book of Snakes and *My Giant Book of Bugs,* and so on. Humour helps of course and Manning and Granström's books explain concepts like time (*Out There Somewhere It's Time to. . .*) and the structure of the earth in layers (*What's Under the Bed?*) with a light touch. It can be tactless to offer older pupils books clearly showing younger children in the pictures, so Macdonald Young Books' *The Drop Goes Plop: a First Look at the Water Cycle* with its animal characters might be a good choice for some children.

Software

A range of software is now available which, while suitable for all children, is particularly helpful to young learners with special literacy needs.

EasyPage (Porters Primary Software) has produced a Windows 1995 version which young learners with special needs find easy to use and flexible. Text can be read, illustrations completed and then the two put together.

Wordshark and *Numbershark*, from White Space, are well-structured programs on spelling, word recognition and number which, while providing a lot of rote practice, also include activities where meaning is important.

Talking computers are liked by teachers and children and they reinforce the efforts of struggling young readers. *Write: Outloud* has a choice of voices and a spell-checker as well as the usual features. The second classroom vignette in this chapter considers the work of Year 1 and 2 children round Sherston Software's *Look! Here! Talking Topics for Infants.* The children were able to control the medium better than if they had been working with information books.

The more imaginative software packages often supply additional material to extend forward young readers and writers and contribute to the teacher's resources for implementing differentiation.

Illustrations to awaken interest

The quality of the illustrations in books and software is important for all children's enjoyment and understanding, but for less forward readers it is often a picture which invites them into the book, as we see in the 'Squirrel' and 'Plague Doctor' case studies 6.4 and 6.6 below. The intriguing, fascinating or even disturbing makes the most impact.

Choosing books and resources for gifted young readers

Just as books with different levels and sizes of text help the less able, they also allow for more flexible reading for gifted readers.

Encyclopaedias, thesauruses, dictionaries and atlases in book and software form often appeal to able readers because of the flexible approach to learning they make possible. The range of reference books suitable at each stage is discussed under the appropriate age-group chapters.

Cliff Moon's 25 *Years of Indvidualised Reading,* approach, already discussed in relation to struggling readers, also helps teachers select books for forward young readers who need the challenge of projects to work on and resources to inspire and stretch them. *The Core Booklists,* from the Centre for Language in Primary Education also provide helpful advice.

Strategies to help

One of the main concerns teachers have about the literacy hour is how to manage a class of children with a range of abilities.

Scaffolding for struggling readers and writers

Reading aloud

This is a good start to any session and links enjoyment with a focus on words and groups of words.

Focus on words

Information books tend to have a technical vocabulary; learning about this can often interest struggling young readers and make them feel in control of the material. Charts can be made of key words in particular books: for example, words about rivers and maps or words about historical periods (clothes, activities, etc.).

It is also helpful to build a sight vocabulary of words to talk about non-fiction contents page, index, heading and so on. The words can be displayed on a white board or flipchart to focus discussion.

Mixed ability groups

Although there is a trend to 'setting' primary aged children for activities, less forward readers and writers benefit from working on the same texts as the other children. They learn from the comments and strategies of their abler peers, as case study 6.6 on Michael and the plague doctor shows.

The very able also benefit from working with children to whom they can explain things for some of the time. Where the atmosphere in a classroom is favourable, I have found able children very willing to develop their ability to describe things clearly for others.

The support computers can provide

With reference to research on Software in Schools, carried out by NFER/NCET, Christina Preston mentions a number of advantages teachers found when using computers with less able readers and writers (Preston,

1995). Children were likely to concentrate on tasks for longer, and the quality and length of their work was improved. Writing of all kinds benefited from the use of the spell-checks. Both teachers and children were pleased with the greatly improved presentation of children's work on the computer and graphics added to the flexibility of the format of the writing and its communicative power. Non-fiction benefits particularly from appropriate formats.

Children with special literacy needs found sound (whether music or the human voice) of great help. (*Write: OutLoud* has a speech module which speaks letters, words or sentences as you type and a useful talking spell-checker.) Greater interest in words was noted through the use of the thesaurus.

Encouraging gifted young readers and writers

Providing extension texts

Teachers generally choose a core of texts to support a topic or series of lessons. I find that some of the books I have used to advance my own knowledge in preparation for work in science, geography or history can be appreciated, sometimes with help, by abler readers. For example, a teacher working with Year 1 children on the topic of 'Spiders' found that all the children, but particularly the abler readers, enjoyed looking at the annotated cross-section of a spider in Dewan's *Inside the Whale and Other Animals* – a book intended for older pupils.

Helping children learn English as a second language

Like all groups of children, these pupils span the full range of abilities from those needing special support to those who are exceptionally able. Not surprisingly, they do seem to flourish in situations where there is a lot of collaborative work. Ten year old Andrew, who had just arrived from Hong Kong, greatly increased his English vocabulary by working with a small group on the topic of 'Bats – an endangered species'. The other children enjoyed showing their communication skills by explaining what 'chemical', 'echo location' and 'habitat' meant.

Practical activities are a good context for learning spoken language, for example while making things in art and technology or carrying out science experiments. This can lead to the more straightforward kinds of non-fiction writing: labels, lists and signs.

The work of researchers like Eve Gregory draws our attention to the cultural knowledge a monolingual learner brings to his or her reading. Phrases like 'safe and sound', 'fish and chips' and 'better late than never' help us predict swiftly when we read. Bilingual children need some help in acquiring this kind of knowledge (Gregory, 1996).

Teachers and researchers have drawn attention to the linguistic and intellectual benefits being bilingual brings. Children with a foothold in more than one language and culture often have greater social awareness and a sophisticated understanding about how language works. Marian Whitehead emphasizes the importance of teachers respecting children's languages and taking the trouble to name them correctly and to learn some greetings. (Whitehead, 1996).

There is increasing awareness that information books should show children from all the groups that make up our multicultural society. Charles Kindersley's *Children Just Like Me*, Ifeoma Onyefulu's *A is for Africa* and Kathryn Cave's *W is for World* all celebrate the diversity of children's lives across the world.

Girls, boys and non-fiction

Several publications suggest that boys prefer non-fiction while girls prefer stories, partly because of attitudes in the wider society and because they model their reading on the parent of the same gender (Millard, 1997; Graham and Kelly, 1998). This is a generalization and many boys enjoy fiction, not least when shared as the class novel (Mallett, 1997b). Girls, too, find satisfaction in reading and writing non-fiction, particularly when this is embedded in sustained work that includes a human and ethical dimension. The teacher can help by making it clear that progress in all kinds of reading and writing is important for all the children.

CASE STUDIES

Over the many years I have worked with children and students some classroom encounters stick in the memory – often because of a special need that was met imaginatively. The following classroom case studies or 'vignettes' show how teachers responded to the needs of gifted young researchers and to those who need some extra help to become interested and to maintain their concentration. Some of these glimpses are from other writers whose work has struck a chord. Readers might also like to return to the account in Chapter 3 about Owen, described by his teacher, with a touch of humour, as an 'expert eggstraordinary' because of his exceptional interest in hens (p. 69).

Case study 6.1: Whales

A group of children in a reception class become young researchers learning about creatures in the sea

Four children worked together with Kathleen Doyle, then a student teacher, to answer their own questions on whales. The work is explained and evaluated in detail in 'Were dinosaurs bigger than whales?' (Doyle and Mallett, 1994). This vignette concentrates on Jason (4 years) who showed outstanding commitment to the work.

He was very interested in the evolutionary aspects of sea creatures and in how we have come to classify sea creatures into those that are fish and those that, in spite of their environment, are mammals that breathe air. Classifying experiences and phenomena is one important way of making sense of the world and is typical of museums, information and reference materials and other resources like wildlife video film. While the children were still in the nursery class they had visited the whale floor of the Natural History Museum. They acted like little researchers, trying to find the answers to some of their questions and asking members of the nursery team to write to their dictation on the clip boards provided.

The children began to ask questions on sea creatures that were beyond the scope of the books available for their age group. Jason had become interested in the environmental issues raised by the killing of whales for food. The teacher's response was twofold. She read Sheldon and Blyth's beautifully written and illustrated picture book *The Whales' Song*. The children's understanding that people have different views on the same evidence was reinforced: Uncle Fred insisted that whales were useful 'for their oil and for their blubber', while Lucy and her grandmother valued them because they were interesting and wonderful creatures. Insight from fiction fed interesting discussion about the ethics of killing whales. Jason thought it would be sad if children in the future could not see whales because they had become extinct. The teacher brought in many other books, some fiction and some informational like Sainsbury's *Animals at Risk* which gave the precise statistics Jason was later to relate to his doctor. Because of their strong interest, the children were able to understand much of the teacher's paraphrased reading of books intended for much older pupils.

All the children and particularly Jason learnt that, as Meek reminds us, facts are not neutral (Meek, 1991). Doyle wrote in her notebook that she had become convinced that

the great vitality of these young learners, their lively sometimes passionate questions – about how big whales were, how did they all fit in the sea, how many babies did they have and why did people kill them – supports the view that the urge to understand precedes literacy.

At the end of the whale work Jason's mother sought out Ms Doyle to tell her that Jason had impressed the doctor when he was taken for treatment for a sore throat. The doctor asked, as doctors tend to, 'And what have you been doing at school?' The doctor was surprised to receive a mini lecture on whales, about how they are sea mammals; that there are different kinds; that they are an endangered species (down from quarter of a million to only a thousand); and that they can shoot water 30 feet from their blowholes.

Case study 6.2: Using the computer – pets

Year 1 and Year 2 children enjoy using Look! Here! Talking topics for Infants[1]

In this vignette from the classroom, simple talking topic books are enjoyed by children of different abilities. We join Joe, who is showing Tim how to click on an icon which activates the 'magic eye' that reads the text aloud as it is illuminated. The context for using the suite of computer programs produced by Sherston Software is a topic on 'Pets'. A strong feature of the work is that the young learners are in control of the medium. They call up an index and then choose 'fish'. The 'magic eye' icon brings an orange waving fish across the screen. Another noticeable aspect is that the children are learning in a social context. This collaborative setting to learning is motivating for all children but particularly helpful to those in the class with special literacy needs. Pagett notes that the children are not reading from cover to cover but much more flexibly, according to need and purpose. The children are being exposed to features of expository text:

> the present tense is used, and there is frequent use of the verb 'to be', no writing in the first person, page numbers are important, there is an index but support is integral for magic ear and eye facilitate comprehension, leaving the readers free to concentrate on their information retrieval strategies.
>
> (Pagett, 1997: 27)

As Pagett points out, less confident readers can sometimes be paired with abler readers and give support. There is additional material to extend the maturer readers who require the manipulation of information, including crosswords, cloze procedures and illustrations to label.

Case study 6.3: Fossils and dinosaurs

Extending and encouraging young experts

Michael and Kieron were in Year 2 at a large suburban junior school when I met them in the context of supervising a student on teaching practice. Michael, aged nine, was reading more than two years ahead of the average for his chronological age and eight year old Kieron was also one of the ablest readers in the class. Their mature interest in how fossil remains are interpreted by palaeontologists came to the attention of the teacher and class when they were studying fossils and bones in science. The boys, not formerly friends, were brought together by this shared interest and expertise. There is a detailed account of the conversations with the children (who brought in fifty books and articles to show me, explaining this was a sample of what was in their joint collection!) in Mallett (1992). The purpose of referring to them here is to consider how best to respond to children whose special need is for advanced work, involving challenging reading and writing tasks.

Strategies here included the provision of resources to keep pace with progress by tracking down books intended for older pupils and adults and magazine articles. Of course, their literacy needs to be extended generally and not just in their area of special interest.

The teacher gave Andrew and Kieron the chance to report to the other children about aspects of fossils and bones that served the purposes of the science project. Andrew, in particular, was beginning to think like a scientist and told the other children that even fossil evidence could offer only partial answers. Both boys were able to evaluate the main books about fossils and dinosaurs on the market and to say why some were better than others. They praised books where authors are advised by experts like the palaeontology department at the National History Museum, looked for double spreads where 'all the information was related and not just a jumble', and recommended books with clear instructions about how to make things (e.g. creating a trilobite or time dial, your own time-line and checklist for identifying fossils). Able people need to be capable of communicating well with those less interested than themselves. Thus the young experts and the other children all benefited.

Enthusiastic and able readers of all kinds of books can help the teacher encourage a culture of research and sharing. In this case other children were asked to let the teacher know if they had a hobby or interest that led to them reading and writing at home and which they could share with others.

Case study 6.4: Squirrel illnesses

Inspiration from a photograph

Andrew, aged nine at the time he carried out this work, found it difficult to concentrate on reading and writing tasks and had a statement of special educational need. I met him in the context of class-based work on the life-cycle of grey squirrels. The work aimed to provide opportunities for learning from a range of secondary sources as well as observation of the creatures.

We had talked about existing knowledge about squirrels and watched a video-film 'Squirrel on my Shoulder' narrated by David Attenborough (BBC Wildlife Project) about an abandoned grey squirrel being nurtured by a cat with her kittens. Most of the children were enjoying finding out the answers to their questions in the books. Andrew had been helped to formulate some questions but was not involved in the task and was beginning to irritate the other children near him.

To focus his work I asked Andrew to find a picture that told us something interesting about squirrels. The breakthrough came when he found a photograph of a squirrel suffering from mange in Susan Coldrey's *Grey Squirrel*, an annotated collection of photographs. The class teacher and I had almost discarded it at an early stage because it had no retrieval devices and was relatively old and out of print. We decided to keep it in the collection for the less forward readers as the photographs were large and showed the creatures in their environment.

Andrew was not inspired by the attractive squirrels shown frolicking in the trees or nurturing their young, but rather by a close-up of a bedraggled creature with bald patches and scabs. Publishers take note – the bland, the cosy and the beautiful often inspire less than the disturbing, the thought-provoking and the grotesque. Andrew asked me to read the text below the illustration out loud. 'This squirrel is suffering from mange, a disease which causes the skin to scab and the hair to fall out.'

The conversation continued and several other children came to see Andrew's squirrel photograph.

ANDREW: Will it die?
TEACHER: I don't know. I think a parasite gets under the skin and makes the hair fall out. Poor creature is probably feeling itchy.
ANDREW: Can another squirrel catch it?
TEACHER: If it got close it might. The parasite might move from one squirrel to another.
KIM: Can people catch it?
ANDREW: People have not got fur!
TEACHER: People can get ringworm on their heads. Where is my big dictionary?

We found that mange is a 'skin disease in hairy and woolly animals, caused by an arachnid parasite' and that it was occasionally communicated to human beings.

Andrew's interest would have been less significant if this had been fascinating but miscellaneous information. In fact, it linked with one of the key areas we had identified in the work: Squirrels' predators and illnesses. Andrew was helped to find those answers to his questions and those of some of the other children and gave a short presentation to the class, using the photograph as the starting-point. The interest of the other children raised Andrew's self-esteem but it is important not to claim too much – Andrew's difficulties were not solved overnight. Nevertheless, he did show more interest in all aspects of the project and particularly enjoyed giving a repeat presentation to the seven year olds who came to hear about the squirrel work at the end of the series of lessons.

Case study 6.5: Dolphins

Ten year old Zoe needed help with focusing the task[2]

Ten year old Zoe had been asked to write about dolphins as part of whole-class work on the subject 'Living Things'. Without support, Zoe, like many other children, tended to copy out huge chunks from the information books provided. She needed to take some focusing questions to the books to give her a sense of purpose and to organise the writing task. To arrive at the questions her support teacher found it helpful to ask Zoe what she already knew about dolphins. A number of scholars stress the importance of ordering and making explicit prior knowledge as a starting-point for acquiring new knowledge (Bransford, 1983; Mallett, 1992; Wray and Lewis, 1994, 1997).

Following Wray and Lewis' KWA grid, the support teacher headed three columns in Zoe's jotter What I **K**now; What I **W**ant to know; What I **L**earnt?

First the teacher scribed the things that Zoe said she already knew, for example that dolphins were clever, related to whales, ate squid, were hunted by fishermen and looked beautiful.

The next stage was to help Zoe write down her questions and to model how she might go about answering them. As the support teacher had only one hour to work with Zoe, it was decided to limit the writing to answering one question: How do they live? Zoe was helped to make a concept map or planning web with the question in the middle and possible subheadings to research: the dolphin's life-cycle and young; the way they dive and swim; and conditions needed to support life.

The subheadings gained from the web provided some key words to take to the indexes of the books and the teacher helped her to scan. The piece of writing that resulted was clearly Zoe's own composition. It began 'Dolphins live in families of about seven. There would be several females but only one male. . .' She is making strides towards controlling her own reading and writing. It occurred to me on considering this case study that Zoe is being helped to go through the same procedures as anyone of any age approaching a piece of research- finding a focus, gathering information and writing an organised account.

Case study 6.6: Plague doctor

A ten year old creates a labelled diagram to enjoy and understand history

Michael lacked confidence and, although not statemented, had some difficulty in completing writing tasks. He was working with a group within

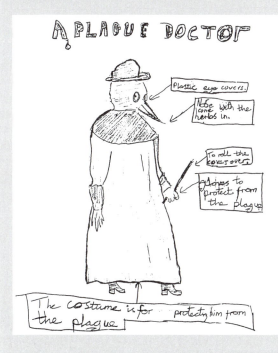

Figure 6.1 Michael's picture of a plague doctor is based on the illustration in Joan Blyth's *Tudor and Stuart Times* (1993) but the labels and information boxes are his own.

his Year 5 class on plague and illness in Tudor times. His contribution was to be an illustration of a Tudor plague doctor in the protective dress of boots, gown and nose cone. He based his drawing on the picture in J. Blyth's *Tudor and Stuart Times* but wanted to make it serve the needs of the group, who expected to make a display of books, drawings and writing and to show their findings to the whole class. There had been a lot of reading and discussion in the group about Tudor beliefs about illness and how the plague doctor greatly feared catching the illness from the patients. Michael hit on the idea of labelling and annotating his picture with his own version of brief notes made (see Figure 6.1). I find that each project or series of lessons in which I have been involved is associated with key images that seem to bring back the essence of the work. Michael's plague doctor became such an image both for me and I believe for the whole class. It somehow stood for the way in which illness was perceived in those times and how people tried to use what knowledge they had to respond to dreadful happenings over which they had little control, like the plague.

His success in designing a striking picture and useful labelling raised his status in the group and showed him how satisfying reading and writing can be when directed towards a worthwhile outcome.

Issues to discuss and reflect on

1   The possible benefits of some work in mixed ability groups for less able readers and writers are recognised. In what ways do you consider abler children might also benefit from contributing to a group made up of children of different abilities?

2   This chapter has recognised the potential of the computer, both for helping struggling young writers and for those able to forge ahead. What, in your experience so far, have been the main advantages of this new transforming technology?

3   With reference to your own work in the classroom, how do you consider children with reading and writing difficulties can be helped to use diagrams and pictures to develop their literacy and motivation?

Notes

1 This vignette is based on Linda Pagett (1997), 'Look! Here's a new idea! Using information technology to facilitate the use of expository text'. *Reading, UKRA*, July 1997, Vol. 31, No. 2.
2 Case study 6.5 based on the work of the EXEL Project, funded by Nuffield, as written up in D. Wray and M. Lewis (1997) *Practical Ways to Teach Reading for Information*, Reading: Reading and Language Information Centre, Reading University.

Further reading

Doyle, K. and Mallett, M. (1994) 'Were dinosaurs bigger than whales? Four year olds make sense of different kinds of text' in *TACTYC Early Years Journal*, Vol. 14, No. 2, Spring.

Gregory, E. (1996) *Making Sense of a New World: Learning to Read in a Second Language*. London: Paul Chapman Publishing.

Mallett, M. (1997) 'Gender and Genre' in *Reading UKRA*, No. 31.

Meek, M. (1991) *On Becoming Literate*. London: The Bodley Head.

Millard, E. (1997) *Differently Literate*. London: Falmer Press.

Moon, C. (1998) *25 Years of Individualised Reading 1973–98*. Reading: Reading University, Reading and Language Information Centre.

Pagett, L. (1997) 'Look! Here's a New Idea! Using Information Technology to Facilitate the Use of Expository Text' in *Reading UKRA*. July, Vol. 31, No. 2.

Preston, C. (1995) *21st Century A–Z Literacy Handbook: Linking Literacy to Software*. London: London Institute of Education, Project Miranda.

Whitehead, M. (1996) *The Development of Language and Literacy*. London: Hodder & Stoughton (see chapter 2, 'Young Bilinguals').

Wray, D. and Lewis, M. (1997) *Practical Ways to Teach Reading for Information*. Reading: Reading University, Reading and Language Information Centre.

Children's books and resources mentioned

Publishers who produce books liked by children with SENs include Dorling Kindersley, Longman (Book Project), Franklin Watts, Cambridge Reading and Oxford Reading Tree.

Blyth, J. (1993) *Tudor and Stuart Times*. London: Ginn & Co.

Cave, K. (1998) *W is for World*. London: Frances Lincoln.

Dewan, T. (1992) *Inside the Whale and Other Animals*. London: Dorling Kindersley.

Godwin, S. (1997) *The Drop Goes Plop: a First Look at the Water Cycle*. Bees series. London: Macdonald Young Books.

Godwin, S. (1998) *A Seed in Need: a First Look at the Plant Cycle*. Bees series. London: Macdonald Young Books.

Kindersley, C. (1996) *Children Just Like Me*. London: Dorling Kindersley.

Hooper, M. (1996) *Dinosaur; Coral Reef*. Cambridge: Cambridge Reading.

Onyefulu, I. (1997) *A is for Africa*. London: Frances Lincoln.

Pipe, J. (1998) *My Giant Book of Bugs* and *My Giant Book of Snakes*. London/ Sydney: Aladdin Books/Watts.

Sainsbury's (1992) *Animals at Risk*. Informational picture book.

Sheldon, D. and Blythe, G. (1990) *The Whales' Song*. London: Hutchinson.

Shuter, J., Hook, A. and Maguire, J. (1995) *Heinemann Our World: History: Tudor Times*. Heinemann.

ICT *for children with special literacy needs*

The software suggested here is suitable for all children and is particularly helpful for children who are struggling with reading and writing. Some items may not be mentioned in the text.

Allwrite from LETSS is an easy-to-use, multilingual word processor with a choice of 19 languages but no spell-checking (0181 850 0100).

An Eye for Spelling is a Word Bank and is customisable from known vocabulary ESM (01945 63441).

CatchWord helps with writing difficulties and has a helpful ideas notebook. Black Cat (01874 636835).

EasyPage. Porters Primary Software. Windows 95 version (1998). The big buttons and ease of use make this suitable for students of all ages with special literacy needs. The computer can be used to make an illustration, write a text and read it, then put them together on a page (0114 258 2878).

Information Workshop is an easy-to-use Windows database program which includes colourful graphs. Black Cat (01874 636835).

Kid Works 2 talking word processor combines skills of publishing and multimedia. TAG (01474 357350).

Landmarks presents interactive adventures linked to the BBC series. The user can talk to a child in the story and explore historical times including The Second World War and The Victorians. Longman Logotron (01223 425558). (From same supplier is *Landmarks Microworlds*).

Look! Here! Talking Topics for Infants. Sherston Software Ltd. Angel House, Sherston, Malmesbury, Wiltshire SN16 OLH. For key stage 1 children of varying ability.

Mapper Series: Body, Weather, Home can be customized for language difficulty. TAG (01474 357350).

Picture Dictionary uses picture scenes and works with any word processor. TAG (01474 357350).

Rainbow is a simple multimedia package. Longman Logotron (01223 425558).

Talking PenDown is an Acorn word processor with wordlists and a talking spell-checker. Longman Logotron (01223 425558).

Talking Word for Windows is an addition to Word for Windows 2 or 6 and simplifies some word options. Longman Logotron (01223 425558).

TalkWrite is a talking word processor with word lists and spell-check. Resource (014469 530818).

Time Detectives . . . The Victorians allows children to learn about the period through following a children's adventure story. Sherston (01666 840433).

Word Bank can be used with word processors to create a dictionary for particular pupils. TAG (01474 357350).

Wordshark and *Numbershark* are well-structured courses which have been particularly successful with young learners with special needs. The stress in both is on skills in number and in spelling and word recognition, but the different activities provide a focus on meaning as well as rote practice. White Space (0181 748 5927).

Write: OutLoud Talking wordprocessor with talking spell-checker and choice of voices. John Johnston (0161 628 0919).

Writer's Toolkit helps older primary children with SEN to self-assess as they try a range of writing including journalism and reporting experiments. SCET (0141 334 9314).

7 Recording progress

Assessment of children's informational reading and writing

Assessing children's knowledge, skills and understanding, as well as their confidence, independence and learning approaches, is not something that can be tacked onto the end of learning.

(Graham and Kelly, 1997: 106)

Introduction

The teachers in the case studies throughout this book were constantly evaluating and recording the progress of their pupils. This chapter provides a more focused consideration of assessment as an integral part of daily practice. Teachers are required to carry out both summative assessments (testing what pupils know at a particular time, for example, the National Curriculum SATs) and formative assessment (evaluating a pupil's strengths and weaknesses to inform their planning). While summative assessments are useful when we need to inform parents or a new teacher of a child's progress, they are less helpful in guiding future planning. They can be one useful way of detailing progress as long as we realise that children's language and literacy development, including their increasing control over informational kinds of reading and writing, is not linear and therefore not easily tested, and that summative tests tend to concentrate on easily measurable skills (Karavais and Davies, 1995).

Formative assessment avoids seeing assessment as bolted on at the end of a phase of work but rather, as The Cox Report advises, as part of a planning, teaching, learning and evaluating cycle (DES, 1989). Like other aspects of language development, progress in informational reading and writing is best assessed in the context of real tasks rather than through contrived exercises. Tools and strategies are acquired to expand children's developing ability to research subjects and communicate their findings. Just as library, computer and book research abilities are learnt about in real situations, so the assessment is best made in context. For example, when children are making notes from resources in a history or geography lesson, the teacher can make a short, dated comment on each child's profile. Progress in the subject and in the note-taking strategy can be assessed at the same time.

This approach to assessment and keeping records is much more economic of teachers' and children's time than more contrived assessments. As the children's abilities are evaluated in context, we do not need to assume there will be transfer from a contrived situation to real tasks. The feedback feed-forward cycle makes it possible for the teacher to think like a researcher. Indeed, one important kind of classroom inquiry, namely action research, is a more systematic form of what the good practitioner does all the time as part of his or her teaching (Bell, 1987). There is much in common between good teaching and good researching.

Non-fiction books and software have tended not to be used as much as stories in the initial teaching of reading. Partly because of the emphasis on genre in the National Curriculum English programmes, a much wider range of material is now used. It has been evident throughout this book that all of the newer reading programmes – *Cambridge Reading, Oxford Reading Tree, Ginn's All Aboard, Nelson's Voyages, Badger's Wonder World, Collin's Pathways, Kingscourt's Story Chest* and *Longman Reading Project* – include different kinds of non-fiction. Teachers can use informational kinds of text to teach the range of reading strategies required by the National Curriculum and the National Literacy Strategy's *Framework for Teaching*. These include strategies to do with phonic knowledge, with word recognition and with grammatical understanding, all of which require good quality reading resources of all kinds (Whitehead, 1996: Graham and Kelly, 1997). But we must remember that the main purpose of non-fiction reading is to nourish the need to find out and make sense of and use new information.

Children's informational writing lends itself well to teaching and assessing handwriting and spelling: there is often a distinctive vocabulary to learn on a topic, and punctuation and paragraphing is needed in writing about findings. Again, attendance to these aspects must not detract from our evaluation of a child's growing capacity to organise information and ideas through writing, with an eye on the purposes of a particular piece of writing and its intended audience.

The teachers whose work has been presented in previous chapters encourage their pupils to be critical thinkers from the earliest stages, evaluating the ideas and information they find and assessing the resources they have used. Indeed, there is increasing recognition of the value of children's own assessment of their progress. *The Primary Language Record* (Barrs *et al.*, 1988) is a major achievement of the Centre for Language in Primary Education and is used (sometimes in modified form) by schools worldwide. It provides space both for children's comments and the comments of parents or guardians.

Children's informational reading and writing not only illuminate their progress in some important kinds of literacy, they also serve as a window into their development as young scientists, historians, geographers and mathematicians. Indeed they reveal progress across the whole curriculum.

This chapter begins by looking at the role of observation in teachers' assessment of reading and writing to learn. It turns next to the other kinds of evidence, including writing samples, which help us to evaluate progress. The potential value of children's self-assessment, both of their own progress as readers and writers of a range of material and their evaluation of the resources they have been using, is then considered. Finally we turn to the role of assessment and record-keeping in the National Curriculum English, including the standardised attainment tests, and the implications of the National Literacy Strategy literacy hour for assessing children's work.

Formative assessment

The role of observation

Observation is an important tool in providing the kind of evidence that informs good assessment. We can learn much from good early years practitioners who are traditionally experts at judging what is significant in illuminating developing literacy as well as other areas of development. Victoria Hurst describes a teacher's careful observation of Kerry, aged three years and two months, making a shopping list as part of role play. Kerry drew some zigzag lines and put some capital Ks and Rs at their side; the use of letters from her own name, something she had experimented with at home, showed the teacher that Kerry was distinguishing between play writing and writing in a public code that others could understand. Not only did this show that Kerry understood the social purposes of writing, it also helped the teacher plan to extend this developing knowledge (Hurst, 1992). This kind of observation informs useful record-keeping.

Children's activities in the reading and writing corners reveal much about their understanding of the purposes of print. We saw, for example, the very young children learning about the topic of 'Journeys' in Chapter 2 writing labels and tickets, making posters and putting up signs during role play. Those of us who work with older primary children need also to make records of our observation of children's reading and writing in the classroom reading and writing area. Although we shall be looking at the progress of pupils who know much more about the kinds of reading and writing valued in our culture because they serve social purposes, observation helps us to plan for individual needs. At every stage we need to support struggling young learners and to extend the abilities of the other children, including those who are ready for more advanced work. One interesting aspect is the progress children are making in the use of the computer, not just as an editing tool, but as a genuine means of redrafting the content of the work and perhaps trying out different formats.

Observation can be planned; for example, the teacher may observe individuals in a group using retrieval devices – making notes on how well they use contents page, index and glossaries. This could take place in the literacy hour or in a lesson across the curriculum. Observation can also be useful when we see something of interest more incidentally; for example, one teacher noted in her records that seven year old Sarah was modelling using an index for another child. Nine year old Ian, who liked Biesty's cross-section books, brought in from home a cross-section of a Tudor ship, showing the ability to label and annotate a diagram.

Teachers in Great Britain have used checklists based on the National Curriculum English orders to guide their observation. They now also take account of the more detailed objectives for non-fiction reading and writing in the NLS *Framework for Teaching* to guide their observations. However, these need not be used mechanistically – after all, teachers were observing and recording children's progress before we had the literacy hour or even the National Curriculum!

Recording progress

Evidence of progress in reading can come partly from focused discussions with a child. Often a review of reading will include both fiction and non-fiction. Some of these discussions could be tape-recorded or brief notes made. Notes can also be made and dated of discussions with parents about their children's informational reading at home. Most schools now have systematic approaches to record-keeping and many find an approach like *The Primary Language Record* comprehensive and flexible. It provides for all kinds of reading and writing (and talking and listening). It makes it possible to see assessment as part of the teaching and learning cycle, and if used as intended, it helps teachers organise the language programme and to feed assessment back into the next round of planning.

There follows a short extract from a much longer discussion by a group of ten year olds with the teacher. Not only does it reveal their growing understanding of some historical concepts, it also shows their increasing control over the information book genre.

Before the discussion began, the children were asked to give book titles and pages to support their comments. I think you can tell from their contributions that the children knew in advance about their task and had prepared for it. The notes the teacher made later mentioned the children's growing grip on what 'chronology' means and their understanding of the need for books which go beyond the superficial and give evidence for historical information.

ADAM: *Kings and Queens* is a general book that I wouldn't buy because it just gives you a list with pictures of all the kings and queens of England in chronological order – but I would want a book just about the Tudors to get the detail. Or even a book just about the *Mary Rose* or just about Henry VIII.

JOANNE: Well my best book is *The Poor and the Wicked* and there is a lot of detail (opens at a double spread) – look at the writing and all the pictures about what the poor ate. Everything was sweetened with honey but that was expensive. And there are pages about the utensils for cooking you used if you were poor and the ones the rich had.

TEACHER: How do we know what people ate then?

ADAM: You might find bones of meat and swans and things under the house that might be dug up and dated. Fossil evidence.

JOANNE: And there are menus for feasts from old books and you can see what people ate in old paintings of families at the table. Christine and I learnt about food and cooking utensils when we were finding out about the *Mary Rose* because the kitchen utensils were brought up from the wreck.

Children's reading diaries or journals

Most teachers ask children to keep their own reading log, diary or journal with the titles of everything they have read at school and possibly at home too. This can make a strong contribution to the teacher's records. Annotations add greatly to the worth of the record. It becomes tedious to expect a full review of every book read. Sometimes just a short comment like seven year old Trevor's on Parson and Young's *Amazing Spiders* – 'good pictures and facts' – is all that is needed.

Occasional detailed reviews of the non-fiction texts children read are helpful indicators of how a child's critical faculties are developing. A selection of these could be photocopied, written out again or copies made using the printer if the work has been word-processed and placed in the child's folder of work. The class could agree on a format for reviews. The title, author and the date the book or resource was read usually head the review. But to ring the changes, children could write brief notes in their reading diary on a text and use these to talk to a group or a class about their opinion, answering the other children's questions. This in an opportunity for the teacher to assess and record a child's progress in spoken language as well as reading and writing.

Collecting examples of children's work

Teacher assessments of a range of different kinds of children's writing, for a variety of purposes and audiences, are made with reference to the National Curriculum writing levels.

As well as writing samples, a full record of a child's non-fiction work would include illustrations: labelled diagrams, charts, graphs, drawings and tables, and annotated photographs taken by the child as part of project work. Brief notes can be made on the back of each item giving the date, child's age, the context, a provisional National Curriculum writing level

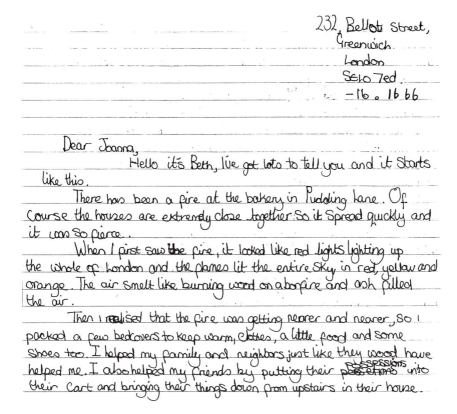

232, Bellot Street,
Greenwich.
London
SE10 7ed
-16.1666

Dear Joanna,
　　　　Hello it's Beth, I've got lots to tell you and it starts like this.
　　　　There has been a fire at the bakery in Pudding Lane. Of course the houses are extremely close together so it spread quickly and it was so fierce.
　　　　When I first saw the fire, it looked like red lights lighting up the whole of London and the flames lit the entire sky in red, yellow and orange. The air smelt like burning wood on a bonfire and ash filled the air.
　　　　Then I realised that the fire was getting nearer and nearer, so I packed a few bedcovers to keep warm, clothes, a little food and some shoes too. I helped my family and neighbors just like they would have helped me. I also helped my friends by putting their possesions into their cart and bringing their things down from upstairs in their house.

Figure 7.1 Letter about the Great Fire of London by ten year old Beth. This is part of a long letter chosen by Beth for her portfolio. It shows that she can transform information successfully from one genre (information books) to another (a letter to a personal friend).

and a brief qualitative comment. Children should be invited to take part in the selection of work for their folder and, as Whitehead reminds us, brief notes on the reasons the child has chosen particular pieces are useful (Whitehead, 1996).

Responding to children's writing

Sometimes teachers give a spoken comment on a child's writing. However, children always appreciate a short written comment. Sometimes teachers can genuinely write that they have learnt something from a child's account. When writing has been displayed I have often heard children reading the piece and the teacher's comments out loud.

The peer group can also be an audience for children's writing and be invited to ask questions or make constructive comments.

Children's self-assessment

There is considerable scope for useful self-assessment in the non-fiction area. We can use opportunities for children to talk to the teacher about their reading and writing discussing problems and successes. Some teachers call these discussions about reading and writing progress 'conferences' after Donald Graves (1983). Reporting back on findings by individuals or groups to the whole class as the children did in the Year 6 work on Tudors (Chapters 5 and 6) is also an excellent opportunity for children to acquire reflective and analytical abilities which will extend their research powers. Where children have been encouraged to think of themselves as a community of young researchers, they will be more likely to appreciate the contributions other individuals and groups have made to the progress of the work.

Summative assessment

At the end of each key stage in Britain both formal assessments (SATs) of children's reading and writing and teacher assessments, related to the National Curriculum level descriptions are required. How teachers observe children's writing strategies and take samples of their work to assess and record progress formatively has been discussed. We turn now to the more formal, timed tests required.

Standard Assessment Tests for reading and writing (SATs)

Although the content of the tests changes each year, the main format and the kinds of reading and writing have remained similar for a year or so. Some changes to the way in which children's language progress is assessed is certain once the literacy hour with its precise objectives gets underway. Full details are provided in the current edition of *Key Stage One English Tasks. Teacher's Handbook* (QCA, 1998). This section gives an outline of what is required together with some discussion of how teachers might respond.

At the time of writing, reading tests for the end of key stage 1 include individual reading to the teacher and an additional comprehension test for children achieving level 2A. The comprehension text is usually a story and the number of right answers decides whether or not a child has reached level 3.

The reading assessment at the end of key stage 2 takes the form of reading a booklet and answering comprehension questions for children at levels 3–5. (Year 6 children who are still reading at level 1 or 2 read with the teacher in the same way as children at key stage 1, but from a different selection of books.) There is 15 minutes for reading the booklet which contains different kinds of writing round a theme, like 'Time' or 'Journeys' and 45 minutes to answer questions in the writing booklet. The extracts are from published works and usually consist of an information text, a set of instructions for making something, and a story. Children who seem to be working at level 6 sit an extension paper which also sets a mix of fiction and non-fiction texts. At the time of writing, the formal writing task at the end of key stage 1 is developed from one of the books from the SAT booklists or from another book related to the work of the class. The teacher may choose to set any appropriate fiction or non-fiction writing task. Informational kinds of writing would include recounts, instructions, factual accounts, letters, diary entries or reviews.

The teacher can discuss the task with the children and they can use dictionaries and other resources they would normally use. Thus it is like other writing tasks except that the first draft is the final draft and the teacher cannot help once the writing starts. Using the QCA handbook for guidance, the teacher assesses the writing. There is a formal spelling test for children whose teacher assessment puts them at level 2.

At key stage 2, there is an hour-long writing test, 15 minutes for planning and 45 minutes for writing. In 1998 two of four titles (from which the children had to choose one) were informational in genre: 'Read All About It!' – an interview; and 'The School Trip' – a newsletter. The audience and purpose of each of these is made clear in the booklet and read out by the teacher. There is no provision for redrafting but children could, if time allowed, check through what they had written and correct spelling and punctuation errors. The writing is marked by externals who have clear criteria in two main categories: Purpose & Organisation and Grammar (the latter is subdivided into Punctuation and Style). Spelling and handwriting are assessed in a separate test in which the children write the words read out by the teacher into the gaps in their version of the text.

What are the implications of these timed tests for our practice? Although efforts have been made to make the test booklets clear and interesting and to illustrate them, the SATs cause some anxiety for children, parents and teachers. While teachers should not narrow their literacy programme, children do have to be prepared for the tests, particularly those on writing. Key stage 1 children may be used to drafting their writing, most probably have experienced teacher support throughout the task and many will have enjoyed shared writing contexts. All these experiences will have helped their development as writers but they will need some practice in writing independently without a first draft before they do the tests.

Informational kinds of reading and writing feature considerably in the key stage 2 SATs and the children will benefit from some experience of identifying writing genres quickly. They will need to think about the organisation of letters, instructions and non-narrative writing. The organisation of a piece of writing reflects purpose and audience, both of which are made clear in the test booklet. Everything they need to know will have been covered in a good programme, but they benefit from some help in responding to the format and demands of a timed test which involves demanding and quick reading and writing.

The National Literacy Strategy and assessment

The National Literacy Strategy *Framework for Teaching* sets out detailed term by term objectives for children's work in the literary hour. Teachers need to show that the objectives have been covered. This has implications for what is included in the children's writing folders as a sampling of their work. For example, a Year 1 child's folder would be likely to include, as part of the non-fiction kinds of writing: some simple lists and instructions (Term 1); some labelled diagrams perhaps arising from science work and some samples of non-chronological reports (Term 2); and evidence that their reading was feeding into the organization of their writing on topics of interest across the curriculum (Term 3). A Year 5 folder might include: recounts for different audiences plus notes from books and for purposes like giving a short talk on a topic to the class (Term 1); expansions of personal notes for others to read plus short non-chronological reports taking account of the features of expositionary texts in their non-fiction reading (Term 2); and a range of letters for different audiences and examples of persuasive writing (Term 3). All the writing can be done in helpful contexts in the literacy hour and across the curriculum.

Good teachers have always invited children to explain and evaluate their work and the plenary session at the end of the literacy hour is a strong feature. Teachers are finding that they would sometimes like more time fully to exploit this opportunity. One idea is to focus on a different group each time rather than every group give a more hasty account.

Issues to discuss and reflect on

1   Many teachers carry out action research projects to develop their professional skills and sometimes to gain a higher degree. Some of the best studies are published in books or articles or appear on web sites on the Internet and so help to further professional knowledge. How might action research help us understand more about children's informational reading and writing and particularly its assessment?

2   With reference to specific non-fiction books, including big books, consider how you would use the text to further and assess children's phonological awareness.

3 With reference to a recent 'conference' with a child about his or her informational writing, evaluate the potential value of children's self-assessment.

4 How might the computer be used as an assessment tool?

Further reading

Barrs, M., Ellis, S., Hester, H. and Thomas, A. (1988) *The Primary Language Record: A Handbook for Teachers*. London: Centre for Language in Primary Education.

Barrs, M., Ellis, S., Kelly, C. and O'Sullivan, O. (1996) 'The New Primary Language Record Writing Scale' in *Language Matters*. Centre for Language in Primary Education, 1995/6, no. 3.

Bell, J. (1987) *Doing Your Research Project*. Milton Keynes: Open University Press.

Graham, J. and Kelly, A. (1997) *Reading under Control*. London: David Fulton Publishers.

Hurst, V. (1992) 'Assessment and the nursery curriculum' in Blenkin, G. and Kelly, V. *Assessment in Early Childhood Education*. London: Paul Chapman Publishing.

Karavais, S. and Davies, P. (1995) *Progress in English: Assessment and Record Keeping at KS1 and 2*. Reading: Reading University, Reading and Language Information Centre.

QCA (1998) *Key Stage One English Tasks. Teacher's Handbook*. London: QCA.

Postscript

Teachers are working in a climate of change, challenge and criticism and ever greater demands are being made on their professional skills and judgement. In a time of change there are some enduring principles. The quality of the materials we provide will continue to be at the very heart of our success. As well as information books of merit, we need to use the fruits of new technology. This means making full and imaginative use of the computer, the Internet, CD-ROMs and a variety of software, tape recordings, video-films and slides. We do not know what further innovations the new millennium will bring, but we know we must exploit the educational potential of new technology in the classroom.

Library and study skills are tools to help young researchers find out and share what they need to know to serve their larger purposes. Direct teaching and modelling of strategies is needed but it is best done in context.

Above all, since language of all kinds is socially situated, children work best collaboratively – taking inspiration from the teacher and from other children. Spoken language has a crucial role in helping children become literate. Talking through developing ideas and new information at the beginning of a new venture energises the work and sustains it. Teachers and the other children are – in the liveliest classrooms – an audience for a child's discoveries both spoken and written.

Any new classroom initiative will only succeed through the skill, judgement, imagination and dedication of teachers. Creative and reflective practitioners will work within the required frameworks to help children make progress in all aspects of literacy, not least in those kinds of reading and writing we call informational.

Appendix

The following telephone numbers of main publishers referred to in the book are correct at the time of going to press.

Addison Wesley		01279 623921
A & C Black		0171 242 0946
Anglia Multimedia		01268 755811
	or	0160 361 5151
Aztec Software		01274 596716
Badger Publishing		01438 356907
BBC Education		0181 746 1111
Belitha Press		0171 978 6330
Black Cat Software		01874 636835
Cambridge University Press		01223 325588
Dorling Kindersley		0171 836 5411
Evans		0171 935 7160
Frances Lincoln		0171 284 4009
Ginn		01296 394442
Granada Learning/Semerc		0161 827 2927
HarperCollins Ed.		0870 0100 441
Heinemann		01865 314301
Kingfisher		0171 903 9999
Letss Software		0181 850 0100
Longman		01279 623623
	or	0800 579579
Longman Logotron		01223 425558
Macdonald Young Books		01273 722561
Microsoft		0345 00 2000
Oxford University Press		01865 556767
Penguin, Puffin, Viking & Hamish Hamilton		0500 807981
Porters Primary Software		0114 258 2878
Ransom Publishing		01491 613711
SCET Software		0141 334 9314

Sherston Software	01666 843200
Storm Educational Software	0193 581 7699
TAG Software	01474 357350
Walker Books Ltd	0171 793 0909
Watts	0171 739 2929
Wayland	01273 722561
White Space Software	0181 748 5927

References

Abott, C. (1994) *Reading IT: a Teacher's Guide to the Use of Computers in Reading Activities*. Reading: Reading University, Reading and Language Information Centre.

Arnold, H. (1992) '"Do the Blackbirds sing all day?" Literature and information texts' in M. Styles, E. Bearne, and V. Watson *After Alice: Exploring Children's Literature*. London: Cassell.

Bage, R. 'History texts in the Literacy Hour', *Times Educational Supplement*, 4 Sept. 1998, p. 22.

Baker, C. D. and Freebody, P. (1989) *Children's First School Books*. Oxford: Basil Blackwell.

Barrs, M. (1987) 'Mapping the world', *English in Education NATE*, Vol. 21, No. 3.

Barrs, M. (1996a) Editorial 'Information Texts' in *Language Matters*, No. 3. London: Centre for Language in Primary Education.

Barrs, M. (1996b) 'The New Primary Language Record Writing Scale' in *Language Matters*. No. 3. London: Centre for Language in Primary Education.

Barrs, M. (1997) *The Core Booklist* (Information Collections, key stage 1 and 2) London: Centre for Language in Primary Education.

Barrs, M. and Pidgeon, S. (1993) *Reading the Difference: Gender and Reading in the Primary School*. London: Centre for Language in Primary Education.

Barrs, M., Ellis, S., Hester, H. and Thomas, A. (1988) *The Primary Language Record: a Handbook for Teachers*. London: Centre for Language in Primary Education.

Bartholomew, L. and Bruce, T. (1993) *Getting to Know You. A Guide to Record Keeping in Early Childhood Education and Care*. London: Hodder & Stoughton.

Barton, D. (1994) *Literacy: An Introduction to the Ecology of Written Language*. Oxford: Blackwell.

Beard, R. (1984) *Children's Writing in the Primary School*. Sevenoaks: Hodder & Stoughton.

Beireter, C. and Scardamalia, M. (1987) *The Psychology of Written Composition*. Hillsdale, NJ: Lawrence Erlbaum.

Bell, J. (1987) *Doing Your Research Project*. Milton Keynes: Open University Press.

Blenkin, G. and Kelly, V. (eds) (1992) *Assessment in Early Childhood Education*. London: Paul Chapman.

Bransford, J. (1993) 'Schema activation – schema acquisition' in R. C. Anderson, J. Osborne and R. J. Tierney (eds) *Learning to Read in American Schools*. Hillsdale, NJ: Lawrence Erlbaum.

Brennan, H. (1998) *The Internet*. 'Talking Point'. London: Scholastic.

Britton, J. (1970) *Language and Learning*. London: Allen Lane, The Penguin Press.

Browne, A. (1996) *Language and Literacy 3–8*. London: Paul Chapman Publishing.

Bruce, T. (1996) *Helping Young Children to Play*. London: Hodder & Stoughton.

Bruner, J. (1986) *Actual Minds, Possible Worlds*. Cambridge MA: MIT Press.

Bruner, J. and Haste, H. (1987) *Making Sense: the Child's Construction of the World*. London: Methuen.

Bruner, J., Jolly, A. and Sylva, K. (1978) *Play: Its Role in Development and Evolution*. London: Routledge.

Butler, D. (1995) *Babies Need Books*. London: Penguin Books.

Calkins, L. (1986) *The Art of Teaching Writing*. Portsmouth NH: Heinemann.

Carthy, R. (1996) 'The impact of word processing on the development of early writers who are using the Foundations of Writing approach combined with the "emergent" writing approach to the writing process'. Dissertation for the degree of Master of Education at the University of Exeter.

Clay, M. (1975) *What Did I Write?* London: Heinemann Educational Books.

Clay, M. (1991) *Becoming Literate: The Construction of Inner Control*. London: Heinemann.

Crompton, R. and Mann, J. (1996) *IT across the Primary Curriculum*. London: Cassell.

Czerniewska, P. (1992) *Learning about Writing*. Oxford: Blackwell.

Dalton-Vinters, J. and Mallett, M. (1995) 'Six year olds read about fire fighters', *Reading UKRA*, April, Vol. 29, No.1.

DES (Department of Education and Science) (1989) *English for Ages 5–16. The Cox Report*. London: HMSO.

DES (1991) *The Parent's Charter*. London: HMSO.

DES (1993) *The National Curriculum and Its Assessment. The Dearing Report*. London: HMSO.

DfEE (1995) *English in the National Curriculum*. London: HMSO.

DfEE (1998) *The National Literacy Strategy Framework for Teaching*. London: HMSO.

Donaldson, M. (1979) *Children's Minds*. London: Fontana Press.

Doyle, K. and Mallett. M. (1994) 'Were dinosaurs bigger than whales?', *TACTYC Early Years Journal*, Vol. 14, No. 2, Spring .

Egan, K. (1988) *Primary Understanding: Education in Early Childhood*. New York and London: Routledge.

Egan, K. (1992) *Imagination in Teaching and Learning: The Middle School Years*. Chicago: Chicago University Press.

Fisher, M. (1972) *Matters of Fact*. Leicester: Brockhampton Press.

Going Places: Library Resource for Geography (1997) Hertfordshire: Schools Library Service

Gorman, T. (1996) *Assessing Young Children's Writing*. London: The Basic Skills Agency NFER.

Graham, J. (1996) 'Using illustration as the bridge between fact and fiction', *English in Education*, Vol. 30, No. 1.

Graham, J. and Kelly, A. (1997) *Reading under Control*. London: David Fulton.

Graham, J. and Kelly, A. (1998) *Writing under Control*. London: David Fulton.

Graves, D. (1983) *Writing: Teachers and Children at Work*. London: Heinemann Educational Books.

Grayson, L. (1998) 'Using drama as a context for writing', BA (Ed.) dissertation, Goldsmiths College.

Gregory, E. (1996) *Making Sense of a New World: Learning to Read in a Second Language*. London: Paul Chapman.

Guha, M. (1996) 'Play in school' in G. Blenkin and A. V. Kelly (eds) *Early Childhood Education: A Developmental Curriculum*. London: Paul Chapman.

Hall, N. and Robinson, A. (1994) (eds) *Keeping in Touch*. Reading: Reading University, Reading and Language Information Centre.

Halliday, M. (1989) *Spoken and Written Language*. Oxford: Oxford University Press.

Hoodless, P. (ed.) (1998) *History and English: Exploring the Links*. London: Routledge.

Hunter, P. (1998) Unpublished dissertation for the BA Ed. Primary with Subject study Course, Goldsmiths College.

Hurst, V. (1992) 'Assessment and the nursery curriculum' in G. Blenkin and V. Kelly (eds) *Assessment in Early Childhood*. London: Paul Chapman.

Hurst, V. and Joseph, J. (1998) *Supporting Early Learning: The Way Forward*. Milton Keynes: Open University Press.

Jessel, J. (1997) 'Children writing words and building thoughts: does the word processor really help?' in B. Somekh and N. Davis (eds) *Using Information Technology Effectively in Teaching and Learning*. London: Routledge.

Jessell, J. and Matthews, J. (1993) 'Very young children and electronic paint: the beginning of drawing with traditional media and computer paintbox', *TACTYC Early Years Journal*, Vol. 13, No. 2.

Johnson, P. (1997) *Children Making Books*. Reading: Reading University, Reading and Language Information Centre.

Jones, N. (1997) 'Beware of the mouse', *Times Educational Supplement*. 'Early Years' section. 23 May 1997, p. 12.

Karavais, S. and Davies, P. (1995) *Progress in English: Assessment and Record Keeping at Key Stage 1 and 2*. Reading: Reading University, Reading and Language Information Centre.

Lewis, M. and Wray, D. (1996) *Writing Frames: Scaffolding Children's Non-fiction Writing in a Range of Genres*. Reading: Reading University, Reading and Language Information Centre.

Littlefair, A. (1991) *Reading All Types of Writing*. Milton Keynes/Philadelphia: Open University Press.

Loveless, A. (1995) *The Role of IT: Practical Issues for the Primary School Teacher*. London: Cassell.

Lunzer, E. and Gardner, K. (1979) *The Effective Use of Reading*. London: Heinemann.

McArthur, T. (ed.) (1992) *The Oxford Companion to the English Language*. Oxford: Oxford University Press.

MacKay, D., Thompson, B. and Schaub, P. (1970) *Breakthrough to Literacy*. London: Longman.

Mallett, M. (1992a) *Making Facts Matter: Reading Non-fiction 5–11*. London: Paul Chapman.

Mallett, M. (1992b) 'How long does a pig live?', *English in Education NATE*, Vol. 26, No. 1.

Mallett, M. (1994) *Non-fiction Reading in the Primary Years*. Sheffield: NATE.

Mallett, M. (1996/7) 'Engaging heart and mind in reading to learn: the role of illustrations', *Language Matters*. CLPE, No. 3.

Mallett, M. (1997a) *First Person Reading and Writing in the Primary Years*. Sheffield: NATE.

Mallett, M. (1997b) 'Gender and genre: reading and writing choices of older juniors', *Reading UKRA*, Vol. 31, No. 2.

Mallett, M. (1998) 'Non-fiction in the literacy hour: staying at the heart of our practice', *Books for Keeps*, September.

Meek, M. (1991) *On Becoming Literate*. London: The Bodley Head.

Meek, M. (1996) *Information and Book Learning*. Stroud: The Thimble Press.

Mercer, N. (1980) *Common Knowledge*. Sevenoaks: Hodder & Stoughton.

Michael, B. and Michael, M. (1987) *The Foundations of Writing Materials*. Glasgow: Jordanhill College of Education.

Millard, E. (1997) *Differently Literate: Boys, Girls and the Schooling of Literacy*. London: Falmer.

Minns, H. (1991) *Language, Literacy and Gender*. London: Hodder & Stoughton.

Moon, C. (1998) *Twenty-five Years of Individualised Reading*. Reading: Language and Information Centre, Reading University.

Moore, P. J. and Scevak, J. J. 'Learning from texts and visual aids: a developmental perspective', *Journal of Research in Reading*, Vol. 20, No. 3, October.

Moyles, J. R. (1991) *Play as a Learning Process in Your Classroom*. London: Mary Glasgow.

Mr Togs the Tailor: A Context for Writing (1987) Scotland: The Scottish Consultative Council on the Curriculum.

NCET (1996) *Early Years Education and ICT*. Information sheet (Internet).

Neate, B. (1992) *Finding out about Finding out: a Practical Guide to Children's Information Books*. Sevenoaks: Hodder & Stoughton with UKRA.

Neate, B. (1994) 'Mining information', *Child Education*, Feb., pp. 12–13.

Nicholson, D. (1996/7) 'Key Stage 2 Information Book Collection, CLPE Core Books', *Language Matters*, Vol. 3, p. 34.

Oxlade, C. (1998) *Virtual Reality: What's the Big Idea?* London: Hodder & Stoughton.

O'Sullivan, O. and Barrs, M. (1998) 'Literacy: Meeting special needs', *Language Matters*, Autumn.

Pagett, L. (1997) 'Look! Here's a new idea! Using information technology to facilitate the use of expository text', *Reading UKRA*, July, Vol. 31, No. 2.

Pappas, C. (1986) 'Exploring the global structure of children's information books,' paper presented to the Annual Meeting of the National Reading Conference, Austin, Texas.

Preston, C. (1995) *21st Century A–Z Literacy Handbook: Linking Literacy with Software*. Project Miranda. London: London Institute of Education.

QCA (1998) *Key Stage One English Tasks. Teacher's Handbook*. London: QCA.

Redfern, A. and Edwards, V. (1997) *Practical Ways to Inspire Young Authors*. Reading: University of Reading, Reading and Language Information Centre.

Rowe, A. and Routh, C. (1997) *Good Ideas for Using Big Books*. Reading: Reading University Reading and Language Information Centre.

SCAA, School Curriculum and Assessment Authority (1996) *Nursery Education Consultation, Desirable Outcomes for Children's Learning on Entering Compulsory Education*. London: SCAA.

Sealey, A. (1996) *Learning about Language: Issues for Primary Teachers.* Milton Keynes/Philadelphia: Open University Press.

Smith, P. (1994) *Through Writing to Reading: Classroom Strategies for Supporting Literacy.* London: Routledge.

Vygotsky, L. S. (1978) *Mind in Society: The Development of the Higher Psychological Processes.* Cambridge MA: MIT Press.

Vygotsky, L. S. (1986) *Thought and Language* ed. A. Kozusin. Cambridge, MA: MIT Press.

Wade, B. (1990) (ed.) *Reading for Real.* Milton Keynes: Open University Press.

Walker, S. (1993) *Desktop Publishing for Teachers.* Reading: Reading University, Reading and Language Information Centre

Weinberger, J. (1996) *Literacy Goes to School: The Parents' Role in Young Children's Literacy Learning.* London: Paul Chapman.

Wells, G. (1981) *Learning through Interaction.* Cambridge: Cambridge University Press.

Wells, G. (1986) *The Meaning Makers: Children Learning Language and Using Language to Learn.* London: Hodder & Stoughton.

Whitehead, M. R. (1996) *The Development of Language and Literacy in the Early Years.* London: Hodder & Stoughton.

Whitehead, M. R. (1997) *Language and Literacy in the Early Years.* London: Paul Chapman.

Whitehead, M. R. (1999) *Supporting Language and Literacy Development in the Early Years.* Milton Keynes: Open University Press.

Wood, D. (1988) *How Children Think and Learn.* Oxford: Blackwell.

Woolland, B. (1993) *The Teaching of Drama in the Primary School.* London: Longman.

Wray, D. (1995) *English 7–11: Developing Primary Teaching Skills.* London: Routledge.

Wray, D. and Lewis, M. (1992) 'Primary children's use of information books', *Reading*, Vol. 26, No. 3.

Wray, D. and Lewis, M. (1997a) *Practical Ways to Teach Reading for Information.* Reading: Reading and Language Information Centre, University of Reading.

Wray, D. and Lewis, M. (1997b) *Extending Literacy: Children Reading and Writing Non-fiction.* London: Routledge.

Name index

Subject index